Haunted Nations

Postcolonialism has attracted a large amount of interest in cultural theory, but the adjacent area of multiculturalism has not been scrutinized to quite the same extent. In this innovative new book, Sneja Gunew sets out to interrogate the ways in which the transnational discourse of multiculturalism may be related to the politics of race and indigeneity, grounding her discussion in a variety of national settings and a variety of literary, autobiographical and theoretical texts. Using examples from marginal sites – the 'settler societies' of Australia and Canada – to cast light on the globally dominant discourses of the US and the UK, Gunew analyses the political ambiguities and the pitfalls involved in a discourse of multiculturalism haunted by the opposing spectres of anarchy and assimilation.

Sneja Gunew is Director of the Centre for Research in Women's Studies and Gender Relations at the University of British Columbia.

Transformations: Thinking through feminism

Edited by

Maureen McNeil
Institute of Women's Studies, Lancaster University

Lynne Pearce
Department of English, Lancaster University

Beverley Skeggs
Department of Sociology, Manchester University

Haunted Nations

The colonial dimensions of multiculturalisms

Sneja Gunew

Routledge
Taylor & Francis Group

LONDON AND NEW YORK

First published 2004
by Routledge
11 New Fetter Lane, London EC4P 4EE

Simultaneously published in the USA and Canada
by Routledge
29 West 35th Street, New York, NY 10001

Routledge is an imprint of the Taylor & Francis Group

© 2004 Sneja Gunew

Typeset in Times by
BOOK NOW Ltd
Printed and bound in Great Britain by
TJ International Ltd, Padstow, Cornwall

British Library Cataloguing in Publication Data
A catalogue record for this book is available from the British Library

Library of Congress Cataloging in Publication Data
Gunew, Sneja Marina, 1946–
    Haunted nations: the colonial dimensions of multiculturalisms / Sneja
Gunew. – 1st ed.
        p. cm. – (Transformations)
Simultaneously published in the USA and Canada.
Includes bibliographical references and index.
    1. Multiculturalism. 2. Postcolonialism. 3. Multiculturalism–Case
studies. 4. Postcolonialism–Case studies. 5. Racism. 6. Ethnicity.
I. Title. II. Series.
    HM1271.G86 2003
    305.8–dc21   2003007487

ISBN 0-415-28482-1 (hbk)
ISBN 0-415-28483-X (pbk)

Contents

Acknowledgements

The seeds of this book began while I was still in Australia and I would like to acknowledge a grant from the Australian Research Council. After emigrating to Canada in 1993 I was fortunate to secure a further grant from the Social Sciences and Humanities Research Council of Canada to complete the research for the book and help me widen the analyses. A fellowship at the Humanities Institute at Irvine, University of California, helped considerably to put many of these questions in their more comparative perspective and I remain indebted to the many spirited conversations I had during the month I was there with the Irvine Comparative Multicultural Group: Allaine Cerwonka (UC Irvine), Elizabeth Constable (UC Davis), James LaSpina (UCLA), John Liu (UC Irvine), Christopher Newfield (UC Santa Barbara), Nan Seuffert (Waikato, New Zealand), Dana Takagi (UC Santa Cruz), Brook Thomas (UC Irvine, Convenor) and Terry Threadgold (Monash, Australia).

My first two years in Canada at the University of Victoria, British Columbia, were a temperate introduction to the culture and I would like to thank Radhika Desai, Smaro Kamboureli, Evelyn Cobley, Misao Dean and Christine St. Peters. In 1995 I moved to the University of British Columbia and my thanks to the following: Mandakranta Bose, Richard Cavell, Mary Chapman, Graeme Chalmers, Gillian Creese, Glenn Deer, Isabel Dyck, Susanna Egan, Sherrill Grace, Rita De Grandis, Tineke Hellwig, Erin Hurley, Anne McKinnon, Kevin McNeilly, Minelle Mahtani, Bill New, Sharalyn Orbaugh, Geraldine Pratt, Leslie Roman, Veronica Strong-Boag, Valerie Raoul and Lorraine Weir.

In Australia my former colleagues kept me up to date with material and my thanks to the following: Ien Ang, Annette Blonski, Marian Boreland, David Carter, Paul Carter, Anna Couani, Elizabeth Gertsakis, Anna Gibbs, Ghassan Hage, Efi Hatzimanolis, Ivor Indyk, Jurgis and Jolanta Janavicius, Mary Kalantzis, Antigone Kefala, Bronwen Levy, Kateryna O. Longley, Mirjana Lozanovska, Peter and Tes Lyssiotis, Susan Magarey, Vijay Mishra, Wenche Ommundsen, Nikos Papastergiadis, Elspeth Probyn, Kay Schaffer, Susan Sheridan, Nick Tsoutas, Irmeline Veit-Brause, Walter Veit and Gillian Whitlock. My particular gratitude to Anna Yeatman.

To friends scattered across Canada and North America my thanks for intellectual stimulus and support: Rey Chow, Elizabeth Grosz, Ann Kaplan, Shirley Geok-lin Lim, Fazal Rizvi, George Elliott Clarke, Aritha Van Herk, Linda Hutcheon, Myrna Kostash, Françoise Lionnet, Kathy Mezei, Roy Miki, Joe Pivato, Sherry Simon and Fred Wah. Particular thanks to the students who have inspired many of the directions this idiosyncratic intellectual journey has taken: Joanna Clarke, Doritta Fong, Gaik Cheng Khoo, Tseen Khoo, Chris Lee, Michelle La Flamme, Kate McInturff, Kara McDonald, Jeff Miller, Debora O, Julie Smith, Shirley Tucker and Mary Zournazi. I am indebted to Kim Snowden and to Bianca Rus for the final checking which they carried out with characteristic efficiency and grace.

Finally my special thanks to Margery Fee and Shirley Neuman, who have been staunch friends during my (not always easy) induction into Canadian contexts and to Terence Greer for his sustaining and irrepressible sense of humour.

Versions of these chapters have appeared in the following journals: *Australian Canadian Studies*, *Australian Feminist Studies*, *Canadian Ethnic Studies*, *International Journal of Canadian Studies*, *Postcolonial Studies*, *Resources for Feminist Research/Documentation sur la Recherche Féministe*, *South Atlantic Quarterly*.

A version of Chapter 4 appeared in W. Ommundsen and H. Rowley (eds) (1996) *From a Distance: Australian Writers and Cultural Displacement*, Geelong, Australia: Deakin University Press. Versions of Chapter 5 appeared in C. Verduyn (ed.) (1998) *Literary Pluralities*, Ontario: Broadview Press and in S. Ahmed, J. Kilby, C. Lury, M. McNeil and B. Skeggs (eds) (2000) *Transformations: Thinking Through Feminism*, London and New York: Routledge.

Introduction
Situated multiculturalisms

Situated knowledges build in accountability.

(Haraway 1991: 111)

This book constitutes an attempt to establish some grounds for comparative studies of multiculturalism, to argue that what appear to be common terms need to be contextualized in relation to local as well as global geopolitical and cultural dynamics. In short, I argue the need for a situated multiculturalism. This book has been produced as discussions about multiculturalism are burgeoning in North America (Willett 1998) and Europe (Modood and Werbner 1997) and are always symptomatic of how various geopolitical interests manifest themselves at local, national and global levels. Such discussions are often framed in terms of a tension between the classic liberal concepts of the private and the public spheres and between concomitantly located group rights and individual rights, though one wonders where one ends and the other begins since the self-formation of the individual draws, usually eclectically, on the accessories and characteristics, the traditions and languages, of various groups.

The material for this book is based on almost thirty years of research and teaching in a number of different countries. While Australia and Canada remain a focus in the study because they were amongst the first nations to constitute models of state multiculturalism, that is, to include multicultural-ism as an official component in their national definitions, at least for a while, the concepts for dealing with multiculturalism often derive from theorists located in the metropolitan centres of the Trans-Atlantic trade in theory. Both the United States and the United Kingdom have also attempted to incorporate versions of multiculturalism within their national fabric. More recently, the European Union is the latest organization attempting to grapple with the questions and tensions untidily grouped together under that unsatisfactory term: multiculturalism.

The title of this introduction signals the need for both detailed and comparative work in relation to the ubiquitous term 'multiculturalism'. My use of the concept of 'situated knowledge' is informed by Donna Haraway's influential writing on this topic. In the process of defining the manner in which feminist theories and methodologies differed from the prevailing paradigms which were organized around the governing logic of objectivity, Haraway proffered an alternative in the following ways:

> Situated knowledges are particularly powerful tools to produce maps of consciousness for people who have been inscribed within the marked categories of race and sex that have been so exuberantly produced in the histories of masculinist, racist, and colonialist dominations. Situated knowledges are always marked knowledges; they are re-markings, re-orientatings, of the great maps that globalized the heterogeneous body of the world in the history of masculinist capitalism and colonialism.
>
> (Haraway 1991: 111)[1]

Haraway argues for the investigator's responsibility to position themselves and to acknowledge that all knowledge is 'interested'. While this declaration has generated accusations of rampant relativism Haraway counters this by stating that: 'The alternative to relativism is partial locatable, critical knowledges sustaining the possibility of webs of connections called solidarity in politics and shared conversations in epistemology' (Haraway 1991: 191). In this era, such a notion of 'dialogue' may sound impossibly utopian, but it does articulate a concept that has guided my investigations in this book, namely, that the meanings of multiculturalism are always deeply enmeshed in constructions of the local, the national, and the global.

In a recent and important essay Marcel Stoetzler and Nira Yuval-Davis re-examine the influential concept of standpoint theory as established through the work of Haraway and others in which the importance of the 'social positioning of the social agent' (Stoetzler and Yuval-Davis 2002: 315) is a primary element in any constructions of 'truth' or 'reality'. Just who comprises the standpoint or location (individuals or groups) and to what degree they are able to embody particular social values and when do these become privileged positions remain some of the complex factors in these debates. The essay reminds us that the imagination is a necessary and often overlooked component in knowledge construction particularly when this is modelled predominantly in sociological ways:

> It is our contention that standpoint theory, in general, and the trans-formation of situated experience into situated knowledge, in particular, are impossible to understand without incorporating a notion of the *situated imagination* . . . Crucially, the imagination in this context is not a straightforward faculty of the individual, but is also . . . a *social* faculty.
>
> (Stoetzler and Yuval-Davis 2002: 325)

And this is where the scrutiny of cultural texts of all kinds becomes, at least in my persepective, authorized even within sociological discursive formations:

Imagination is situated; our imaginary horizons are affected by the positioning of our gaze. But, at the same time, it is our imagination that gives our experiences their particular meanings, their categories of reference. Whether it is 'borders', 'home', 'oppression', or 'liberation', the particular meanings we hold of these concepts are embedded in our situated imaginations.

(Stoetzler and Yuval-Davis 2002: 327)

To attempt a book such as this might understandably be perceived as an act of hubris that deserves criticisms. Such a comparative study reaching across the globe will inevitably raise expectations that all and not merely some of the local differences will be taken into account. In a sense it will please no one because there will always be gaps – by definition. The reviewers of the initial book proposal confirmed this. Indeed, there should be a name for the kind of fallacy involved. The central rationale for the book is that it reiterates a simple point – the need for sensitivity to the situatedness of a multicultural dynamics. While those located in the various contexts where multiculturalism is a term used can indeed learn from each other, the point remains that these principles cannot be universalized because this inevitably flattens or blunts the analytical value of the concepts used. Thus the book is not an attempt to produce comprehensive accounts of the workings of multiculturalism in the various sites mentioned: Canada, Australia, the United States and the United Kingdom. It uses particular sites, particular events or examples, in order to show the complex and nuanced workings of what is (at times perversely) named multiculturalism. The underpinnings of my own academic nomadism are used merely to exemplify the mechanism of an inherent resistance to the over-arching claims offered in the name and on behalf of 'multiculturalism' in each site where I have worked. I have also retained use of a first-person speaking position because the (at times) idiosyncratic choice of examples and locations have been governed by my own peripatetic pedagogical enterprises. I have, however, endeavoured to be as scrupulously self-reflexive as possible concerning the 'interested' positioning of this organizing persona.

Some people seem destined to be nomads, perpetually in exile, always maintaining a critical distance from any society of which they are, for a time, a part.[2] While I cannot claim agency over my initial migration to Australia at the age of four, thereafter a pattern of movement was undeniably established. In my early twenties I moved to eastern Canada (Waterloo and Toronto) and subsequently lived in Manchester, United Kingdom for a few years. Then back to Australia for another fifteen years. My move from Australia to western Canada (Victoria and Vancouver) ten years ago was accompanied by a belated and self-conscious disciplinary redefinition. From being involved for fifteen years or so in the kind of literary studies which merge uncontroversially into cultural studies in the Australian context and being, moreover, immersed in 'critical multiculturalism,'[3] I found myself back in an English department in a country that takes its disciplinary boundaries more seriously than I had expected.[4] Within that discipline I was categorized as a postcolonialist since my teaching and publishing records were most easily accommodated in a context where the word 'postcolonial' had only recently overturned 'Commonwealth Literature' in university calendar entries. Now while I had eagerly searched out and used postcolonial theory as it slowly emerged in the 1980s, I had not actually labelled myself a postcolonialist, in part, perhaps, because I was uneasy about the speed with which some Australian theorists in the field were applying the term to Australian culture in general.[5] As well, my own affiliation with the postwar migrants who changed the face of Australian culture meant that I was thoroughly immersed in various attempts to make visible and to ensure the archival survival of the cultural contributions of these groups. These battles were conducted under the ambiguous sign of 'multi-culturalism' and included many kinds of institutional politics.[6] Attempts to ensure that the many writings and histories which fell outside the major 'ethnic' groups (Anglo-Celtic) in Australia did not disappear without trace (what might be considered an unproblematic commitment to historical preservation), and trying to introduce it into the various debates around what counted (as literature, as theory) in the emergent discussions around the national culture were successful only in limited ways.[7] Over the years since I left Australia many of the state institutions (such as the Office for Multi-cultural Affairs) have been progressively dismantled and abolished.[8]

Something that also became clear to me as I was researching this book is that generational differences inform this text in ways I saw more clearly as the work advanced. While the perception of these debates around 'difference' has been explored in recent feminist writings[9], comparable analyses in postcolonial and multicultural studies do not, to my knowledge, exist. Reading Hage (1998), Ang (2001) and Ahmed (2000) for example, all of whom comment on the Australian situation, defined for me quite starkly that their perception of the complex dynamics concerning the workings of particular terminology, the concepts that were available in more general theory and, in sum, the ways in which relations between cultural minorities and majorities operated, were embedded in specific moments in history. For example, the manner in which the postwar, older ethnic groups are characterized in their texts would not have been possible (or conveyed the appropriate meanings) when I was beginning my own work in these areas.[10] My observations therefore acknowledge, somewhat ruefully, that events have moved on and I am glad they have done so but, more seriously, and in the spirit of this book in general, I am also suggesting that an awareness of such historical contexts will always be a useful element to bring into play in these comparative studies. In their absence, retrospective essentializing, or characterizing one's precursors as being simply crippled and compromised by false consciousness, is all too easy.

While my relations with Canada took a somewhat different line, I know enough to realize that Canada has its own generationally distinct and idio-syncratic history of multiculturalism, colonialism and empire, and North

America in general has a different history again of the institutionalization of knowledge which we associate with disciplinarity. For example, the very existence of so-called 'ethnic studies' in both Canada and the United States meant that the kind of basic multicultural archival work I and others had been pursuing would have been less controversial in North America than it proved to be in Australia.[11] Of greatest interest to me was to note how in Canada, often seen as the pioneer of state multiculturalism, the meaning of this term varies considerably from the Australian context in its foregrounding of racialized differences.[12] As in Australia, a distinction exists in Canada between multiculturalism as a set of government policies designed to manage cultural diversity and multiculturalism as an attempt by various groups and individuals to use these policies to achieve full participatory cultural democracy. In ways similar to Australia (though to a greater and more nuanced extent) Canadian critics have revealed that official multicultural policies often produce restrictive notions of ethnicity which continue to be fuelled by assimilationist and often racist principles (Blodgett 1990; Kamboureli 2000; Mukherjee 1994, 1998; Bannerji 2000). As the noted Canadian writer M.G. Vassanji put it in the preface to a recent collection, anxious attempts to define a cultural core may have deleterious effects:

> The problem is, what constitutes that core; and in the demographically changing society doesn't its definition end up being exclusionary and divisive, potentially destructive and ultimately redundant? I believe that if such an essence exists . . . it is or will be more subtle than being comprised of a mere response to nature, making a fetish out of low temperatures, or turning away and looking north out of a mule-headed defiance of the south . . . Every year between two and three hundred thousand immigrants arrive in this country, which depends on such influxes to stay healthy in a number of ways. No longer do a majority of these newcomers come from Great Britain or Europe. The Bible is not their Great Code, the Mahabharata or the Arabian Nights or the Hadith or the Monkey King inspire them more than Homer, and if they are Westernized it is often through the medium of America.
>
> (Vassanji: vii–viii)

The elements preventing the consolidation of a 'cultural core' have been present from the beginning. In addition to treaty settlements surrounding the First Nations or indigenous peoples, Canadian nationalism has always been effectively split between two founding powers: England and France. Thus from the outset while the Anglo element has been a dominant feature of the hegemonic group it has never been as superficially seamless in character as in Australia because of the historically divided cultural reference points functioning in Canada. What has on the other hand served without doubt as a unifying force has been the American cross-border presence in relation to anxieties concerning economic, cultural and other takeovers. Canadian discussions have also been affected by the cross-border PC (Political Correctness) debates that code multiculturalism in terms of racism, that is, signal an emphasis on so-called visible minorities (Corelli 1991; Smith 1991). Increasingly there have been charges comparable to the ones operating in the United States debates that multiculturalism, circulating as liberal pluralism, focuses too much on the older ethnic groups who have long managed to secure a footing at the expense of newer groups who are perceived as being more difficult to 'assimilate'. Thus multiculturalism in terms of official policy is seen as a covert form of assimilationism and even of white supremacism (Onufrijchuk 1988; Brand 1990; Bannerji 2000). As one critic put it:

> Multiculturalism to me is a way of managing seepage of persistent subjectivity of people that come from other parts of the world, people that are seen as undesirable because they have once been colonized, now neo-colonized. So we are not talking about Germans or Finns and Swedes or the French . . . We are talking about the undesirables. It is southern Europeans, sometimes, and Third World People who have to be ethnic.
>
> (Bannerji 1990: 146–7)

In the perception of many, there appears to be as much racism and occlusion of these groups in Francophone as in Anglophone Canada (*Tessera* 1992).

Insofar as multicultural literatures are concerned, there has certainly been more official activity in Canada; for example, the Secretary of State's commissioned bibliographies on specific language/cultural groups or attempts to produce comprehensive bibliographies (Miska 1990). It is noteworthy that poststructuralist and postmodernist approaches were initially condemned by a number of critics as being inappropriate for looking at such texts. Instead their major contribution was identified by such critics as that of bearing witness (Blodgett 1990: 19; Dimic 1990: 18; Loriggio 1990a: 25) and of linking history to fiction (Padolsky 1990: 26) particularly insofar as this concerns the history of a community or the fictional representation of a community (Onufrijchuk 1988; Chao 1997). These debates have also been associated with the 'appropriation of voice' controversies, where the rights of mainstream writers to create minority characters from another minority culture or race have been challenged (Maracle 1990; *Books in Canada* 1991; Stasiulis 1993).

Other critical turns have included the reconfiguration of the status and function of the so-called ethnic community in relation to diasporic histories and to differences within such notional groups linking them, for example, to other traditional categories of difference such as gender and even region (Minni 1990: 101). Literature is conceived here as a set of relations (Dimic 1990: 9) rather than simply a list of texts, whether canonized or not. Rather than amounting to the conveniently marginalized study of ethnic literatures, ethnicity functions here to signal the ethnic component permeating literature in general (Padolsky 1990: 26ff). Both approaches helped unsettle the cultural and linguistic reference points of traditional literary studies (Blodgett 1990;

Loriggio 1990b). However, more recent studies such as those by Kamboureli (2000) are more systematic in their exposure of the commodification of ethnicity within Canadian cultural frameworks.

When we consider the United States, the term multiculturalism most persistently permeates debates around education rather than being harnessed to centralized state (in the sense of federally propelled) policy, as is true of both Canada and Australia.[13] On the other hand, during the PC (Political Correctness) debates in the United States the term 'multicultural' was bandied about in all kinds of contexts. The history of the PC controversy is conveniently detailed in two publications (Aufderheide 1992; Berman 1992a). In these volumes are arrayed the major statements, individuals and organizations, revealing that what was initially perceived as a binary structure is now a more complicated spectrum of positions in which the Left can sometimes sound like the Right and vice versa. There was also the realization that far from being a recent phenomenon these controversies, one way and another, were at least a decade old even at the beginning of the nineties (Berman 1992b: 4). In the PC context the multicultural factor comprised an array of assaults on cultural norms as defined within a national context. Joan Scott contended: 'If "political correctness" is the label attached to critical attitudes and behavior, "multiculturalism" is the program it is said to be attempting to enact.' (Scott 1992b: 13). The Chicago Cultural Studies Group defined multiculturalism as 'a desire to rethink canons in the humanities – to rethink both their boundaries and their function . . . to find the cultural and political norms appropriate to more heterogeneous societies within and across nations, including norms for the production and transmission of knowledges' (CCSG 1994: 114). While the terrain and terminology were much contested in the context of the PC debates (Berman 1992b: 6), multiculturalism appeared to include: ethnics (including Hispanics and Asians), Blacks (pertaining to the African Americans who are united by their common history of slavery which has in turn functioned as an excuse for occluding their contribution to the construction of the nation), indigenous peoples, feminists, gays and lesbians, ecologists, deconstructionists (by which was usually meant anything post-structuralist or postmodernist) (Bérubé 1992:143) and a generalized Left. These motley groups were apparently united by their opposition to the West or Western values, also defined as Eurocentrism, and by a framework in which universal propositions or truths are intoned from positions which remain immune from being defined as positions. Given this restrictively coded and to some degree metaphoric meaning for the 'West', we encountered the absurd situation, for example, that Hispanics were at times arrayed against the West and outside Eurocentrism (Fernández 1992). To comprehend this, one had to realize that the defining element in such formulations was oppositionality and the substantive nature of the opposition remains valid whereas the terms used are often misleadingly ambiguous, or, at the very least, function meta-phorically.[14]

Those who represented dissident 'minority' groups, critiqued multiculturalism differently. Some of the most powerful oppositions emanated from African-American theorists situated in Black Studies who saw it as a deflection from dealing with racism (Asante 1992: 303; Carby 1992; Wallace 1992: 232) in that multiculturalism focused on the older ethnic groups who had by this stage been thoroughly assimilated to 'white privilege,' for example, Italians and Jews and various Northern Europeans. In such a framework hegemonic America was constructed as a movement from Anglocentrism to Euro-centrism (Spivak 1992a: 10) which effectively left out the other minorities such as African, Indigenous, Hispanic and Asian Americans. In other words, embraced in this version of multiculturalism was an apolitical smorgasbord of cultures where everyone was free to either offer tit-bits or taste them (Gitlin 1992: 188). Indeed, the smorgasbord approach is echoed in a more sophisti-cated form by David Hollinger's influential *Postethnic America* which argues for a model of 'rooted cosmopolitanism,' a phrase which resonates in disturbing ways with the Nazi term for Jews as 'rootless cosmopolitans'.

The existence of 'area studies' and 'ethnic studies' in the United States, and to some extent in Canada, has both enabled and put particular kinds of restraints on the teaching of multicultural studies. As Rey Chow points out, the historic Cold War underpinnings of 'area studies' are simply too imperial-istic to 'acknowledge, if not directly address, the exploitative, assymmetrical relations inherent in the Western studies of non-Western cultures . . . Once these relations are acknowledged, the paths of inquiry taken by cultural studies towards its objects are bound to be different from those historically adopted in area studies' (Chow 1998: 6). Chow goes on to sound a cautionary note to those who pit a non-Western cultural studies against 'Western theory': 'In the name of studying the West's "others," then, the *critique* of cultural politics that is an inherent part of both poststructural theory and cultural studies is pushed aside, and "culture" returns to a coherent, idealist essence that is outside language and outside mediation' (Chow 1998: 9). As these debates gather force once again in the post-9/11 era, it becomes even more imperative to develop their strategic power by embedding them in comparative studies and so this book constitutes a plea for a comparative Multicultural Studies which remains situated in relation to both globalization and the local.

In Chapter 1, 'The terms of (multi)cultural difference', I speculate in a kind of ground-clearing process as to how we might analyse the local meanings and global resonances of terms such as 'race' and 'ethnicity' which continue to provide the discursive limits of multiculturalism. What is the history of each? Did ethnicity take over from race because there was a retreat from the 'scientific racism' of an earlier era or does it in fact represent a new racism (as argued by Balibar and others) where the focus on culture (designated culturalism) serves to camouflage issues to do with unequal power relations? In North America, ethnicity has a tradition of theorization (notably the work of Werner Sollors) which derives from the largely European immigrants to the United States in the immediate postwar period, but more recent analyses have been influenced by the changing patterns of migration with respect to 'economic' migrations and the identification of what are perceived to be 'visible minorities' or 'people of colour' who are seen as somehow breaking up a supposedly homogeneous nation. Debates are often conducted in terms of the 'ethnic' and 'civic' nation but, as one might expect, these binaries are not necessarily as neat as they imply. As well there is the rise of horrific terms such as 'ethnic cleansing' in recent history. How self-evident are these differences and what does an emphasis on naturalized visibility function to hide? Are the categories 'black' or 'white' or 'European' or 'Asian' indeed self-evident or transparently self-explanatory?

Furthermore, what role does the rise of postcolonial studies play in these debates? What indeed is the relationship between postcolonialism and multi-culturalism? The former has served to shed light on the histories of imperialism and colonialism (often seen in North America as beginning with the work of Edward Said) but how do these legacies structure current cultural concerns? And where do we place the even more recent development of diasporic and transnational studies? These last two categories have emerged to enable the analysis of those tremulous ties to language, to religion, and to more diffused cultural mores which haunt some ethnic groups even over generations as well as clarifying the intrinsically porous nature of all such group identities. How might we theorize these elements when they are severed from the ostensibly more clear-cut histories of colonialism or migration from somewhere else?

In Part I, 'Haunted nations', I consider the ways in which various histories, and in particular colonial histories, haunt and structure current debates around immigration and diaspora. In Chapter 2, 'Colonial hauntings: the colonial seeds of multiculturalism', I suggest that the further analysis of the relationship between postcolonialism and multiculturalism depends on when and where one is posing these questions. While both multiculturalism and postcolonialism have indeed been recognized as floating signifiers there is necessary work to be done in looking at their interactions and mutual exclusions in various nation states. The chapter poses a cautionary note regarding critics like Robert Stam in the US context who, in a relatively recent discussion, displays a tendency to project a particular US resonance for terms such as 'multiculturalism' and to infer that these meanings have a wider (universal?) application than may indeed be the case. Stam's equation of the 'multicultural project' with a generalized anti-Eurocentrism is undone by the Australian and Canadian examples analysed. The problem with his approach is the assumption that Eurocentrism, and even European, have a fixed meaning instead of being unstable terms whose meaning changes radically in specific contexts (as examined further in Part III). Indeed, the war over who may claim 'European' values is at the heart, for example, of Australian multiculturalism. This analysis will highlight the fact that racialization is always an arbitrary process and that charged terms belonging to the rhetoric of nationalism are always part of a discursive chain of difference (Hall 1996a) rather than being rooted in any 'natural' referential system.

In his detailed review of some attempts to canvass and deliberate on the various definitions of the postcolonial, Stuart Hall ('When was "the Post-Colonial"?') suggests that colonialism structures both colonizer and colonized in a process whose stakes are organized around claims to modernity read as European civilization. The Other, who is constructed in and by such mechanisms, rather than having essential alterity, may more correctly be perceived as being located in difference as part of a signifying chain. In the specific context of the settler colony of Australia this chapter argues that, following Stuart Hall, the legacies of British colonialism haunt contemporary Australian debates around the nation, citizenship and multiculturalism so that who owns modernity (and inherits European civilization) instigates a process of racialization in which the descendants of European postwar immigrants are aligned with indigenous and 'Asian' settlers. The contention is that this chain of signification around difference as modernity and European civilization has, in the Australian context, allowed the Anglo-Celtic descendants of the settler colonizers to construct their English ethnicity as European modernity and civilization against the differences of not only the indigenous peoples and those in the surrounding Asia-Pacific but, as well, and paradoxically, those 'multicultural others' many of whom in the wake of postwar migration came precisely from what is traditionally cited as continental Europe or the West. Those NESB (non-English-speaking-background) Europeans are situated in this relay as being outside European modernity and part of a grouping of subaltern subjects who remain in need of enlightenment and civilization.

In Chapter 3, 'Corporeal choreographies of transnational English', I analyse a different kind of haunting, the ways in which specific languages, in this case English, inscribe and produce particular bodies. The chapter begins by looking at the diversification of globalization into debates around internationalization and new definitions of cosmopolitanism described by James Clifford, for example, as a 'discrepant cosmopolitanism' which takes into account the transnational experience whose meaning is defined by localized, and contradictory contexts which may or may not be 'post-nationalist'. While English has indeed become a global language it is clear that different versions of E/englishes exist in the world. Meanwhile in the wake of the work of Said, Viswanathan and Gikandi it is clear that English Studies have been implicated in imperial histories but that they have in turn helped redefine their metropolitan origins. The chapter looks at the ways in which English and English Studies have functioned in a somatic and affective sense to inscribe and animate particular bodies in specific ways. By examining the memoirs of Edward Said, Shirley Geok-lin Lim and Eva Hoffman it analyses the ways in which English Studies inscribed them as particular subjectivities in both British and US pedagogical regimes.

Part II, 'Abjected bodies', comprising Chapters 4 and 5, are case studies in 'ethnic transvestism' where I ponder whether, indeed, all displays of ethnicity might be perceived as performative. If so, for what kind of audience/desire? How does one move beyond notions of 'visible minority' or 'skin' as the primary marker of naturalized racial differences, a task which becomes even more urgent in this new era of 'racial profiling'? Chapter 4, 'A text with subtitles: performing ethnicity', examines the elements in a curious case of 'ethnic passing' in which what appeared to be a young Ukrainian Australian writer, Helen Demidenko, produced a first novel about the complicity of Ukrainians in the Holocaust. She was praised for her 'courage' and 'honesty' in revealing the existence of war criminals among the postwar immigrant communities and won every major literary prize in the country. It subsequently emerged that the writer, Helen Darville, was the daughter of British immigrants and that she had a history of right-wing political activities. The ensuing debates and soul-searching among Australian cultural pundits raised many issues about the national culture's expectations around 'authentic' ethnicity and the ways in which this could be expressed in writing and how this in turn constructed both abjected subjectivities and sites which functioned to maintain the dominant cultural paradigms. Using various theories of performance, including those developed by Marjorie Garber and the more abstract ones developed by Judith Butler around speech act theory, the chapter also makes comparisons with the well-known play and film of *M. Butterfly* to argue a case for evidence of the melancholia of the dominant Anglo-Celtic group which, by means of Demidenko's 'performance', mourns (rather than acknowledges as loss) its own suppressed 'ethnicity'.

Chapter 5, 'Acoustic transgressions and identity politics: a translated performance', considers the necessary tension between global diasporas, with their networks and coalitions, localized manifestations and negotiations, and asks how one might locate or construct intellectual and pedagogicial interventions that avoid the pitfalls in the compromised categories of community and of identity politics. Because the 'new racism' and attendant discourses of difference are primarily organized around an economy of the visible (as in the Canadian term 'visible minorities') the chapter attempts to sketch a theory for an alternative 'aural' or acoustic reading of texts which are too easily slotted into the category of 'ethnic minority' where 'ethnic' is often a code word for an occluded process of racialization. Using the work of Canadian poet and short story writer Evelyn Lau, who is often criticized for refusing the so-called 'empowering' racial categories with which critics were eager to provide her, the chapter situates Lau's first novel *Other Women* within a framework of desire and symbolic identification informed by the work of Slavoj Zizek. A psychoanalytic framework is used because redefinitions of identity have often pursued these paths; for example, the notion of 'ambivalence' in the work of postcolonial critic Homi Bhabha and recent feminist debates around the vexed question of identity politics which has led to terms such 'intersectional identities' or 'differential consciousness' as a way of moving beyond the paralysing binaries which are often an inescapable part of identity politics. Slavoj Zizek's work, furthermore, suggests itself because of his consistent attempt to bring the insights of psychoanalysis to bear upon the social and political dimensions. The chapter foregrounds the importance of the aural dimension by linking it to a conference performance at which it was first staged in a spoken rather than written form.

In Part III, '(Un)civilized communities', Chapters 6 and 7 offer perspectives on the following: Who are the heirs to the European Enlightenment's 'civilization'? Who 'belongs' to modernity? Who is part of 'community'? And what are the effects of globalization on national cultural/literary (and their internal) differences? In Chapter 6, 'Somatic choreographies: public spaces; private belongings', I take up once again the issue of language and cor- poreality in different ways from earlier chapters. To what degree can we speak of 'bodied language' in spatialized terms? These languages may comprise a repertoire of gestures which indicate belonging, or otherwise, as they move through public urban spaces. What kinds of bodies are permitted to register or 'sign' their spatial entitlement in public spaces? And what occurs when what is assumed to be a universal language of gesture does not in fact communicate in anticipated ways? The chapter looks at the work of a variety of writers and thinkers including the philosopher Charles Taylor's concept of the politics of recognition and the anthropologist Ghassan Hage's critique of multicultural- ism in Australia as forming part of a white supremacist discourse. It also considers the work of Australian writer David Malouf and Canadian poet Fred Wah, the latter dealing in his latest collection of prose poems with what he terms 'hyphenated transpicuities' or the ambiguities surrounding hyphenated identities.

Chapter 7, 'Can ghosts emigrate? Diaspora, exile and community', returns to the thematics of haunting and considers how we might think about the diasporic poet-pedagogue in terms of a discursive economy which splits open, or at least rearranges, cultural orthodoxies. Beginning with the model of Edward Said's intellectual (itself very influenced by Gramsci's concept of the organic intellectual) it examines examples of 'poet-pedagogues' who used their 'hyphenated identities' as bases for exploring new models of weaving community in diaspora. The late Roy Kiyooka was born in Canada but experienced a sense of internal alienation when the Japanese Canadian community was uprooted from the west coast of Canada and interned in various parts of the country, east of the Rockies. The chapter examines the memoir of his mother, instigated by him but published after his death. The memoir comprises a series of translations since Kiyooka's Japanese was not good enough to speak with any complexity to his mother and her English, in turn, was not adequate to convey her feelings fully. The translation was edited by Kiyooka's friend, the feminist writer Daphne Marlatt, to produce a complex, many-layered text. This text is placed alongside the memoir of Japanese American poet Garrett Hongo who examines his long and often painful process of rediscovering the history of his family, a journey which takes him to the Hawai'ian island of Volcano and the remnants of a scattered family and community whose lives had been completely disrupted by the internment of Japanese Americans during the Second World War. Finally, the chapter considers once again the memoir of Shirley Geok-lin Lim. Lim, poet, short story writer and a pioneering force in the setting up of Asian American literature, charts her impoverished upbringing in Malaya/Malaysia, her journey through a colonial education and as a Fulbright graduate student in the United States. Her further intellectual trajectory is informed by her various experiences teaching in community colleges and finally entering the university system as a professor. All these memoirs are used to illustrate some of the contradictions involved in artists who are also teachers who become the focus for creating and maintaining an intellectual community informed by the diasporic histories of its constituent members and enmeshed in contradictory relations with the dominant cultural paradigms. The various forms of un-belonging and belonging and the tensions between an 'abjected' community, for example the Japanese Canadians/Americans and the national culture, are juxtaposed in a further comparison with the Italian Canadian community in Montréal. Using the example of the small publishing house Guernica it shows how their valiant attempt to be the mediators in the bicultural/bilingual struggle in Canada resulted in their recent withdrawal from Montréal and their relocation in anglophone Toronto, marking a further stage in the chequered history of the French–English divide and the complexities of the resonances of 'multiculturalism'.

Finally, in the conclusion, possibilities for future directions for a comparative situated multiculturalism are suggested within the framework of 'transcultural' studies which to some extent represent a tension within nation states in the localized politics of multiculturalism and a globalization which, to some degree, renders the nation state irrelevant as an autonomous self-legislating cultural body.

1 The terms of (multi)cultural difference

The relationship between multiculturalism and postcolonialism is an uneasy one. Multiculturalism deals with theories of difference but unlike post-colonialism, which to a great extent is perceived to be defined retroactively by specific historic legacies, multiculturalism deals with the often compromised management of contemporary geopolitical diversity in former imperial centres as well as in their ex-colonies. It is also increasingly a global discourse since it takes into account the dynamics of diasporas and their relations with nation states and other entities (such as transnational corporations), and the flow of migrants and refugees. The reason for continuing to focus on *critical* multiculturalism is precisely because multiculturalism is so intimately bound up in many parts of the world with those practices and discourses which manage (often in the sense of police and control) 'diversity'. Within critical theory it was an embarrassing term to invoke partly because it was perceived as automatically aligned with and hopelessly co-opted by the state in its role of certain types of exclusionary nation building. As a result, for example, it was consistently rejected by anti-racist groups in Great Britain (Hall 1995). In theoretical debates it was often associated with an identity politics based on essentialism and claims for authenticity which automatically reinstate a version of the sovereign subject and a concern with reified notions of origins. Thus it became difficult to mention multiculturalism and socially progressive critical theory in the same breath. But because it is a contested term it is crucial to continue to scrutinize the discourses and practices mobilized in the name of multiculturalism. This chapter will briefly consider some of the different interpretations of multiculturalism in various parts of the world and will then consider the ambiguous function of the key terms 'race' and 'ethnicity' within its deployment. Consideration for the most part will be given to debates within Australia, Canada, the United States, and the United Kingdom.

Multiculturalism means different things in different contexts and in Canada, the United States and the United Kingdom, the term is intertwined with questions of racialized differences that have so far not been given sufficient prominence, for example, in Australia. While there have always been migrations and disaporas, after two world wars and many other conflicts

last century, the mix of people within borders increasingly rendered traditional national models anachronistic. Multiculturalism has been developed as
a concept by nations and other aspirants to geopolitical cohesiveness who are
trying to represent themselves as transcendently homogeneous in spite of their
heterogeneity. For cultural analysts the politics of representation are at its
heart while for sociologists the specificities of legislation, public policies and
their often arbitrary implementation are major concerns. Multiculturalism
may also be invoked as a way of signalling divergence from a notional mono-
culturalism often too glibly identified with the 'West' or 'Europe' and here it
overlaps significantly with postcolonial concepts and debates.

Multiculturalism purports to deal with minorities and thus implies a
relation with a majority, but how these two categories are defined and wielded
in relation to each other is highly contested and further complicated by
differences in articulation between advanced capitalist countries and the so-
called Third World; between 'settler societies' and, for example, the European
Union. In general, the organizing factor for the minorities are such terms as
'race', 'ethnicity' and 'indigeneity' while their origins are causally linked to
migration, to colonization and various forms of subjugation. With respect to
'race' it would be more accurate to refer to the processes of racialization
involved in representing minorities than to the existence of unproblematic
racial categories. 'Ethnicity' as a defining category was initially employed as a
differential term to avoid 'race' and its implications of a discredited 'scientific'
racism. Ethnicity was more easily attached to the European migrations which
proliferated around the two world wars. In Canada, phrases such as 'visible
minorities' were developed to categorize non-European immigrants who
formed part of mass diasporas and neatly encapsulated as well the indigenous
groups and those descendants of African slaves who had been an uneasily
acknowledged part of the 'nation' for many centuries.[1] Hence multiculturalism is often perceived as a coded way to indicate racialized differences. The
need to deconstruct the 'natural' facade of racialization is clear when one
notes that groups such as Ukrainians in Canada and Greeks and Italians in
Australia were designated 'black' at various historical stages (Kostash 1994;
Gunew 1994a). Further difficulties encountered by indigenous groups are
highlighted in Australia, for example, where the Aborigines prefer not to be
included in multicultural discourses on the grounds that these refer only to
cultures of migration, whereas in New Zealand 'biculturalism' is the preferred
official term because multiculturalism is seen as a diversion from the Maori
sovereignty movement (Greif 1995). In Canada, 'First Nations' (as they are
known) are occasionally included in multicultural discourses and practices
and are also consistently trapped between the French–English divide.[2] These
factors have complicated continuing debates on cultural appropriation
(Crosby 1994).

Discussions must also distinguish between state multiculturalism, dealing
with the management of diversity, and critical multiculturalism used by
minorities as leverage to argue for participation, grounded in their differ-

ences, in the public sphere. Minorities use a variety of strategies to overcome the assimilationist presumptions of most state multiculturalisms. Crucial to both areas is the notion of 'community' and here women, for example, are particularly affected. State multiculturalism followed 'assimilation' (a term deriving from digestion and indicating 'becoming the same as') and 'integration' (separatism in association with some common values) and represents a kind of liberal pluralism which implies both a hidden norm from which minority groups diverge while failing to recognize prevailing power differentials (Goldberg 1994). State multiculturalism operates most clearly in the discourses and practices of education, sociology, the law and immigration and is always contradictory in its application and assumptions. In educational discourses it is often framed by a liberal pluralism where cultural differences are paraded as apolitical ethnic accessories celebrated in multicultural festivals of costumes, cooking and concerts. A relatively recent example of schoolgirls being barred from attending French schools if they wore head scarves has precipitated major debates in which the traditional Left was aligned with the far Right because both identified Islam with religion and bigotry, supposedly at odds with the secular and rationalist republican values constituted by the French nation (Silverman 1992). In sociology and immigration the 'migrant or minority as problem' is a prevailing trope and emphasis is consistently placed on compatible differences and the need to obey the laws and conform to the mores of the new country. In contrast to supposed Western tolerance the minority is often represented as primitive or uncivilized, importing its social pathologies (such as criminal gangs, or 'uncivilized practices', such as arranged marriages or clitoridectomy).

In the terms of this logic, the 'community' becomes the representative of and reference point for cultural difference and women rarely have gender-specific agency within these frameworks. In the exceptional instances where they do, for example in the women's movement, other internal differences, such as class loyalties, often create insufficiently unacknowledged tensions (Ali 1992). In a diasporic situation minorities become characterized externally as static and ahistorical (Anthias and Yuval-Davis 1992) and internally often suffer from compensatory nostalgias which can lead to rather rigid constructions of and adherence to purported traditions, particularly when associated with the struggle for maintenance of religious beliefs. Women in these situations are often designated the bearers of these traditions without having agency in terms either of their interpretation or as community leaders (Saghal 1992). A particularly telling example was provided by the Shahbano case in India where a 73-year-old Muslim woman was awarded maintenance by the High Court of India after a ten-year battle. This in turn led to accusations by the Muslim minority that their rights under the Muslim shariat law (personal laws governing the family within a religious framework) were being undermined by the Hindu majority. Shahbano herself rejected the decision in what was interpreted as an act of Muslim solidarity. As Pathak and Rajan point out, such apparent respect for minority rights repeatedly trap women between the private and the public spheres, in this case, the family and the state (Pathak and Rajan 1992). Clearly the legal contradictions in and limits to multicultural policies exist in all contexts. It remains to be seen how the European Union will legislate to deal both with minorities within their separate nations and with the differences between the various European nations (Modood and Werbner 1997).

Even within supposedly more enlightened contexts, such as universities or academic feminisms, one encounters the phenomenon of the token 'woman of colour' invited to conferences (Trinh 1989; Chow 1993) or equally tokenistic cross-cultural work which repeatedly uncovers the usual round of stereotypes (Nnaemeka 1994). There is also the problem of conflating minorities through the use of terms such as 'women of colour' or 'visible minorities' which once again serve to reinforce the notion of a legislative centre or norm (Bannerji 1993). Multiculturalism's implied focus on culture can also occlude or minimize specific political activisms and their histories. Hazel Carby (1992) has noted that literary/cultural emphasis on black women's texts often functions as a substitute for actual social relations or the continuing work of desegregation and anti-racism.

However, even these complicit practices have become the target of what became known as the 'PC' (Political Correctness) debates. Following the implementation of multicultural policies and programmes, including such tactics as affirmative action, a number of conservative commentators began to refer to the suppressive reign of the 'thought police' and 'biopolitics' (Fekete 1994). The latter is a reference to the further issue of identity politics – that in the name of political agency people are identified with and reduced to their assumed sex, race, or ethnicity. As Ella Shohat and Robert Stam state wryly (1994: 342), 'theory deconstructs totalizing myths while activism nourishes them'. This formulation can lead both to a backlash from the wider community and to minorities competing with each other to build hierarchies of legitimation based on oppression.

While Canada has to some degree pioneered the concept of multiculturalism as part of state policy in dealing with minorities, there is a plethora of studies focusing on multiculturalism in the United States. It is clear that racialized differences are at the heart of these debates, but there has been an interesting historical shift in the wake of the demise of the Cold War. As Rajeswari Mohan puts it:

> In its incarnation in the 1980s, multiculturalism was a code word for 'race,' yoked to signifiers that included 'affirmative action' and 'quotas', among others. Since the 1992 controversy over New York City's rainbow curriculum, the term has become a code word for lesbian and gay issues. Despite shifts in the ideological freight carried by the term, what remains constant is its connotation of 'special interest' that supposedly weighs against an implied general interest.
>
> (Mohan 1995: 374)

The notion that multiculturalism could be coded to register a variety of oppositional minority positions is also taken up by George Yúdice (1995) in relation to Jewishness. The defining reference point for all these is a consolidated and hegemonic 'whiteness' as the encompassing sign for all forms of socio-economic and political privilege.

While multiculturalism is now often perceived as an empty signifier onto which a range of groups project their fears and hopes, the future for critical multiculturalism lies in an alertness to the inherent 'hybridity' and diverse affiliations of all subjects which may be mobilized in varying combinations by particular projects or events. Coalitions may be built around 'mutual and reciprocal relativization' (Shohat and Stam 1994). Critical multiculturalism may still be usefully invoked to counter exclusionary hegemonic practices or appeals to nostalgic histories in a bid to return to 'basics' and the reinstatement of the conservative status quo suggested by such recent examples as the efforts to abolish affirmative action policies in the United States and in Canada.

In Australia, the legacies of multiculturalism are too often ignored as significant factors in the proliferating work in cultural studies or as part of socially progressive critical theory. The example provided by the Republican debates in Australia (whether or not Australia should cut itself free from constitutional adherence to the British monarchy) includes numerous dismissive references to so-called 'multicultural orthodoxies' (Docker 1994; Curthoys and Muecke 1993) which indicated a 'straw' position in which the repeated injunction that everyone participates in ethnicity is used to obliterate considerations of Australia's diverse histories of migration. The attempts to give a presence to 'multicultural others' were misrepresented as striving to create a binary logic in which a hegemonic and homogenized Anglo-Celtic centre was supposedly always placed in contrast to an equally homogenized multicultural ideal. One could argue against this that the references to 'Anglo-Celts' in the work of multicultural theorists (Gunew and Longley 1992) are not simply concerned with depicting historical continuities but are often attempts to highlight a language of representation dealing with inclusions and exclusion in the narratives of the nation. In other words, who is included in those various narratives of Australia's cultural traditions or other collective histories? The history of Australian immigration has been a very diverse one over two centuries but these nuances are not foregrounded when various compilations attempt to depict or characterize the nation.[3] Of particular concern are the ways we are enmeshed in and positioned by discourses of nationalism with all their contradictions, tensions and exclusions. The Australian caricatures of multicultural critical theory recall a timely warning contained in Paul Gilroy's study *Black Atlantic* in which he mentions, in the British context, 'a quiet cultural nationalism which pervades the work of some radical thinkers' (Gilroy 1993a: 4) who prefer not to deal with the influences of forces (such as non Anglo-Celtic nationals and their concerns) they consider to be outside the national imaginary. The various incarnations of radical nationalisms in

Australia could also be perceived at times as falling into these conceptual traps.

Australian usages of multiculturalism tend not to signal overt articulations of racialized differences and this may in part be because the category represented by race is often reserved for the Aboriginal peoples who in the Australian context (unlike indigenous peoples in North America) have succeeded in dissociating their concerns from discourses of multiculturalism (in the sense of immigration or ethnic diversity). But these obvious ways may be deceptive for I would argue that by privileging 'ethnicity' as an organizing term Australian discourses of multiculturalism represent the erasure or evasion of race (race being used here in the sense of racialized groups, concepts and forms of power). The racial other is always a shifting concept but this aspect is not clearly indicated in the contemporary Australian focus on depicting the category exclusively in terms of the indigenous peoples. As Ien Ang and Jon Stratton have argued, in Australia 'the category of race should be seen as the symbolic marker of unabsorbable cultural difference' (Stratton and Ang 1994: 155).

For example, a dominant rhetorical pattern in the debates surrounding Australian republicanism suggests that Australia is borrowing to some degree from New Zealand in that it appears increasingly to be embracing a politics of biculturalism. The brave new republic is re-narrativized on the basis of reconciliation with the indigenous peoples and while this is admirable in itself, it is interesting that this process is framed in terms of a binary opposition which homogenizes both sides and leaves little room for their internal differences, much less for other locations of difference. For example, a collection titled *Being Whitefella* (Graham 1994), modelled on New Zealander Michael King's famous anthology *Pakeha*,[4] attempts to scrutinize and deconstruct the norm of whiteness or Europeanness. This represents a timely move in line with comparable directions elsewhere (R. Young 1990; Frankenberg 1993; Morrison 1992; Ware 1992) but in Australia these efforts once again appear to consolidate Australianness as synonymous with Anglo-Celticism, albeit without acknowledging this.[5] For example, here is a comment from the introduction: 'Ireland, and having an Irish ancestry feature in the backgrounds of other contributors. . . . Perhaps because the Irish understand oppression, love the land and know what it's like to live on the fringe. Booker Prize-winning author Roddy Doyle commented that the Irish are the blacks of Europe. A number of prominent Aboriginal people have also noticed the shared experience' (Graham 1994: 23). It is clear from this who is being constructed here as part of what the back cover describes as 'non-indigenous Australians'. We are confronted with 'blacks' versus 'whites' in the familiar contexts which derive from the scientific racism of an earlier period. Where does that leave 'ethnicity', the code name given for those more recent immigrant settlers who do not conveniently derive from Britain or Ireland and who interrogate these neat categories? And where does that leave Aboriginality for that matter, aspects of which can arguably also be constructed in terms of ethnicity? Aboriginality is also a matter of intersubjective relations as Marcia Langton notes, '"Aboriginality", therefore, is a field of intersubjectivity in that it is remade over and over again in a process of dialogue, of imagination, of representation and interpretation. Both Aboriginal and non-Aboriginal people create "Aboriginalities"' (Langton 1993: 33–4).

As a plethora of books suggests, the distinction between race and ethnicity is increasingly a blurred one (Anthias and Yuval-Davis 1992; Essed and Goldberg 2002; Frankenberg 1993; Goldberg 1990, 1993; Morrison 1992; West 1993). Both are, it seems, invented in ways that accord with the particular traditions they are asked to shore up. It becomes a matter of historical specificity in relation to particular groups as to where they have been placed on those axes of nationalism or globalization which contextualize both race and ethnicity. In an earlier era ethnicity was seen as a way of circumventing the racist history of 'race' and was associated with apparently cultural choices; in other words, that one could choose the groups to which one belonged and within them could also choose what to preserve as part of an imagined past. Ethnicity was also largely conceived in cultural terms as a matter of the rituals of daily life, including language and religion, where culture supposedly operated as a place distinct from the political, a kind of safe haven from its exigencies. Race on the other hand has been associated with irreducible difference (akin to representations of sexual difference) often located in what have been termed 'visible differences' (for example, skin colour) which gained their legitimation through associations with so-called biological givens. This meant that choice was suspended in the face of racist projections emerging in response to some aspects of these arbitrarily chosen visible differences. It also means that visible differences often amount to a coded way of referring back to those apparent biological essences that formed the grounds for scientific racism. While concepts of irreducible differences can be said to work in two directions by conferring legitimacy on both racism, on the one hand, and on attempts to forge radical communities which subvert those agendas, modern theorists have increasingly undermined the bases for arguing for race as predicated on absolute differences. As David Goldberg puts it, 'race is arbitrary . . . were one to line up all the individual members of the human species according to any usual racial criteria like pigmentation, there are no non-arbitrary points at which one might draw the lines of racial distinctions' (Goldberg 1993: 83).

Models attempting to locate the absolute grounds of racial difference have been displaced by analyses establishing the mechanisms of racism and racialized forms of power which result in certain groups gaining 'race privilege' (Frankenberg 1993). As Goldberg states, 'race is irrelevant, but all is race' (Goldberg 1993: 6), that is, irrelevant because, while there are no non-arbitrary or absolute markers of race, 'debates about and struggles around race in a variety of societies are really about the meaning and nature of political constitution and community: Who counts as in and who out, who is central to the body politic and who peripheral, who is autonomous and who dependent?' (Goldberg 1993: 83). Another way of putting it is to see it in this period of history as a struggle over who controls the codes and practices of nation-building and other forms of legislated belonging.

Constructions of nationalism are traditionally predicated on formulating both cohesiveness within the borders of the nation and on instituting absolute differences from adjoining states, so they borrow their structures from, and indeed incorporate concepts pertaining to, racialized differences (Goldberg 1993: 4). Therefore it is much easier to stage a national history, founded on Ernest Renan's 'moments of forgetting' (Renan 1990: 11), in terms of cohesive autochthonous peoples displaced by equally cohesive colonizing powers. In the event, those other groups, with their different legacies from those who settled and displaced the 'original' inhabitants, are left out of the drama, particularly when they are associated with another supposed 'race', as 'Asians' are often deemed to be, in the settler colonies of Canada, New Zealand and Australia. Where are the histories and analyses of 'first contact,' for example, with those many non-Anglo-Celtic settler others? While the European immigrants could (with some effort and strain perhaps) be amalgamated with the Anglo-Celts or 'whites', it proved rather more difficult to do this with the so-called Asians. In other words, while there is no 'natural' logic which orders racialized discourse, it is made to appear as though there were.

If one were to attempt to continue to differentiate race and ethnicity it could be suggested that, while race is structured by the desire to be considered human, ethnicity is structured by a concomitant desire for citizenship, that is, to be a legitimate part of political structures. This does not constitute an absolute difference but one of emphasis. It has also been argued by Goldberg that *racial* differences are in fact determined by *ethnic* choices, that is, that the arbitrary markers by which means race is constructed are based on ethnic choices, whether this be religion, skin colour or the wearing of headgear. As he puts it, 'invoking the concept of race is invariably ethnocentric. Ethnicity is the mode of cultural identification and distinction . . . assigning significance to biological or physical attributes . . . [it] is a cultural choice' (Goldberg 1993: 74–5). This is illustrated for example in Myrna Tonkinson's contribution to the collection *Being Whitefella*. Tonkinson, an anthropologist involved in Aboriginal land claims, is from Jamaica via the USA and describes herself as of African-Caribbean origin (Graham 1994: 162). Presumably, after years of living as 'black' in a highly racialized society, she finds herself in the interesting position of being designated 'white' by the Aborigines she encounters who clearly displace the supposedly 'natural' markers of skin-colour for those designating 'race privilege'.[6] By making Tonkinson an honorary white, the Aborigines, according to Goldberg's analysis, have exercised the kind of ethnic choice which traditionally, but invisibly, structures discourses of race.[7]

Turning now to another example of the processes which choreograph the relations between race and ethnicity, in Canada there was a considerable controversy about whether or not the 'Legion' clubs of returned soldiers would allow Sikhs wearing turbans to enter their sacred precincts where the dominant activity seems to be the very secular one of consuming alcohol and where the European convention, that men should remove their headgear, prevailed (Smyth 1994). One presumes the Sikhs were less interested in alcoholic rites than in fighting for the right to enter these clubs, to be included in this nationally significant community. In the midst of these debates it was revealed that Canadian-Jewish veterans, to preserve the right to wear the yarmulke, had discreetly formed a separate chapter and that this 'choice' was of course also open to the Sikhs – indeed, they were strongly encouraged to exercise it. The controversy was organized around a rhetoric of 'respect' both for the war dead and for the dominant cultural conventions of a country into which one was being 'assimilated' (marked culturally by not wearing headgear in hegemonic European-Canadian culture and the opposite in a branch of Asian-Canadian culture). Thus the logic appeared to be governed by ethnic choices rather than racism.

The example illustrates once more that we are dealing with who belongs to the nation and who does not and that this may be organized around quite arbitrary markers. Ironically this dispute took place in the midst of com-memorative D-Day celebrations, thus producing a spate of letters in the press asking in bewilderment how this could happen in the face of a war in which the forces of enlightenment and tolerance had won, after all, over the forces of intolerance. This was set in the context of a recurrent and heated nationalist discourse surrounding the question of whether or not Quebec would finally separate from Canada. It may well be that the debate around soldiers and headgear was in fact a diversionary tactic or displaced symptom produced by the heightened emotions surrounding the possibilities of Quebec's imminent secession. But the fact remains that Canadian nationalism (like any other) finds it difficult to sustain the protocols of a non-contradictory nationalist discourse which attempts to maintain, as Homi Bhabha has argued, the ambiguous task of representing the-people-as-one at the same time that they affirm cultural differences within the nation (Bhabha 1990: 291–322).

In an earlier era, dominated by critics such as Werner Sollors in the United States, ethnicity was perceived as shaping the discourses of consent rather than those of descent (relating to race in the model of genealogy) which were seen as structuring an earlier period of narratives of nationalism. It amounted to the desire to be a citizen in one's differences which, being based on a *choice* of the rituals one wished to continue, tended to work towards avoiding those anxieties provoked by cultural difference in the sense of fragmentation and dispersal. Ethnicity was of course not able to deal with the characteristics pertaining to visible minorities; in other words, it only functioned as an organizing rhetoric for a predominantly European settler population. This 'whiteness', as Toni Morrison has eloquently demonstrated in her book *Playing in the Dark*, was never able to deal consciously, for example, with African-American differences. The more recent era which attempted to establish multiculturalism as a token acknowledgment of these other differences also strenuously side-stepped a recognition of power differentials among competing minority groups (a recognition significantly absent in the 'Political Correctness' backlash discussed in the Introduction). Thus a profoundly conservative pluralist model of state multiculturalism has arguably always prevailed in the United States, Canada and Australia. It is useful to note that in his more recent compilations of debates in the field of 'ethnicity', Werner Sollors points out:

> The belief in a deep divide between race and ethnicity that justifies a dualistic procedure runs against the problem that the distinction between ethnicity and race is simply not a distinction between culture and nature . . . What seems to be the case then is that in societies that cherish racial and ethnic distinctions, ethnicity and race will interact in complex ways, and that in some societies the belief that they are completely separable will emerge so that certain ethnic conflicts can come to be understood as 'racial'.
>
> (Sollors 1996: xxxiv–v)

While 'race' has no basis in fact, racism does. Thus analyses of race have attempted to distinguish themselves from the scientific racism prevailing last century which in turn, according to analysts such as Gilroy and Goldberg, have served to structure both nationalism and modernity. As part of this analysis Goldberg argues that, far from being inherently irrational, 'racist exclusions throughout modernity can and have been rationally ordered and legitimated' (Goldberg 1993:11) and indeed, that racism has always structured the Enlightenment legacy of the 'man of reason'. Therefore the notion that racism is irrational, that it falls outside the mechanisms of reason, is questionable. The fact that racism is indeed 'reasonable' returns agency to individuals who are therefore once again made responsible, at least to some degree, for their racist actions. Prevailing models analysing systemic and discursive racism have tended to remove the emphasis from individual responsibility and Goldberg suggests that there needs to be a corrective to this trend. Similarly, Ruth Frankenberg's analysis, based on numerous interviews, in *White Woman, Race Matters*, also argues that responsibility for certain racist actions must be maintained in what she designates as the three areas of racism: essentialist racism, colour- and power-evasiveness, and race cognizant reassertions (Frankenberg 1993: 140).

In these models of inclusion and exclusion one notes that constructions of both race and ethnicity have the following features: they are structured in relation to an economy or logic of the 'natural' linking family, community and the nation, in other words, maintaining the apparent homology and cohesiveness of such 'natural' ties. While all are discrete they are also seen as leaking into each other. In relation to this point, Gilroy's critique of the essentialist nature of American Africancentricity shows how 'the trope of the family which is such a recurrent feature of their discourse is itself a characteristically American means for comprehending the limits and dynamics of racial community' (Gilroy 1993a: 191). Meanwhile Ruth Frankenberg's chapter on 'interracial' marriages clearly reveals how these supposed continuities and homologies are in fact structured in terms of *irreconcilable* contradictions. The family of the nation is clearly at odds with the nation of families.

Such figurative logic also informed (albeit in idiosyncratic ways) a news item referring to the Bosnian war (Toronto *Globe & Mail* 1994). It was reported that a United Nations panel had found that Bosnian Serbs had pursued 'an overriding policy of advocating the use of rape as a method of "ethnic cleansing" against Bosnian Muslims'. How might one unpack the signification of 'ethnic cleansing' here? One surmised from the many reports that 'ethnic cleansing' was powered by the desire to align groups conceived as ethnically absolute or homogeneous with particular territories. In this instance, how those ethnic groups were chosen seemed to be predominantly based on religion rather than 'blood ties', since there had been considerable genealogical intermingling amongst the peoples of this area, and presumably language (another of the privileged markers of ethnic difference) was not as clear-cut an issue as religion. Religion, embedded in history, dated back to the Turkish conquest of 1389 at Kosovo, which is one of the rallying historical moments for Bosnian Serbs (Kostash 1993). Thus Muslim victims *now* were refigured in terms of Muslim aggressors *then*. Ethnic absolutism is therefore not con-structed in the expected racist model of the racially pure family (in the sense of bloodlines), otherwise how would one offer the logic of rape as a means of ethnic cleansing? Rape, a violent genealogical intervention in many imperialisms (including of course African-American ones), here interrupts a symbolically pure genealogy on both sides. It was constructed in this case, however, not as genealogical contamination but as blasphemy, if religious difference is the prime referent for each group. Thus the bodies of Muslim Serbian women were figured as the reliquary of the 'ethnically homogeneous' family and, coherent with this figurative logic, as the sanctuary of the Muslim faith.

When Michael Ignatieff concluded his series of television programmes *Blood and Belonging* which examined various nationalist trouble spots (including the Kurds, Quebec, Northern Ireland, Germany, the Ukraine and the former Yugoslavia), he stated that there were two concepts of nation: the ethnic one (for 'us' only) and the civic one (an alliance based on consent rather than descent).[8] In the example above, the publicly witnessed withholding of consent (the accounts suggested the women and girls were deliberately and repeatedly raped in front of their families) meant that we were dealing with the 'ethnic' nation here. Genealogically speaking, the rapes ensured that there would be continuity between the 'them' and 'us' in the future. In other words, Ignatieff's ethnic model of the nation is perpetuated into a bloody future of continued ethnically based contention. There appeared to be no room for civic consent here. Blood (in the sense of genealogy and religion) underwrites belonging in the sense of legitimating territorial aspirations. The future bloodlines injected into these bodies, as genealogy and blasphemy, established the corporeal continuum of a past dating from presumed comparable actions by the Muslim Turks in 1389. One assumed that this overdetermined chronology served to justify the atrocities of that contemporary war. The absolutism projected onto ethnicity in this scenario matched the absolutism associated with race in a previous age. The mechanisms relating to both race and ethnicity are therefore used interchangeably in this new rhetoric of constituting and managing the nation.[9]

David Goldberg suggests that 'if we see race as a fluid, fragile, and more or less vacuous concept capable of alternative senses', then instead of talking in terms of theories of race, as though 'race' were a given, 'we will take them alternatively as transformed and historically transforming *conceptions* of race, subjective identity, and social identification' (Goldberg 1993: 80–1). Race, as he points out, naturalizes 'the groupings it identifies in its own name' (Goldberg 1993: 81) including those pertaining to the nation. As we know from studies in nationalism, notably Benedict Anderson's (1983/1991) work, the assumed natural and primordial homogeneity of the nation is actually the result of much labour to cover over the differences and disparate elements. It can take as given neither language, genealogy nor territory and is instead sutured by specific rhetorical structures of icons and symbols that construct notions of both borders and belonging.

To what extent can cultural critics analyse the models of culture emerging from these deployments of race and ethnicity? Culture, as we have observed in these debates, too often represents a retreat from the political and clearly this is one element to bring to crisis. A prevailing trend in these debates is that of self-consciously employing a differently situated perspective to deconstruct the dominant, indeed, to show whether and how there is such an object as the dominant in representation, in a variety of discourses. For example, Ruth Frankenberg suggests how 'to speak of whiteness is to assign *everyone* a place in the relations of racism. It is to emphasize that dealing with racism is not merely an option for white people ... ' (Frankenberg 1993: 6). And later, in an interesting echo of Marcia Langton's statement quoted earlier, '"whiteness" is indeed a space defined only by reference to those named cultures it has flung out to the perimeter. Whiteness is in this sense fundamentally a relational category' (Frankenberg 1993: 231). In other words, it is the 'white gaze' or position which we can usefully define (Frankenberg 1993: 18) at this point. And, like blackness, whiteness is a shifting term as we have seen in the case of Tonkinson. Indeed, a Canadian example was precipitated by the relatively recent 'Writing Through Race' controversy[10] when Myrna Kostash made the following pronouncements in the *Globe & Mail*:

> In 1908, Ukrainians were not white. Two generations later we are. How can this be? For one thing we learned to speak English. My parents, born in Canada, acquired the status of loyal British subjects – honorary whiteness, if you like. By the time I was in school in the 1950s and 1960s,

Ukrainian Canadians had become part of the Canadian 'mosaic', colour-
ful nuggets decorating the two 'founding nations'.

(Kostash 1994)

Appeals to the facts of a nation's history are not really at issue here, since we
are dealing rather with metaphors and signifying systems mobilized as part of a
rhetoric of the national culture concerned with identifying insiders and
outsiders.

In relation to teasing out the salient features of minority perspectives, the
founding study for the construction of alterity is Said's *Orientalism*. Its later
and local applications are many but Toni Morrison's study is an outstanding
example. Morrison's organizing question is: 'how is "literary whiteness" and
"literary blackness" made, and what is the consequence of this construction?'
(Morrison 1992: xii). She then goes on to examine the creation of 'Africanism'
(an invented Africa) in American literature and finds, for example, that early
American writing is 'in large measure shaped by the presence of the racial
other' (Morrison 1992: 46). In a parallel development in the United States,
increasing scholarly work around the construction of 'Asianness' is gathering
pace: the work of Shirley Geok-lin Lim (1993, 1994), Rey Chow (1991, 1993,
1998, 2002) and a whole new generation of critics, often drawing upon their
own personal histories of being Asian-American (Hagedorn 1993; Wong
1993; Cheung 1993). In Australia such work serves as a useful corrective to the
oversimplified biculturalist oppositions mentioned earlier, for example, the
work of Ghassan Hage.

Homi Bhabha, a critic who embodies Trans-Atlantic comparativism in his
move from the United Kingdom to the United States, is particularly relevant
in attempts to think about borders and hybridity. He defines 'hybridity' as 'the
construction of cultural authority within conditions of political antagonism or
inequity. Strategies of hybridization reveal an estranging movement in the
"authoritative", even authoritarian inscription of the sign' (Bhabha 1993:
212). We should also note that there is a suggestion in some criticism, based on
classic deconstruction, that such analyses in the name of hybridity might be
perceived as dependent on the very boundaries they seek to cross or blur
(Jagose 1993). Such formalist dangers bedevil any counterdiscourse, hence
the intellectual purchase of theories such as Judith Butler's notion of performativity which constructs the subversive in terms of repetitive stagings.[11] One
thinks also of Paul Gilroy's brilliant study of jazz as the detailed workings of a
hybrid culture flowing in two directions of mutually beneficial 'contamination'
in *Black Atlantic*.

Where does this leave multicultural critical theory? For one thing it remains
a useful discourse adjacent to and partly overlapping with postcolonial theory
in particular. While postcolonialism is sometimes defined as studies in
Eurocentrism, it should not be confined to this and one has to be alert to its
usage and claims in specific instances. As Arif Dirlik has pointed out, there are

problems with its deployment as being both too general and too particular: too general when used by First World thinkers 'who apply concepts of First World derivation globally without giving a second thought to the social differences that must qualify those concepts historically and contextually' (Dirlik 1994: 340) and too specific when non-First World intellectuals generalize from the local to the global. As Dirlik points out, there is 'a contradiction between an insistence on heterogeneity, difference, and historicity and a tendency to generalize from the local to the global while denying that there are global forces at work that may condition the local in the first place' (Dirlik 1994: 341).

In relation to this critique, multicultural critical theory can serve to remind one of both the local and the global in that it introduces minority perspectives as well as suggesting diasporic networks. It continues to be a way of situating subjectivities outside certain nationalist investments and hence may be used as a way of paying attention to minority perspectives, using them to critique dominant discourses and practices. There seems some truth in Ruth Frankenberg's suggestion that minorities see the elements which structure the dominant more clearly than do those at the 'centre' (Frankenberg 1993: 5; 206). At the same time the caution always remains that minority perspectives are neither free of their own investments nor do they automatically retain a hold on some kind of privileged moral capital. For example, in relation to the question of ethnicity it is interesting to note that Frankenberg's analysis shows her subjects signifying their cultural belonging in terms of 'heirlooms' or annual celebrations of certain genealogies. This brings to mind the Australian-Vietnamese writer Uyen Loewald's (1994: 78–81) character-istically acerbic designation of ethnic groups in Australia as comprising a 'museum culture' relevant to the cultural tourism industry rather than to themselves as part of a struggle for gaining political legitimacy in their differences. This version of, or complicity with, a type of all-too-prevalent construction of ethnicity is hardly radical in either a cultural or socio-political sense and serves merely to reinforce dominant structures which always perceive the minority as consigned to a past which is rich and diverse but always safely in the past (Anderson 1983/91). In ways that we have traced in relation to race and ethnicity, multiculturalism is now, according to Bhabha (1993), a kind of floating signifier which gains both meaning and strategic capabilities only in a specific context. It is available for use by any faction and has no privileged or unchanging meaning. These decentred perspectives can also be used to demonstrate the ways in which certain discursive traditions haunt the new; for example, the new racism referred to by Goldberg and Gilroy or the continuing covert racism hiding at the heart of modernity and at the heart of liberalism (Frankenberg 1993). This in turn may lead to the refiguring and rehistoricizing of modernity and the various 'posts' that follow,[12] including postmodernism and postcolonialism.[13] In the Australian context, for example, there are the thoughtful reminders put forward by Wayne Hudson and David Carter in the introduction to their anthology on the republican debates:

Often the history of Australian republicanism is narrated as if it were a purely English–Irish drama. Such narration tends to ignore the ethnic diversity of the peoples living in this country and the diverse republican traditions of which many have had direct or indirect experience.

(Hudson and Carter 1993: 7)

However one notes as well Gassan Hage's equally thoughtful and thought-provoking analysis of these republican debates which reveal them to serve the interests of an Anglo-Celtic hegemony, in spite of their use of an inclusivist rhetoric of multicultural tolerance. In his detailed examination of the workings of the multicultural spectacle of the nation, the organizing tropes derive from the classificatory systems of collections and zoology which 'belong to a long Western colonialist tradition of exhibiting the national self through the exhibiting of otherness' (Hage 1993: 123).

Once again we return to the question of belonging and note that these interrogations of the national emerge from both local communities and global diasporas. They can have outcomes as murderous as those of the old national-isms but at the same time a retreat into nostalgias for some putative lost coherence of the nation does not appear to be an answer. Nor does the imposition of binary oppositions that trivialize the interactions of complex and non-homogeneous groups, reducing them to 'black and white', seem to be the solution. The way ahead in terms of analysing cultural texts of any kind seems to be to denaturalize the classificatory categories invoked to stabilize and legitimate all types of nation-building and here the constellation of terms – multiculturalism, ethnicity, race, postcolonialism – all have their shifting and shifty roles to play.

Part I
Haunted nations

2 Colonial hauntings

The colonial seeds of multiculturalism

As various nations around the world compete to claim the status of post-coloniality, there is the increasing recognition that migratory diasporas have cut across many nation state boundaries and that multicultural societies are an empirical reality in most parts of the world. But, as discussed in the previous chapter, while postcolonialism as a concept has a certain cachet in academic circles, multiculturalism is viewed with some suspicion as tarnished with a history of coming into being as a state apparatus designed to manage variegated demographies. This chapter explores some of the issues associated with the complex dynamics between postcolonialism and multiculturalism[1] in Australia and Canada and shows them to be at odds with generalizations contained in contemporary analyses emanating from the United States. Broadly speaking, this is intimately tied to the different colonial histories of these settler colonies from that of the United States.

Included in a relatively recent compilation of postcolonial essays, Robert Stam's piece 'Multiculturalism and the Neoconservatives' (Stam 1997) usefully delivers a summary of what contemporary multiculturalism means within the United States. In brief, he defines it as being primarily concerned with anti-Eurocentrism; in other words, as questioning the universalism of European norms. The problem with his approach is the assumption that Eurocentrism, and even European, have a fixed meaning instead of being floating signifiers whose meaning changes radically in specific contexts. Indeed, the war over who may claim 'European' values is at the heart of Australian and Canadian multiculturalism, as this analysis demonstrates.

In his detailed review of some attempts to canvass, and deliberate on the various definitions of the postcolonial, Stuart Hall ('When was "the Post-Colonial"?') suggests that the major contribution of postcolonialism has been to destroy forever the distance (temporal and geographic) that has been perceived to exist between the colonial centre and its colonized peripheries, 'one of the principal values of the term "post-colonial" has been to direct our attention to the many ways in which colonisation was never simply external to the societies of the imperial metropolis' (Hall 1996a: 246). Colonialism, he goes on to argue, structures both colonizer and colonized forever, breaking down the supposed distinction between inside and outside. He suggests that this process is one whose stakes are organized around claims to modernity read as European civilization. The Other, who is constructed in and by such mechanisms, rather than having essential alterity, may more accurately be perceived as being located in difference as part of a signifying chain: 'The Other ceased to be a term fixed in place and time external to the system of identification and became, instead, a symbolically marked "constitutive outside", a positionality of differential marking within a discursive chain' (Hall 1996a: 252).

This chapter explores some of the ramifications of posing the question 'Who counts as European?' within the so-called multicultural nations of Canada and Australia as a way of registering the importance of the question for *all* analyses of multiculturalism. In the Australian context the chain of signification around difference as modernity and European civilization has allowed the Anglo-Celtic descendants of the settler colonizers to construct their English ethnicity as European modernity and civilization against the differences of not only the indigenous peoples and those in the surrounding Asia-Pacific but, as well, and highly paradoxically, those 'multicultural others' who, in the wake of postwar migration, often came precisely from what is traditionally cited as Europe or the West. Those NESB (non-English-speaking-background)[2] Europeans are situated in this relay as being outside European modernity and part of a grouping of subaltern subjects who remain in need of enlightenment and civilization. This symbolic process serves as a reminder that there is no inherent content in such floating signifiers as 'postcolonialism' or 'multiculturalism'. They are constituted in relational negotiations around certain reference points; in this case 'European', read as modernity, read as civilization, read as English. In this movement 'European' is glossed as 'English-speaking' and, in constitutional political terms, as deriving from the British Westminster system. In cultural terms it comprises a tradition emanating from Britain though including as well (in a move that might surprise Tom Nairn and other analysts of the divided nature of the United Kingdom) the cultural productions and various colonial histories of the Irish and Scots in particular. One notes that in both the Canadian and Australian postcolonial peripheries a history of those internal English colonizations (in relation to Ireland and Scotland) is being endlessly replayed, but that would be another book.[3]

Some of these tensions are usefully displayed in an address delivered (11 December 1997) by the Australian Prime Minister John Howard. Howard is infamously associated in the global media with his refusal to apologize to the indigenous peoples of Australia for the evils perpetrated by the settler colonizers, including the kidnapping of their children, a process which ended only in the 1970s,[4] well within the lifetime of John Howard and his colleagues. The occasion for the speech was a reaffirmation (repetition with a difference) of Australia's commitment to being an officially multicultural nation. It is necessary, alas, to quote extensively from his speech in order to make the point. Readers will note the slides between Australian, European and British:

One of the great things about the Australian achievement has been our special skills to take the good bits of the various elements of our heritage and put them beside the not so good bits. Because every heritage has good and bad bits. We have brought from our *British and European heritage*, we have brought the great building blocks of parliamentary democracy and the rule of law, free press and the respect for civil attitudes on many issues. But we have been careful . . . to reject the class consciousness and the stratification of society and the disdain for people, according to where they were born or their class, that was sometimes a feature of *European* societies . . . Now none of that suggests that our history has not been without a blemish. We did, as I'm sure we all recognise, generations ago, treat our indigenous people appallingly and much remains to be done to achieve a complete reconciliation between various sections of the *Australian* community. And I am conscious, as an *Australian* of several generations back and having *British and Irish descent*, I'm conscious of the fact that some years ago, newly-arrived people of this country were perhaps not treated with the welcome and as tolerantly as might have been. That was not always the case but it was sometimes the case and there's no point in pretending otherwise.

(Howard 1997: 9. My emphasis)

Directed at appropriate cultural insiders, these seemingly bland words contain highly coded distinctions between various groups. This piece may be juxt-aposed with another written by a very differently located Australian pundit as a way of providing a further example (this time from the political 'left') of the ways in which these floating signifiers ('multicultural', 'Australian' etc.) are attached to implicit assumptions concerning the nature of European modernity and civilization. The contextualizing material is quite lengthy and the need for such situational narratives is of course a sign that one is outside Trans-Atlantic metropolitan debates.

In 1995, one of Australia's leading contemporary women writers, Helen Garner, published a 'faction',[5] *The First Stone*, based on a case of sexual harassment involving the Master of a residential college attached to the University of Melbourne, one of Australia's oldest universities. Garner, a writer who came to fame on the crest of second-wave feminism, took the controversial line of arguing that feminism had gone 'too far' and that the young women involved had over-reacted to what she depicted as the rather pathetic 'gropings' of a middle-aged male. The young women went to the police because there were no policies or mechanisms in place for dealing with sexual harassment at the college at that time. The legal case which ensued deprived the Master of his job and effectively cast him on the unemployment scrapheap, an outcome effectively mined for its pathos in Garner's account. Garner had insinuated that the young women, who refused to speak to her, had been mentored by a 'coven' of feminist advisers.[6] It emerged in fact that this supposed 'coven' was really one woman who had been split into several characters to avoid libel suits, or so Garner argued in a later essay (Garner 1996). This woman also subsequently lost her job at the college and eventually published an edited collection refuting Garner's book on many counts (Mead 1997).

Within that collection is a piece by Rosi Braidotti, an international feminist academic now based at the University of Utrecht, is that, now firmly ensconced in continental Europe. In the Australian reviews of the collection, Braidotti's piece was singled out by a number of commentators as being 'off the wall' in that it comprised a misguided rant. In her contribution she deals not so much with the controversy around *The First Stone* as with another moment in Helen Garner's history, one which took place when she was a junior teacher in the 1970s in an inner-city secondary school in Melbourne, a school where Braidotti was a student, and whose demographic make-up consisted overwhelmingly of the children of recent Italian and Greek immigrants. In Braidotti's account, Garner felt she needed to enlighten her students about sex:

> . . . she depicts her migrant subjects as not being leading lights intellectually, as speaking bad English and having brutally ill-educated parents. This catalogue of miseries, let alone the generous spirit of the revolution that blows through Garner's words, justifies the need to give them sex education against their deprived and repressive background . . . Garner is utterly ethnocentric and blissfully unaware of her own ignorance about those 'others' . . .
>
> (Braidotti 1997: 135)

Garner was subsequently dismissed from the school and became a *cause célèbre* taken up by the libertarian left of the time. Braidotti's piece delineated how at that moment the school's students and their parents had been fighting to gain academic credibility (that they too were the heirs to European modernity) and how the media scandal around Garner had served to derail this struggle. One should note in this context that, as is the case in other parts of the world, Australian second-wave feminism had also been fielding many accusations of excluding the full range of women's voices, including non-Anglo-Celtic ones (Gunew and Yeatman 1993).

The quotation now juxtaposed with John Howard's speech is from a review in the national newspaper by Beatrice Faust, a revered liberal feminist spokesperson particularly on matters to do with sex education. Once again readers will note the relationship between 'European' and, in this instance, the terms 'migrant'[7] and 'Australian':

> [Braidotti] has two bob each way on exactly what culture and how much of it, the *migrants* had: they were notable only for 'good soccer and bad English', but they simultaneously possessed, all unrecognised, 'a classical European education'. More particularly, *migrant* parents were not

'backward and ignorant'. My narrative of the period, which differs greatly from Braidotti's and somewhat from Garner's, begins with a *migrant* girl in one of my classes at Sunshine High School who was shunned by the *Australians* because, not being allowed to wash during her periods, she regularly stank . . . At the time I helped relieve the girl's misery by initiating some quietly subversive guidance in hygiene through the senior female teacher . . .

(Faust 1997. My emphasis)

Not much has changed since the 1970s. What is of interest here in both the Prime Minister's and Faust's speeches is the chain of terms signifying multicultural difference. Both depict comparable alignments between 'Australians', who are constructed as able to choose from their heritage (forgoing class hierarchies but retaining enlightened liberalism) and those others who are trapped by their heritage in what is, in effect, a combined cultural and class difference illustrated by good soccer, bad English and bad hygiene. The reference to class, oddly, in the Prime Minister's speech is associated not directly with the British heritage but with a slide to 'European societies'. In Faust's piece we are never told the putative cultural affiliation of the 'migrant girl', though we know she is from Melbourne's West, traditionally a less affluent area, but we *are* informed she is not 'Australian' and that she and her parents belong to a class and culture that require remedial training in sex education (and no doubt in other everyday practices). On the face of it, this discussion belongs to the discourses and practices of multiculturalism rather than postcolonialism, but the argument in this chapter is that, following the guidance of Hall's analysis, the mechanism of the one, colonialism, covertly structures the other, multiculturalism.

While postcolonialism to some degree merges into discussions of 'globalization', multiculturalism tends to be reserved for what are perceived (implicitly and explicitly) as racialized interactions within the boundaries of nation states. In a reductive schema one might imagine that postcolonialism and multiculturalism are related in terms of the global and the local. Oddly though, the specificities of these local multicultural interactions are often mapped onto adjacent countries with some curious and problematic results, as this chapter demonstrates. A relatively new term which perhaps mediates both postcolonialism (global) and multiculturalism (local) is that of diasporic studies (Chow 1993; Radhakrishnan 1996) and it may be that, given the historical linking of multiculturalism to state policies and to traditions of conservative liberalism, diaspora has become a preferred term for examining the local inflections of global movements – not least because it resonates more satisfyingly with recent analyses around multinationals and the discrediting of nation states as meaningful entities.[8] Even more recently, terms such as 'transnational' and 'transcultural' (as I suggest in the Conclusion) attempt to capture the ebb and flow of these dynamics.

Colonialism as a moment in the history of imperialism (of which contemporary global capitalism is often seen as the most recent manifest-ation) has unleashed a series of migrations and displacements (some voluntary, most not) across the globe and rearranged the various nation states in its wake.[9] While postcolonial studies can account for an emphasis on historical dimensions (though the question needs always to be posed: from whose perspective?) and for the fact that the colonizing country and its colonizing language remain sustained reference points for these histories, it cannot really account for the local negotiations with these complex elements. How do these histories play themselves out in a particular time and place? To give one example, Homi Bhabha's scrutiny of the well-known territory of 'minority languages' finds that: 'Minority writing emerges from its uneven and unequal cultural locations with a fierce, anxious time lag that effects an anachronous displacement upon the majority, making it confront its own precarious peripheral existence' (Bhabha 1997: 440). In the Australian context the usual invocations of postcolonialism depict Australian writing in general *vis-à-vis* British writing in such an 'anxious relationship'. Instead one might pose the supplementary question of what happens when we invoke those multicultural or ethnic minority writings (non-Anglo-Celtic) which, in turn, trouble a particular nationalist history in Australia (Gunew 1994a)? The anxieties and temporal dislocations are then displaced to another locally circumscribed scenario.

As described in the Introduction and Chapter 1, multiculturalism as part of a national definition has long been regarded as tainted with state concerns and perceived as a strategic 'top-down' imposition of state policies and narratives when viewed in relation to Canada and Australia. Those two countries differ from others in that they have used the term as part of their rhetoric of the nation for some decades, that is, they describe themselves as multicultural countries with multicultural policies (Gunew 1996b). In the United States, multiculturalism is not attached to national definitions but permeates the various separate state discourses on education and clearly signals a way of managing diversity, particularly in the sense of controlling racism (Edgerton 1996; B. Mukherjee 1997). What has not been noted as readily is that the suspect rhetoric of the state has a supplement which functions in the usual troubling way that supplements do; various groups have taken up this discourse and these policies as a lever for local struggles around cultural citizenship and the attainment of cultural franchise. For example, in the midst of her scathing critique of Neil Bisoondath's controversial critique of Canadian multiculturalism, *Selling Illusions*, Canadian critic Marlene NourbeSe Philip concedes the following:

> Multiculturalism may have been a cynical ploy by Liberal politicians to address the balance of power in Canada, but the creativity and inventive-ness of the people in being able to turn to their own advantage policies that may not have their interests at heart can never be underestimated. Throughout the former British Empire black and brown subjects would

use the very precepts employed in governing them against their rulers to
gain independence.

(Philip 1995: 10)

It is clear that many have borrowed their postcolonial theoretical concepts
from the British cultural studies of Raymond Williams and Stuart Hall,
particularly as these were imbricated in the ferment surrounding the arrival of
the British empire back home, that is, the remarkable demographic change in
the English heartland over the last few decades, with its profound implications
for multicultural matters and for English Studies in their hegemonic form.
From the work of Marxist-inspired cultural studies and, more recently,
postcolonialism, we have been given conceptual models for dealing with issues
concerning so-called minorities, or as permeated by what Avtar Brah
characterizes as the 'minoritarian impulse'. This recent discourse intersects
with older debates around ethnicity, such as Werner Sollors' work in the
United States around descent and consent.[10] This intersection has to some
extent caused confusions, in part because the issue of race was central to the
later debates but differently posed in the earlier ones which were the result
of studying largely European migration patterns. But the ways in which
England and Englishness have been redefined and confounded at their roots
(Gilroy 1987; Talib 2002) do provide important reference points for those who
are working to find new ways of defining national cultures which take into
account internal cultural and ethnic complexities. The nostalgic investments
in, and other forms of referencing which take place in relation to, England are
necessarily at the heart of any discussion of the postcoloniality of British
settler colonies.

These concerns emerge directly and indirectly out of debates in postcolonialism since this is the privileged academic domain where issues to do
with cultural hierarchies and investments and debates around who owns
modernity (civilization) are addressed. While both multiculturalism and
postcolonialism have indeed been recognized as floating signifiers, there is
necessary work to be done in looking at their interactions and mutual
exclusions in the settler colonies. For example, whereas postcolonialism
almost never makes the daily press in Canada and Australia, debates around
multiculturalism constantly erupt; but in academic conferences the situation is
reversed.[11] Why is that? Postcolonialism took over very quickly in academic
circles as a privileged site for debates around difference once these had moved
from the Black movement and Civil Rights in the United States through to
First World feminism and the critiques offered by Third World feminists (e.g.
Mohanty, Trinh, Spivak, etc.). Multiculturalism as a way of complicating these
debates by lifting them, in some cases, out of an assumed racialized binary
opposition was a comparative blip on the horizon in terms of metropolitan
theory, at least initially. As US critics Gordon and Newfield admit in their
wide-ranging collection on multiculturalism, Canada is mentioned twice
whereas neither New Zealand nor Australia are mentioned at all (Gordon and

Newfield 1996b: 94). This limited geopolitical perspective is also true of David Goldberg's influential *Multiculturalism: A Critical Reader* in which the Canadian philosopher Charles Taylor, at least, is included. Thus a major challenge of the present exercise is to present alternatives to the metropolitan versions in the United Kingdom or the United States of multicultural debates; some comparative work is well overdue.

Critical multiculturalism: between state and community

For many working within critical multiculturalism, 'multiculturalism' itself (like any other 'ism') represents a site of multiple ambiguities whose critical edge is clearly very dependent on the historical and socio-political particularities of the specific state formations which produce multiculturalism. In all of these, multiculturalism on the one hand can mean simply a way of managing or controlling diversity and, on the other, might at times signal more democratic participation by minority groups constituting, notionally, as NourbeSe Philip contends above, a utopian move. In public populist discourse (exploited by politicians at strategic moments) it is perceived as running counter to the interests of the coherent nation state with its allegiance to core values and institutions, and many progressive political analysts perceive it as a sleight of hand by the state functioning to perpetuate dominant interests under the guise of extending political and cultural suffrage to minority groups. What is not in doubt is that state multiculturalism serves to construct dominant versions of multicultural difference (Derkson 1997–8) and, as this chapter emphasizes, these mechanisms are informed directly by the legacies of specific colonialisms.

One issue to emerge over the last decade is the charge of culturalism, a charge levelled as much at postcolonialism as at multiculturalism.[12] The focus on cultural issues within the broadly defined field of cultural studies has been linked by some social scientists to the general trend towards what has been termed 'cultural racism' or the charge that, whereas in the past racism was constructed around notions of biological determinism, now we have the idea of cultural difference as incommensurability, when argued in a post-structuralist sense, and as simply constituting 'lifestyle' incompatibilities when argued in a commonsense manner. As Stephen Castles puts it :

> Fixation on older definitions of racism as notions of biologically based hierarchies allows more subtle racisms based on cultural markers to claim to be benign and progressive ... The 'new racism' is a 'racism without race' (Balibar 1991: 23). It no longer speaks of superiority, but rather of immutable differences that make coexistence between varying cultural groups in one society impossible.
>
> (Castles 1996: 29)

This prejudice may, in part, be traced to a long-standing debate that initially took place in leftist circles around 'culturalism'. The argument was that a focus on culture had been used in the past to divert attention from historical inequities in power relations.[13] For example, Himani Bannerji maintains with respect to Canadian multiculturalism that it represents simply a ploy to shore up and perpetuate European colonialism: 'The nation state's need for an ideology that can avert a complete rupture becomes desperate, and gives rise to a multicultural ideology which both needs and creates "others" while subverting demands for anti-racism and political equality' (Bannerji 2000: 97).

As a counterbalance to this summation one could point out that in the wake of postcolonial and cultural studies there have been determined efforts by critics to politicize the history of representation. It is not a question of *either* culture *or* politics but of retaining an alertness to the importance of cultural materialism[14] so that questions of representation always remain linked to material conditions, including power inequities and their histories. Avtar Brah reminds us that it is the *meanings* attached to culture that are the decisive factor in socio-political relations: 'Cultural specificities do not in and of themselves constitute social division. It is the meaning attributed to them, and how this meaning is played out in the economic, cultural and political domains, that marks whether or not specificity emerges as a basis of social division' (Brah 1996: 235). Brah also argues that the 'minoritising move' inherent to multiculturalism often serves to reinforce literal readings that minorities are positioned as children or that they are minor cultural players, or that at the very least it functions to erase the histories of colonialism, settlement and migration of various groups. These legacies are flattened into an amnesiac and exclusive concern with the present as well as occluding prevailing power inequities. That process becomes clear when we are dealing with indigenous groups but functions as well for others, particularly highly racialized groups sometimes referred to as 'visible minorities'.[15]

Locating politics: multiculturalism and anti-racism

Pnina Werbner argues in the 'Afterword' of the collection *The Politics of Multiculturalism in the New Europe* that 'multiculturalism without anti-racism does not make sense as a radical political programme' (Werbner 1997: 262). The relationship between multiculturalism and race is also raised by Gordon and Newfield who describe multiculturalism in the US context as to some extent serving to camouflage or exclude references to race: 'It had the air of pleading for a clean start' (Gordon and Newfield 1996a: 3), as they put it in their introduction, with its suggestions of granting an amnesty to the dominant group concerning the history of slavery in the United States. Avtar Brah, in the British context, remarks on the polarization in the 1980s between proponents of 'multiculturalism' and 'anti-racism': 'The confrontation was generally perceived as an opposition between the woolly liberalism of multiculturalism and the Left radicalism of anti-racism' (Brah 1996: 230).

In North America (the United States and Canada) now, multiculturalism has almost become a code word for racialized differences. This has not always been the case in Australia. Until recently, invocations of racialized differences were reserved for referring to the history of colonialism *vis-à-vis* the indigenous peoples. What was eclipsed in the process was the history of racism against varieties of immigrant groups who followed hard on the heels of the first settler colonizers. With the appearance of the Australian collection edited by Ellie Vasta and Stephen Castles, *The Teeth Are Smiling: The Persistence of Racism in Multicultural Australia*, we encounter belated attempts to consider the history of racism in Australia in relation to a variety of groups. Vasta and Castles argue rightly that analyses of racism against indigenous peoples have for too long been separated off from considerations of immigrant communities. What became lost in this somewhat simplistic oppositional categorization were historic alliances made amongst the various groups. The recent 'Demidenko' scandal (analysed in Chapter 4), for example, revealed the dominant group's suspicion that there were all kinds of subversive racist alliances operating amongst the various 'ethnic' groups and that these could not be discussed in the hierarchically conceived politically correct framework of old and new Australia; not, in other words, within the official state framework of multiculturalism. Vasta and Castles argue that there need to be coalitions between Australian Aborigines and non-Anglo-Celtic groups but that these remain difficult. Australian Aboriginal groups have preferred to distance themselves, politically, from multiculturalism which they see as pertaining to immigrant groups, whereas they wish to dissociate themselves from all notions of migration. Their desire, insofar as one can generalize, veers more towards a politics of biculturalism as exists in New Zealand or towards the kind of separate 'nation within' status that is put forward by First Nations groups in Canada (Kymlicka 1998).

Like Werbner, Himani Bannerji argues that multiculturalism in Canada is in effect, 'a form of bounty or state patronage [which] is a managed version of antiracist politics' (Bannerji 2000: 118). Marlene NourbeSe Philip also contends that 'multiculturalism, as we know it, has no answers for the problems of racism, or white supremacy – unless it is combined with a clearly articulated policy of anti-racism, directed at rooting out the effects of racist and white-supremacist thinking' (Philip 1992: 185). Indeed Philip argues that Canada is founded on the principles of white supremacism; and that indictment has been made against Australia as well (Irving 1997; Hage 1998). Such legacies do not disappear although they may well become camouflaged, and many critics in the Canadian context argue that state policies of multiculturalism constitute one such camouflaging device. Indeed Jeff Derkson contends that:

> . . . multiculturalism . . . has remained merely symbolic, reducing ethnic and racialized cultures to folklore and sponsoring celebrations of 'red boot' ethnicity while never actually alleviating the real inequalities within Canadian society. This criticism of multiculturalism charges that it cannot forcefully address racism . . . precisely because, as a policy and a law,

multiculturalism fails to recognize race and ethnicity as socially constructed and, rather, deals with them as natural.

(Derkson 1997–8: 61)

Thus, on the one hand, multicultural policies are often seen to be complicit with racist structures while the project of critical multiculturalism continues to argue that to be effective these policies need to be tied to explicit anti-racist activism.

Multiculturalism and indigeneity

Vijay Mishra's and Bob Hodge's distinction between what they term complicit and oppositional postcolonialisms arises out of debates around whether or not settler colonies such as Australia, New Zealand and Canada are entitled to call themselves postcolonial. Mishra and Hodge would prefer to reserve the term postcolonial for the struggles of the indigenous peoples in such countries who continue internal battles against the descendants of settler colonizers. In the current debates around citizenship and whether or not Australia will become a republic, severing itself from the British monarchy, the grounds on which these debates are conducted are charged with old histories referring back to colonization. The 'unfinished business' with the Australian Aborigines continues to surface – most recently in the wake of the Mabo and Wik High Court decisions recognizing native title (Perrin 1998; Bartlett 1993) and following a recent report on the 'stolen generations' (Aboriginal children removed from their families). What has not perhaps been observed as readily is that Australian multiculturalism itself can be productively analysed as an idiosyncratic manifestation of (rather than a departure from) this colonial history.[16]

These various elements come together in a recent book published by American anthropologist Elizabeth Povinelli. Povinelli argues that indigenous citizenship is undermined by multiculturalism; in other words, that the kind of principled adherence to postcolonialism as being reserved in settler colonies for indigenous struggles is being eaten away by a state rhetoric of multiculturalism. The argument in the rest of this chapter is that the effectiveness of Povinelli's subtle argument in relation to postcolonial ethics is limited because her interpretation of multiculturalism is based on some questionable assumptions. Povinelli formulates her central argument in the following manner:

. . . the state and public lean on a multicultural imaginary to defer the problems that capital, (post)-colonialism, and human diasporas pose to national identity in the late twentieth and early twenty-first centuries. How do these state, public, and capital multicultural discourses, apparatuses, and imaginaries defuse struggles for liberation waged against the modern liberal state and recuperate these struggles as moments in which

the future of the nation and its core institutions and values are ensured
rather than shaken . . .

(Povinelli 2002: 29)

While I agree with much of what Povinelli is arguing here, I would wish to
suggest further that the Australian state fails its 'multicultural' subjects as
much as it does its indigenous ones.

Using the familiar example of clitoridectomy as marking the limits of multicultural tolerance in the United States and elsewhere, Povinelli describes the
affect of 'national nausea' which structures a battle about the moral high
ground: who owns modernity, humanism and democracy? While clitoridectomy is one such instance (often invoked in such debates), I would argue
that these limits in the Australian context are played out also with respect to
non-Anglo-Celtic subjectivity in general, for example, in the case of Helen
Garner, Rosi Braidotti and Beatrice Faust to which I have alluded and the
even more spectacular and much commented upon case of Helen Demidenko/
Darville (see Chapter 4). Demidenko/Darville's depiction in her novel, *The
Hand That Signed the Paper*, of Ukrainian complicity in the Holocaust and
its further life within the Ukrainian diaspora certainly functioned to induce
the affect of 'national nausea'. In the Australian context it reinforced the
prevailing belief (as shown in Beatrice Faust's comment on personal hygiene)
that the ethnic ghettoes harbour unspeakable atavistic pathologies, outside
modernity.[17]

It is in her interpretation of Australian multiculturalism that Povinelli
places too much emphasis on a limited textual rhetoric. As she puts it:

> The Australian juridical, state, and public commitment to multicultural-
> ism provides an especially interesting example of the role a multicultural
> discourse and fantasy play in cohering national identities and allegiances
> and in defusing and diverting liberation struggles in late modern liberal
> democracies . . . Australian nationalism came to mean something other
> than descent from the convict, ruling, or immigrant classes who arrived
> from Britain and western Europe . . . Multiculturalism is represented as
> the externalised political testament both to the nation's aversion to its past
> misdeeds, and to its recovered good intentions.
>
> (Povinelli 2002: 17–18)

On the contrary, recent events have shown the fissures in this rhetoric and
indeed there never was any widespread or substantive commitment, even
under the previous Labour administration, to this rhetoric as set out by
Povinelli. One also needs to point out that immigrants from Britain and those
from 'western Europe' *cannot* be linked in an unproblematically naturalized
sequence as Povinelli claims. While those distinctions are not made in the
United States perhaps, they are most emphatically, and have always been,
present in Australia.

Indeed the rhetorical logic is undone even by the time we get to the last sentence cited. The nation invoked here is clearly and exclusively the Anglo-Celtic one and elsewhere in the book Povinelli does recognize this (Povinelli 2002: 19ff.). The shame and sense of history are felt by and are addressed exclusively to those initial Anglo-Celtic colonizers.[18] The failure to address or include those multicultural others in whose name the multicultural rhetoric supposedly speaks is partially measurable in the shifting register of the 'European' as argued in the beginning of this chapter. Povinelli rightly argues that: 'The court's use of the shamed Anglo-Celtic Australian fixed the ideal image of the nation as a white, First World, global player in the national imaginary' (Povinelli 2002: 182–3). The ways in which 'European' is invoked hearken back as much to the US register (a white supremacist discourse marshalled against an African-American history of slavery, as argued in Gordon and Newfield (1996b: 86ff.) as to the more recent 'Australia as a part of Asia' which had been introduced by the former Labour government. Povinelli's very fine account of the tensions between indigenous Australians and Anglo-Celtic Australian liberalism and their crucial metaphysical as well as direct political implications needed to be troubled by a much more nuanced and differentiated account of those Australian multicultural others to which she refers in somewhat essentialist ways. In these Australian discourses, European is a shifting register and often means British. In her riveting history of the Australian constitution, Helen Irving states: 'It might be thought that to be British was to be white. This was . . . much more literally true for Australians than it was for Britons. There were shades of 'whiteness' for the British with the English themselves being as 'white' as possible' (Irving 1997: 73).[19] As well, Alistair Davidson has shown that much has been invested in keeping a continental European distinct from the British political legacy because adherence needs to be maintained to Westminster's democratic constitutional practices rather than to the very different form they took on the European continent.

Povinelli makes the further mistake of assuming that state documents capture the reality of state policy as it is implemented. For a very different viewpoint one might recommend the archive of documents produced by the many who were involved in trying to implement such multicultural cultural (and other) policies who ran up against their limitations very quickly (Gunew and Rizvi 1994). Those who attempted to use these policy documents as leverage for introducing a greater variety in state funding for the full range of artists from many backgrounds became very aware of how the rhetoric served to camouflage a very different hegemony in this particular arena. It is also in the territory of culture that one is likely to find the most vehement statements by 'old Australians' of their refusal to redefine themselves in the 'multicultural' ways suggested by Povinelli (Gunew 1993c; Hage 1998).

There are also further implications relating to the whole nature of Australian citizenship, as has been argued by Davidson who reveals that there has been a deliberate attempt, behind the facade of multiculturalism, to exclude any deviation from the British Westminster model of citizenship which authorizes elected representatives rather than referring to the sovereignty of the people themselves. While the US model is akin to the European one in that authority is invested in the people, Lisa Lowe's analysis of American citizenship reveals comparable hidden limitations when she points out that in a constitutive sense the abstract notion of citizenship cannot inherently deal with diversity: 'In being represented as citizen within the political sphere . . . the subject is "split off" from the unrepresentable histories of situated embodiment that contradict the abstract form of citizenship' (Lowe 1996: 2). She argues that citizenship in the United States has been defined precisely against the border threat of the 'Asian' in various guises as a way of defining itself. It *cannot* include a difference against which it defines itself. The logic she mobilizes echoes Homi Bhabha's more abstract and influential essay on the pedagogical and performative nation where he suggests that pedagogical inclusiveness cannot deal with the everyday iterative performances of difference (Bhabha 1994: 145). Davidson reveals that it is the legitimation of the British Westminster system that is being invoked in Australia rather than any attempt to find the best model for the repository of sovereign authority. In comparable terms Helen Irving traces a history of Australian federalism in which she identifies 'the function played by the Chinese of identifying a community by what it is not. The white populations of Australia metaphorically became British together' (Irving 1997: 114).[20] One could also suggest that the rhetoric clearly shifted once again under the Liberal government and that its masked intent is even more clearly revealed, for example, in the Prime Minister's speech quoted above. At the launching of the National Multicultural Advisory Council Report *Australian Multiculturalism for a New Century: Towards Inclusiveness* (5 May 1999) the Prime Minister's speech echoed the earlier one, but there was significantly less emphasis on the British heritage of Australians.[21] The new report offered a renewed commitment to multiculturalism with the proviso that it always be prefaced by the modifier 'Australian'.

Like Povinelli, one could cite Zizek here when he states that what you see is the opposite of what you get: 'The problematic of multiculturalism – the hybrid coexistence of diverse cultural life-worlds . . . is the form of appearance of its opposite, of the massive presence of capitalism as *universal* world system: it bears witness to the unprecedented homogenization of the contemporary world' (Zizek 1997: 46). While Zizek's argument pertains to the machinations of multinationals one could, cautiously, suggest that a similar process occurs with this particular version of Australian nationalism, that the fervent invocation of multiculturalism cited by Povinelli as evidence masks its very absence from national practices.[22]

Who counts as European?

Eclipsed in these Australian accounts of citizenship and the nation are the structurally aligned 'others', those multicultural and indigenous others, who also have an unacknowledged *mutual* history. Whereas the imbrications of 'whiteness' and 'Aboriginality' or the issue of 'white Aboriginality' (McLean 1998) have been traced in some of their complexities, the history of Aborigines and non-Anglo-Celtic settlers has yet to be systematically collected.[23] There is, for example, the controversial case of 'Wongar', the pen name of a Serbian immigrant who, as an amateur anthropologist, identified strongly with Aboriginal groups, lived with them and produced several novels and poetry and short story collections drawing upon his experiences. The most recent, *Raki*, draws parallels between the experience of Serbian peasants under successive waves of colonization dating back to the Ottoman empire (the defeat at Kosovo) and the treatment of Australian Aborigines. Because it was felt that Wongar did not make sufficiently overt his non-Aboriginality and was indeed initially perceived as an indigenous writer (for example, in Germany where his work circulated in translation), he was repeatedly vilified in the Australian press over the last few decades rather than being perceived to be part of a long tradition of 'white indigeneity' (Goldie 1989). There is an interesting footnote to this history in that recently a plethora of tales emerged concerning the 'authenticity' of several famous Australian Aboriginal writers, including Mudrooroo (the best known of these)[24] and the long-time Black activist Roberta (Bobbi) Sykes.[25] While the example of Mudrooroo has generally been met with uncharacteristic media tact,[26] this was certainly not the case for the Serbian Wongar who was accused of attempting to cheat the Australian cultural funding bodies and of obtaining writers' fellowships under false pretences (Gunew 1993b). There appears to be an interesting battle here around who may lay claim to 'our Natives' where debates are conducted in terms of 'who gets it right', that is, who 'owns' or is able to legislate upon the representations of the 'Native'.

The further aspect which needs to be emphasized here is that there is nothing natural about processes of racialization. Avtar Brah points out that different groups are differently racialized (Brah 1996: 228); and Roxanne Ng in the Canadian context argues that 'while racism today is seen in discriminatory practices directed mainly at coloured people (the Black, South Asian, Native people, for example), skin colour and overt physical differences were not always the criteria for determining racial differences. The racism directed toward the Acadians by the Scots and Irish is no less abhorrent as that encountered by Native people and today's ethnic and racial minorities' (Ng 1993: 207). In Canada there has also been a history of seeing Ukrainians as 'black' in the sense that they were not perceived to be part of the English/ French European axis.[27] The Canadian writer Myrna Kostash contends: 'I may be European, but what kind of European? Ukrainians, I would argue, are not European Europeans. We have never had a Renaissance, Reformation or Industrial Revolution. We never spoke French. We didn't live in cities. (The Jews and the Poles were the Europeans in our midst.) The ideas of Enlightenment, Revolution and National Liberation were a kind of *dementia praecox* afflicting our housebound intelligentsia. So, if you're going to accuse me of Eurocentricity, you'd better be specific' (Kostash 1991: 41).[28] Canadian critic Janice Kulyk Keefer also feels the need to identify the prevalent 'myth of the "white monolith" ' (Keefer 1996: 251) currently being constructed by some activists working within anti-racist frameworks.

In Australia there is a comparable history of seeing Southern and Eastern Europeans as 'black' (Gunew 1994a) whereas Western (particularly Northern) Europeans were relatively quickly accepted. More recently some of these other histories are being represented, ranging from the work of David Malouf whose Lebanese antecedents appear in his autobiographical collection *12 Edmonstone Street*, to the more recent controversial work of the Greek-Australian writer Christos Tsiolkas whose first novel, *Loaded*, deals as much with discrimination against Greek Australians as against gays and lesbians. What constitutes 'white' or 'Europe' or the 'West' in Australia is a whole other dilemma, as I have indicated in the first part of this chapter. Too often in postcolonial critiques, European immigrant groups are homogenized and made synonymous with a naturalized 'whiteness' or with various imperialisms. But at the same time different nations or groups within Europe had very different histories relating to colonialism and imperialism. In the anglophone world of postcolonial theory, European and Western in fact often slide directly into English or British and no distinctions are made amongst these categories. Apart from the Garner/Faust/Braidotti cluster cited earlier, there is an interesting moment in the Vasta and Castles collection when Kalpana Ram, an immigrant South Asian academic, suggests the following in her analysis of the term NESB:[29] 'On the one hand, we have English and English literature celebrated as the language of British *and, increasingly, of Western identity*. On the other hand, postcolonial immigrants are fashioned in opposition to knowledge of English . . . ' (Ram 1996: 140. My emphasis). For postcolonial immigrants like Ram who bear the legacy of British education, this constitutes one kind of anomaly. For those immigrants who locate their ancestry in European cultures and languages other than the British, another kind of absurdity is set up in that notions of the European, made synonymous with Englishness, exclude continental Europe. Thus non-English becomes non-European and non-Western. Echoes of this occur in Canada also as may be seen in Francesco Loriggio's example of Southern European immigrants, in the introduction to a relatively recent collection, where he states: 'Theirs was an "imperialism of the powerless", "of the poor" . . . which had survival as its aim, not the carrying of the White Man's Burden. The idea of Europe was probably more of an abstraction to them than the idea of America' (Loriggio 1996: 13). And yet, one needs also to bear in mind Canadian writer and critic Dionne Brand's contention that 'whiteness' as a category does have a certain elasticity over time, but only for some: 'One can enter not only if one belongs to the so-called founding nations – the English and the French – but also other European nationalities like the Germans or Ukrainians. Its flexibility and its strength allow it to contain inter-ethnic squabbles . . . without rending the basic fabric of white entitlement' (Brand 1994: 174).

From a different perspective located in European Union politics, Stephen Castles speaks of a 'growing cultural diversity [which] . . . feeds into a moral panic which portrays "Fortress Europe" as under threat by unpredictable influxes from the East and the South, evoking the "Mongol hordes" of a distant past' (Castles 1996: 36). The Hungarian political scientist László Kürti's study of the contemporary tensions between 'western', 'central' and 'eastern' Europe reveals it to be a highly ideological project:

> . . . the making of Central Europe and the discrediting of an Eastern Europe has been a curious blend of historical revision, fiction and intellectual contestation between national identities . . . This sort of scholarly reconstruction of a new Europe solidifies the primacy of Western European capitalism and, to some, it stands for western European democracy of the liberalist kind. For many, Europe continues to be what it once was: a developed north and west in opposition to the underdeveloped south. Sandwiched between the two are the undemocratic, unruly, and backward states of eastern Europe.
>
> (Kürti 1997: 31)[30]

In other words, within Europe itself cultural and political analysts would not be quite so quick to homogenize 'European', much less see it as British. But in English-identified settler colonies there appears to be a clear tendency (imperialist in itself) to assume a totalizing move where the border is between the English (and even British) and the rest, not between Europeans (or the West) and the rest. When Ram goes on to argue that Australian multiculturalism continues to foster core values through its persistence in assigning peripheral values to minorities she is correct, but these are often very culturally specific English values and not pan-European ones. While her terms suggest that English has become a global language, that is quite a different line of argument from one that equates the English language with traditional British culture. The various literatures in English constitute their own oppositional terrain to the univerzalising notions of English canonical literature (Gunew 1994a and Chapter 3). Recent work by Australian critics such as Ghassan Hage (1998) and Ien Ang (2001) indicates that Australian cultural debates are also being inflected by the 'whiteness' debates proliferating in North America and in Europe. The project of tracing a white supremacist discourse and history in Australia reinforces the recognition that 'whiteness' and 'Europeanness' are not givens and that the specific historical and colonial dimensions (the differences within) of the term need to be uncovered. Within Canada the continuing split between English and French Canadians clarifies this further. Given the presence of the French tradition, it is more difficult to slide from European to English or British equivalence in Canada or, more accurately, one needs to bear in mind that 'European' also has a very specific colonial history in Canada, as Bannerji, amongst others has shown.

One is reminded of Dipesh Chakrabarty's much quoted 'postcolonial' injunction to 'provincialise Europe', that is, to deconstruct the universalist claims of European modernity. It is not a matter of turning our backs on modernity or the Enlightenment, he argues, but of making visible within this history European modernity's 'own repressive strategies and practices, the part it plays in the collusions with the narratives of citizenship in assimilating to the projects of the modern state all other possibilities of human solidarity' (Chakrabarty 2000: 45). The meanings of 'Europe' and its supposed counter-term 'Asia' or adjacent pairs such as 'globalization'/'Americanization' are productive ways of instigating this process. This chapter, situated within comparative critical multiculturalism, offers a note of caution for assuming that common terms have common meanings. In the specific context of the settler colony of Australia, I have been arguing that, following Stuart Hall, the legacies of British colonialism structure contemporary Australian debates around the nation, citizenship and multiculturalism so that who owns modernity (and inherits European civilization) instigates a process of racialization in which the descendants of European postwar immigrants continue to be aligned with indigenous and 'Asian' settlers. I have also posed a cautionary note regarding critics like Robert Stam and Elizabeth Povinelli in the US context who have a tendency to project a particular US resonance for terms such as 'multiculturalism' and imply that these meanings have a wider, even universal, application than may indeed be the case. Stam's equation of the 'multicultural project' with anti-Eurocentrism is undone, as has been argued, by the Australian example which reveals the historical fissures within that term. A contemporary populist expression of these debates appeared in Canada's national newspaper the *Globe and Mail*, a rather sardonic piece speculating about the current popularity of East Coast Celtic music in this country:

> Celtic roots music to call our own – a Canadian home-grown phenomenon bubbling out of the East Coast. Our own, that is, if you define 'our' as Scots, Irish, hybrid, and even English (so they oppressed everybody, but let's face it, they like their bagpipes too). It's ethnic music for white folks – but *'mangiacakes'*[31] only, Ukrainians and Italians need not apply.
>
> (Roy 1998: A14)

This analysis generally serves to highlight the fact that racialization is always an arbitrary process and that charged terms belonging to the rhetoric of nationalism are always part of a discursive chain of difference rather than being rooted in any 'natural' referential system.

3 Corporeal choreographies of transnational English

> To move past speaking foreign words to taking them into your body –
> absorbing their meanings into who you are – feeling the grain of the language
> rough against your skin – that is the most difficult of all.[1]

> I felt very strongly that the body was somehow styled differently and that I was
> required to move differently . . .[2]

Growing up in Australia in the 1950s on the outskirts of Melbourne, where land was cheap enough to be settled by the postwar immigrants 'flooding' into the country, we struggled to acquire English, a notoriously difficult enterprise since, according to my parents, it did not abide by the usual linguistic rules of logic. There were far too many exceptions, for example, in the disjunction between pronunciation and spelling. In revenge my mother informed us, only semi-humorously, that the idiosyncratic Australian intonation would result in thin lips and protruding chins – as we could easily observe everywhere around us. Thus my first exposure to the idea that there could be affective[3] and even somatic attributes of language – one might be outwardly marked by the embodiment of a language.

This slight anecdote functions as a kind of *mise en scène* to the chapter in which the English language as a strand in globalization is examined in relation to other components: diasporic movements as linked to debates around corporeality. The argument is that while English as such does not automatically convey an imperial or colonial charge, its embededness within various pedagogical and disciplinary regimes of subjugation (whether these relate to colonization, neo-imperialism or migration) and its attachment to a tradition of English Studies mean that it cannot function neutrally as a worldwide *lingua franca* (Talib 2002; Willinsky 1994; 1998). More particularly the chapter examines the somatic effects and affects of English when it is acquired within an immigrant context and displaces other prior languages. Globalization is often glibly invoked as an homogenizing force but, paradoxically, it yields useful meanings only when analysed within very specific locations. Similarly, the ways in which individuals narrativize the process of acquiring English as a foreign language lose their particularity in the wake of decades of debates around corporeality. After Foucault, we have learnt that the body is both unique as well as being caught up within broadly generic accounts of regimes of disciplinarity.

English as world language, a force undermining the linguistic and cultural diversity of the world has functioned as a given in many debates dealing either with postcolonialism (Phillipson 1992) or as subsumed in overarching conceptions of globalization. At a tangent to such assumptions, it becomes increasingly clear that any residual notions of English itself as constituting a unified language have been changed completely by the various 'englishes'[4] proliferating around the world, whether these be part of the ex-Empire and thus harnessed to a spectrum of distinctive programmes of education, or not. Something not examined as closely are the details of what it means, corporeally and viscerally, to speak these englishes at the same time that one is encouraged to pursue English (in its received standard form), and to register these effects in narrative texts. How, more precisely, does English/english write on the body in ways that may be decoded from written texts? Is it possible to map this process as a technology of subjectivity and a disciplining of bodies in quite specific material ways outside the more general means by which bodies have traditionally been marked or disciplined by educational institutions? Indeed, is it even possible to isolate the effects of a particular language from a programme of studies imbued with an imperial history as has been the case with English and English Studies?

The concept of a technology of the self derives from the work of Michel Foucault.[5] Foucault glosses this notion in a number of ways: as 'the history of how an individual acts upon himself', and more elaborately as 'technologies . . . which permit individuals to effect by their own means or with the help of their own bodies and souls, thoughts, conduct, and way of being, so as to transform themselves in order to attain a certain state of happiness, purity, wisdom, perfection, or immortality' (Foucault 1988b: 18–19). Foucault traces this procedure through various ethical frameworks, ranging from the Platonic dialogues to the Christian era and finally to the Enlightenment. In work tantalizing in its brevity and suggestiveness he describes the constitution of subjectivity, plotted through the care of the self, as moving among various models which include consideration of the intersection between the political and the pedagogic, the latter involving a relationship to a master or mentor, as well as becoming enmeshed in a regime writing which takes on increasing importance 'in the culture of talking care of oneself' (Foucault 1988b: 26–7). With the advent of Christianity, knowledge of the self, in which the confessional plays of course a major role, becomes synonymous with the renunciation of the self. By the eighteenth century a new regulating ethical model comes into being in which 'the techniques of verbalization have been reinserted in a different context by the so-called human sciences in order to use them without renunciation of the self but to constitute, positively, a new self' (Foucault 1988b: 49). That care of the self by means of which we cultivate an 'art of living' generates a lifelong duet between our bodies and their contexts. And as recent debates on corporeality have taught us, the body is far from being a blank slate comprising neutral or inert matter on which events and habits are simply inscribed (Grosz 1994; Gatens 1996). But the nature of those corporeal registers of and resistances to its contexts remains somewhat mysterious and this chapter begins to explore aspects of this conundrum, particularly as they relate to English language acquisition within a diasporic context with its attendant induction into the further mysteries of the transmission of English Studies and Englishness.

It is generally understood now that just as linguistic English functions differently in its various global locations (Fishman *et al.* 1996), English Studies, comprising the acquisition of a robust and complex literacy by means of studying both the language and its attendant literature, is no longer perceived as a monolithic entity. Two decades at least of postcolonial studies, preceded by Feminist, Black and Commonwealth Studies, have ensured that we now speak of literatures in English and that we recognize, indeed, that English Studies never were quite as unified as they were once assumed to be or perhaps even endeavoured to be (Colls and Dodd 1987; Doyle 1989). The work of Edward Said (1993), and Gauri Viswananthan (1989) and Simon Gikandi (1996), has meant that we now often perceive English and the promulgation of its literature as being embedded in an imperial history operating with differing protocols attuned to the exigencies of localized contexts and their demands. But other consequences, less easily classified than those linked simply with legacies of colonial subjugation, follow. Gikandi, for example, articulates the paradox that those formerly colonized by English – as language and culture – remain obsessed by some of its idiosyncratic cultural fixtures, the cultural and linguistic accessories that comprise everyday life: 'Why did formerly colonized people . . . seem to invest so much in cultural institutions . . . that were closely associated with imperial conquest and rule?' (Gikandi 1996: ix). What effect does this apparently reactionary predilection have in a local context on fledgling postcolonial nationalisms? As well, there is the embedding of imperializing English within the larger concerns of Eurocentrism where it functions as one of a number of colonizing languages and cultures which have emanated from what has been loosely called Europe. In the words of Walter Mignolo, 'Europe as the locus of enunciation and other civilizations of the planet as the locus of the enunciated' (Mignolo 1998: 33). In an adjoining area of power relations we encounter the rise of communication technologies and the rule of American transnational corporations (TNCs) which have disseminated a renewed dominance of a particular version of English over other European languages and cultures. How has this in turn affected our sense of English Studies in their globalized incarnations? Given its dominance as a worldwide language, to what extent indeed are these views of English at the core of structuring our very perception of globalization (Holborow 1999)? Since globalization can mean so many things, it might be useful to pause here and consider briefly some of the terminology surrounding debates around globalization, culminating in a consideration of the model of a 'discrepant cosmopolitanism' as possibly the most useful way to approach the implications of English and English Studies.

Globalization itself may be defined as the manner in which one is rendered an object/abject in the face of the forces of globalized capital, communication systems and TNCs, which tend to disseminate American, rather than British, language and culture. Masao Miyoshi, for example, perceives TNCs as the most predatory incarnation of late capitalism and feels that all our critical energy should be directed at exposing their machinations which pervade, not least, the very universities we all inhabit, fundamentally structuring what scholars may, or not, research. As he puts it:

> Global corporate operations now subordinate state functions, and in the name of competition, productivity, and freedom, public space is being markedly reduced. And the university that was at times capable of independent criticism of corporate and state policies is increasingly less concerned with maintaining such a neutral position. The function of the university is being transformed from state apologetics to industrial management . . . an unmistakably radical reduction of its public and critical role.
>
> (Miyoshi 1998: 263)

In the introduction to the volume containing this essay, Frederic Jameson, in a more guarded manner than Miyoshi, raises a paradox which recurs in the debates that describe globalization as source of both transnational domination and, at the same time, the liberation of local cultures from the nation state (Jameson 1998: xiii). Whether or not and to what degree globalization functions as a liberating force for *local* cultures remains a point of contention. However it is undoubtedly true that globalization appears to cover a range of contradictory meanings, although it often continues to be rather glibly and emptily invoked as the foundation or cause in discourses attempting to analyse cultural crises.

An adjacent term 'internationalization' could perhaps be reserved for the ways in which each nation state (and smaller groupings) chooses to respond to globalization, as far as possible, on its own terms. Jonathan Rée, on the other hand, considers internationalization, deriving from an emphasis on the nation at the core of this term, to be quite illusory:

> Before the establishment of internationality as a world system, politics presented itself as the somewhat abstruse concern of a small political class, rather than the supreme form of human association, and it is only in the twentieth century that it has become compulsory for everyone to have a nationality, an "identity" that is supposed to assign them to the jurisdiction of a particular political power.
>
> (Rée 1998: 88)

One might consider as well the fraught arena of the international selling of education, particularly the profit-rich field of transmitting English itself, where the perception is that versions of 'authentic' English compete with one another and that ultimately they will all be swallowed by the sophisticated US- and UK-based communication companies, who are producing online education at an alarming rate and simply buying up the diversified talent peddling its wares in the world in general. The prevailing belief is that while at present one can buy one's ESL courses from a smorgasbord offered by Australia, the United Kingdom, or Canada, ultimately these will become part of Disney or Microsoft packages and their usefully jarring local inflections will be smoothed out by the processes of capitalist commodification. The extent to which English Studies functions as handmaiden to these enterprises is a complex question and one beyond the scope of this chapter but one bears in mind Said's contention concerning English as 'worldwide *lingua franca*. This all but terminally consigned English to the level of a technical language almost totally stripped not only of expressive and aesthetic characteristics but also denuded of any critical or self-conscious dimensions' (Said 1992b: 5).

With reference to globalization, particularly when one is focusing on neocolonial or diasporic issues, it might be more useful to invoke the term 'cosmopolitanism' which has a long history not unrelated to the previous term 'internationalization'. As Bruce Robbins, quoting anthropologist Paul Rabinow, succinctly put it: 'In the past the term has been applied, often venomously, "to Christians, aristocrats, merchants, Jews, homosexuals, and intellectuals . . . "' (Robbins 1998: 1). It was often coupled with the adjective 'rootless' and became a code phrase used to designate those whose allegiance/ patriotism were seen to be withheld or in doubt. Initially it was also associated with class mobility and only recently, as Robbins points out, has it been widened to include all those diasporic or transnational subjects who criss-cross the globe (Robbins 1998: 5). Influential social analysts such as the historian David Hollinger now call for a 'rooted cosmopolitanism' as part of the changing emphases in what he designates 'postethnic' America (Hollinger 1995: 5).

Bruce Robbins also takes issue with the homogenizing impetus in the term 'citizen of the world' and argues that there are now many forms of cosmo-politanism which are subject, as one might expect, to complex geopolitical orderings (Robbins 1998: 5). With respect to its relation to the nation state, Robbins suggests that cosmopolitanism need not be inherently post-nationalist, as some have argued, and that, for example, a community in diaspora may well be functioning in a situation of 'long-distance nationalism' as has been demonstrated in the recent upheavals in the former Yugoslavia or, for that matter, in the Rushdie case (Robbins 1998: 11). James Clifford's term 'discrepant cosmopolitanism' is a useful one because it avoids 'the excessive localism of particularist cultural relativism, as well as the overly global vision of a capitalist or technocratic monoculture' (Clifford 1997: 36). Pheng Cheah, refining Jameson's contention quoted above, suggests that cosmopolitanism is inherently opposed to nationalism only when the latter is conceived in terms of territoriality, in other words, when it is equated with 'exilic migrancy' from a particular homeland, increasingly not the case for groups associated with serial migrancy.[6] Cheah also speculates about the degree to which transnational migrants feel that they do indeed belong to the world in general rather than identifying with particular localities.[7]

Following the contemporary recognition of the force of diasporic movements within globalization, does it ultimately make more sense to speak of cosmopolitan English Studies or is it the case that Clifford's notion of a 'discrepant cosmopolitanism' refers more accurately to our current perception of English Studies since this recognizes, to some degree, that a British *ur*-version of English Studies is no longer an automatic reference point? While there remain conferences and networks which bind together the transnational diaspora of English Literature scholars, the bases for their existence are hugely varied and not necessarily dominated by questions revolving around nationalisms or processes of decolonization. One might indeed argue that their practices are increasingly recognized to be situated ones and that local exigencies set up the terms under which English Studies may be carried out (Rajan 1993). The abundant historical studies dealing with specific institutions charged with the promulgation of English Studies appear to support this thesis.[8] Looking more closely at the imperial history attached to projects of Anglification one would tend to agree with Gikandi's suggestion that the margins have transformed the centre: that 'in inventing itself, the colonial space would also reinvent the structure and meaning of the core terms of Englishness' (Gikandi 1996: xviii). As exemplified in the work of Bhabha there is general agreement that the colonizing masters were inextricably bound up with their colonized subjects and that a mechanism of mutual constitution was involved. In her painstaking analysis of the workings of English Studies in India, for example, Gauri Viswanathan uncovers an imaginary Indian subject produced by the colonizer and thus clearly serving the colonizer's interests. She depicts the curriculum itself as 'process and discourse' rather than an 'essentialized entity' and points out that 'English literature as subject existed in the colonies long before it appeared in at home' (Viswanathan 1989: 3). The ideological baggage carried by these curricula and texts served to camouflage the imperial process: 'The English literary text, functioning as a surrogate Englishman in his highest and most perfect state, becomes a mask for economic exploitation, so successfully camouflaging the material activities of the colonizer . . .' (Viswanathan 1989: 20). Simon Gikandi goes so far as to suggest that these implications are with us still and that even the supposedly oppositional 'postcolonial project seeks, unconsciously perhaps, to complete the project of colonialism' (Gikandi 1996: 16). This approach has been offered by a number of critics of postcolonialism who see the fixation on the colonial moment inherent in postcolonial studies as precluding any recognition of truly independent decolonization or the emergence of unique national cultures and languages. Hence, perhaps, the contemporary shift to analytical frameworks of globalization and diaspora in which the imperial, colonizing agents are displaced by transformed and hybrid nation states in turn to be shunted aside by transnational corporations who prefer to invest in 'flexible citizens' (Ong 1999).

Whereas Viswanathan exposed the mechanism of historical English Studies in India, one might speculate as to how such a process functioned in the settler colonies. While English, and particularly English Studies, consistently remain an ideological technology, the material upon which they were imposed was clearly not quite the same as in India or Africa. What, in particular, might the experience of English mean to those who migrated out of England, whether as convicts or free settlers, and were caught up in the imperial process to some degree after it had lost its purpose and purchase? That process is described by Edward Said as the final convulsions of 'a wounded colonial power' where the arbitrariness of the technology was exacerbated by the fact that its teleology had vanished (Said 1999: 186).

In an interesting contrast to postcolonial studies which, in their analysis of ethnography and anthropology, helped identify the visual register as dominant in the colonizing process,[9] it was clear that this ideological technology of subjectivity did not necessarily appear in the visual register; it dealt with the censorship or shaping which continued below the surface of the skin, the abrasive grain of English on a colonized body which had been structured by another language producing in turn the array of 'dialects, creoles and pidgins' which have more recently and respectfully been resurfacing as 'englishes'. Here we return to the question of somatic affect. One of the ways to approach English from another angle than the manifestation of the visual is to consider it as a type of technology, not simply of subjectivity in general but of corporeality in a specific sense. The argument in the remainder of the chapter is that learning to speak English structured, or at least choreographed, bodies in certain ways. This approach can take a variety of forms, for example conjures up the relatively familiar territory, to those teaching postcolonial studies, of the absurdities of imposing a foreign poetics or imaginary landscape on whatever outer reaches of the empire one inhabits. Edward Chamberlin provides an excellent encapsulation of this psychic colonization:

> . . . the Windermere I knew well, high in the Rocky mountains, was nothing like the place that Wordsworth wrote about, and certainly had never seen a daffodil. All of the institutions that influenced me, from the schools I attended to the radio programs I listened to, were part of a language located somewhere else: in southern England, for my teachers; somewhere in the middle of the Atlantic, for the announcers on the Canadian Broadcasting Corporation, who spoke a language never heard elsewhere, or since . . . Some of these languages did not belong to anybody. None belonged to me.
>
> (Chamberlin 1993: 272)

Jamaica Kincaid's essay 'On Seeing England for the First Time' gives an account of a complementary physical colonization: the material effects on the body of this impulse to civilize the recalcitrant colonial subject by replicating it out of 'English' ingredients, no matter how unsuitable:

> The very idea of the meal itself, breakfast, and its substantial quality and quantity was an idea from England; we somehow knew that in England they began the day with this meal called breakfast and a proper breakfast was a big breakfast. No one I knew liked eating so much food so early in the day; it made us feel sleepy, tired. But this breakfast business was Made in England like almost everything else that surrounded us, the exceptions being the sea, the sky, and the air we breathed.
>
> (Kincaid 1991: 33)

Indeed, it was probably the very unsuitability of these ingredients that helped render them more mysteriously tyrannical and authoritative.

Focusing on the diasporic subject cut adrift from the naturalized bonds of city or nation state helps isolate the concerns of affect, the psychic phenomena which are linked to corporeal reactions (Green 1999). While it is inherently impossible to gain direct access to unconscious processes, there exists quite a complex variety of narratives dealing with linguistic affect, often, though not exclusively, contained in autobiographical texts. I turn now to three memoirs written by quintessentially globalized exilic subjects who experienced their learning of English in tandem with exposure to English Literature: Edward Said, in Egypt and Palestine and then the United States; Shirley Geok-lin Lim in Malaysia and then the United States; and Eva Hoffman in Poland, then Canada and the United States. All three subjects endure ambivalent responses to the experience, comprising a rebelliousness against the ideological impulse behind the induction into English, more precisely into an imperially-derived pedagogy, at the same time that they are seduced by the aesthetic power of both the language and the texts it has produced. All three express the psychic and the physical effects/affects of exposure to a foreign body of language and writing.

At quite an early point in his recent memoirs, Edward Said makes the telling comment, 'I have never known what language I spoke first, Arabic or English, or which one was really mine beyond any doubt' (Said 1999: 4). He goes on to rationalize this fact as the reason for the pervasive sense throughout his life that he had been forced to move among various identities. Attending an English prep school in Cairo he is instilled with the certainty that 'school teachers were supposed to be English' (Said 1999: 36). He receives there a grounding in what he somewhat sardonically terms 'English glory', comprising English history, at the expense of his own Arabic traditions (Said 1999: 39). The results at that early stage of education are a fatalistic recognition of a racialized hierarchy in which his own inferiority is established (Said 1999: 44–5). As a teenager, attending Victoria College in Cairo, he finds that Arabic becomes a refuge in which to exercise rebellion, an outlaw language, in the face of a continuing indoctrination in the English language and Englishness:

> The students were seen as paying members of some putative colonial elite that was being schooled in the ways of a British imperialism that had already expired, though we did not fully know it . . . We were tested as if we were English boys, trailing behind an ill-defined and always out-of-reach goal from class to class, year to year, with our parents worrying along with us . . . we felt that we were inferiors pitted against a wounded colonial power that was dangerous and capable of inflicting harm on us, even as we felt compelled to study its language and its culture as the dominant one in Egypt.
>
> (Said 1999: 185–6)

Said's father attempted to instil notions of an alternative American identity, since he himself had spent time in the United States and established a business enterprise there. Later, indeed, Said continues his education in the United States and discovers a different technology of subjectivity, one not so clearly linked to an imperial tradition of colonial repression but without a doubt directed towards assimilation to a specific cultural model, 'a more subtle form of moral pressure than what I had encountered in years of often brutal confrontation with British authority in my Egyptian and Palestinian schools. There at least you knew *they* were your enemies' (Said 1999: 229). Insofar as a body is deployed in those memoirs, it is one rendered out of place (as the title of the memoirs emphasizes) and made timid by encounters which include being caned as a bewildered eight-year-old by the Headmaster of the prep school. The reminiscence is oddly tied to Said's later discovery that the man was a minor poet, which led him to track down some of his rather sentimental poetry – an early link between linguistic, cultural and corporeal disciplines in which assumptions concerning the civilizing effects of poetry are undercut by the memory of corporeal punishment. It includes being accused of trespass (when he cuts across the outer fields of the British Gezira Club) by the father of a school mate and being informed that Arabs were not permitted on the premises (Said 1999: 44). The Althusserian interpellation 'Arab' structures subjectivity in mysterious and compelling ways thereafter.[10] There are further numerous episodes of bullying whose idiosyncratic details add to the many accounts of the English public school experience so successfully transplanted into the various outposts of the English empire.

Like Said, the academic and poet Shirley Geok-lin Lim describes in her memoirs a pedagogical formation which passed through both British and American stages. Her early education took place in Malaya, initially in a convent school where, as with Said's education in 'English glory', the British readers distributed to the class formed the first building blocks in producing those 'mimic men' famously portrayed, as Lim notes with a later consciousness, by V. S. Naipaul (Lim 1996: 65). Very soon the young Shirley internalizes an understanding of a racialized hierarchy in which the Malayans were at the bottom and the Eurasians, particularly if they were fair-skinned, were closer to the British pinnacle: 'To every schoolgirl it was obvious that there was something about a white child which made the good nuns benevolent' (Lim 1996: 69). Realizing early that her only way out of the constraints of gender and poverty were to excel in scholastic endeavours, she discovers that, for better or worse, this obstacle course was ultimately in the hands of a set of distant legislators: 'The national standard examinations were set by British teachers and professors and were administered from Cambridge University' (Lim 1996: 84). Although Malaya received its independence in 1957, the change from British Empire to British Commonwealth appeared to be more a continuum than a break (Lim 1996: 117). At the same time that she recognizes, with the knowledge of hindsight, an innate intellectual rebelliousness, she also recalls developing a love of words, even in this language, and that this expresses itself in physical ways: 'The physical sensation of expansion in the chest, even in the head, as I read a profoundly beautiful or mindful poem was conclusively and possessively subjective. The literature may have been of Britain, but my love of literature was outside the empire' (Lim 1996: 120). The seduction of the language itself, a point reiterated by Said in his memoirs as well, is further emphasized in Lim's short essay on Brewer's *Art of Versification*, a book which provided her with an induction into the craft (the animating discipline) of verse (Lim 1994: 3–7). None the less, in spite of the pleasures of language, Lim regrets the 'loss of the potential Malaysian intellectual' (Lim 1996: 87) she might have been able to become; the intellectual possibilities she and others like her possessed were lost to the fledgling postcolonial culture for several generations. In a telling and rhetorically violent passage she describes the ways in which she and her peers were forced to become derivative subjects whose abjected[11] lives were 'mismatched to the well-oiled machinery of the English-language essay. The irony was not that my companions were uninteresting or unlearned but that what they learned was so far removed from their senses that the learning remained separate, unvivified, and undigested: many of them did regurgitate class notes, lectures, and globs of memorized passages for the exams, an undifferentiated vomit of words, dates, ideas and scrambled facts' (Lim 1996: 85–6).

Struggling to gain the cultural capital, in Bourdieu's sense (Bourdieu 1986), of English and Englishness, Lim and her colleagues are constantly reminded that 'this language did not belong to us . . . English was only on loan' (Lim 1996: 121). Embedded in the turbulent politics leading to the 1969 race riots in which her ethnic group, the Chinese Malaysians, were targeted, Lim hangs onto the aesthetic core of art as a way of transcending the continuing and brutal pressures of the political (Lim 1996: 137). In her account the English language provides an alternative to the problematic relations she has with the Hokkien Chinese dialect of her father's family, a language in which she feels alienated and forever trapped in infancy (Lim 1996: 10), and the Malay transmitted by her mother, who eventually abandons the family and becomes erased from its collective history. Malay is thus an abjected mother-tongue and the young Shirley is dubbed a 'Malay devil' by the paternal extended family with whom her own stranded and bankrupt family take refuge briefly during her childhood.

As in the case of Said, circumstances lead her to the United States where she is drawn to study American literature as a way to self-consciously avoid or mediate the imperialist burden associated with English literature in its British incarnation. Paradoxically, she does become embroiled in politics once again when her innate rebelliousness leads her to become a cultural activist as a result of her experiences in the United States as a 'resident alien':

> Unlike the happy immigrant who sees the United States as a vast real-estate advertisement selling a neighborly future, the person who enters the country as a registered alien is neither here nor there. Without family, house, or society, she views herself through the eyes of citizens: guest, stranger, outsider, misfit, beggar . . . A resident alien has walked out of a community of living memory, out of social structures in which her identity is folded . . .

> (Lim 1996: 160)

Isolated and feeling invisible without the anchor of community and family which confers social identity, Lim slowly forges an academic career at the same time that, like Said, she uncovers in the United States a parallel system of assimilatory practices. One of her earliest positions teaching composition at a community college in the Bronx leads her to confront the ways in which the college was 'a holding pen that kept black and brown students out of the established campuses of The City University of New York' (Lim 1996: 170). Eventually she faces the reality that 'I could not reconcile English literature and the deprivations of black and brown students . . . I did not believe that teaching them English grammar was what they deserved' (Lim 1996: 183).

Lim's awareness as cultural activist is nourished by a recognition that, even in the United States, English was employed as a technology which structured the cultural terrain so that the self-defining gaze was always mediated by a cultural legacy which rendered one's own immediate context alien and unworthy. But what about the deeper somatic layers exposed by her account? What corporeal effects does one encounter in English when English becomes a kind of virus inhabiting the body?[12] As Lim puts it: 'Every cultural change is signified through and on the body. Involuntarily the body displays, like a multidimensional, multisensorial screen, the effect of complicated movements across the social keyboard. . . . My Westernization took place in my body' (Lim 1996: 89). Said too speaks of such corporeal manifestations as the resistant movement between languages and notes that it takes him until his sixties to return to Arabic and to take pleasure in it (Said 1999: 198). Such multilingualism establishes a kind of bedrock of resistance in relation to all language or, at least, to the pre-Babel dream of a 'natural' language encompassing and communicating all the nuances of experience which is more easily enjoyed by those who remain monolingual. But multilingual consciousness has its costs, as is more clearly illustrated by the third example.

In the third case we move away from English as linked with a specific imperial history to the manner in which English and English literature function as technology in a more diffused globalized context. Eva Hoffman grew up as a Jew in Poland and eventually moved to Vancouver in her teens. In her memoirs English materializes initially as a kind of fog, preventing access to her precociously developed private self whose interior language increasingly evaporated: 'I'm not filled with language anymore, and have only a memory of fullness to anguish me with the knowledge that, in this dark and empty state, I don't really exist' (Hoffman 1989: 108). As in the case of Lim's experience in the United States, she feels her substance slipping away so that she becomes confined to a spectral existence – both for herself and others. The use of English, located within a particular version of Canadian Englishness, animates her body in new ways where she learns not to gesticulate too much, to sit on her hands when she's talking and to tone down her expression of emotions (Hoffman 1989: 146). Well-meaning older women take her aside and teach her to groom and dress her body in a particular manner and to assimilate to the local ways of being 'feminine' (Hoffman 1989: 109). At the same time a kind of linguistic corporeal violence is being registered: 'My voice is doing funny things. It does not seem to emerge from the same parts of my body as before. It comes out from somewhere in my throat, tight, thin, and mat – a voice without modulations, dips, and rises that it had before, when it went from my stomach all the way through my head' (Hoffman 1989: 121–2).

Once again, as in the texts of Lim and Said, the inner music of the language eventually exerts its seductions so that gradually Hoffman succumbs to it, though this occurs somewhat belatedly, at the end of successfully completing graduate school. Contemplating T. S. Eliot's 'The Love Song of J. Alfred Prufrock', 'my eye moves over these lines in its accustomed dry silence; and then – as if an aural door had opened of its own accord – I hear their modulations and their quiet undertones . . . now, suddenly I'm attuned . . . to their inner sense' (Hoffman 1989: 186). And this recovery of the lilt or inner music establishes, temporarily at least, the glimpse of a psychic wholeness in which the body moves once more with the easy grace of dance.

The memoir comes full circle when English finally does become the narrator's interior language:

> So that those moments when I'm alone, walking, or letting my thoughts meander before falling asleep, the internal dialogue proceeds in English. I no longer triangulate to Polish as to an authentic criterion, no longer refer back to it as to a point of origin. Still, underneath the relatively distinct monologue, there's an even more interior buzz, as of countless words compressed into an electric blur moving along a telephone wire.

> Occasionally Polish words emerge unbidden from the buzz. They are usually words from the primary palette of feeling.
>
> (Hoffman 1989: 272)

It is a bitter-sweet triumph because in many ways it measures the success of the somatic technology constituted by the learning of English.

What remains? Languages all function as somatic or corporeal technologies and at times, unbidden, the old and discarded spectre of a prior language surfaces in the form of a recurrent fear of speechlessness arising to threaten and, on occasion, to overcome the narrator (Hoffman 1989: 219). Those are the psychic costs whose nature we do not entirely know. Thus it is not simply that (British?) English still functions as reference point for all the 'englishes' operating in a global context rendering them, often, as something which at best provides the exoticism of cultural tourism and at worst furnishes evidence that their version is always dis-eased, inadequate or two-dimensional. As Fishman (1996) points out in the introduction to a recent collection, languages themselves are arguably neutral. However, it needs to be pointed out that one does not ever acquire them outside of social and psychic relations and it is here that matters become more complicated. The somatic affects of discrepant English Studies effect a specific kind of consciousness, particularly when imposed on the existing bedrock of another language and its cultural entourage, of a consciousness of the fragility of all these linguistic symbolic structures. The phobia of aphasia and muteness lurks as a result of this exposure or submission to another language and culture. The unconscious ease of moving within a language and culture can never be recovered, although, somewhat enviously, one imagines that one glimpses it at times:

> Apparently, skilled chefs can tell whether a dish from some foreign cuisine is well cooked even if they have never tasted it and don't know the genre of cooking it belongs to . . . As I listen to people speaking that foreign tongue, English, I can hear when they stumble or repeat the same phrase too many times . . . I can tell, in other words, the degree of their ease or disease, the extent of authority that shapes the rhythm of their speech. That authority – in whatever dialect, in whatever variant of the mainstream language – seems to me to be something we all desire.
>
> (Hoffman 1989: 123–4)

The Lacanian linguistic turn in psychoanalysis has focused attention on the psychic and corporeal effects of language. But the universalizing impulse of psychoanalysis has made it difficult to analyse the affect of specific languages. This chapter is a modest attempt to suggest that these details may have more importance than we imagined. While the psychic and corporeal splits occasioned by the acquisition of a second (or more) language have a general effect of the kind which haunts Eva Hoffman's narrator, these cannot be attached to English alone. However, as this chapter argues, there are also very particular effects and disjunctions caused by the learning of English and its attachment to the ideological baggage of English Studies. As we contemplate the global future of English, in the wake of all we have learnt about its colonial history, it may now be the time to delve more profoundly into the local and somatic affects of discrepant English Studies and the detailed ways these function as technologies of subjectivity across all those multicultural societies haunted by their specific colonialisms.

Part II
Abjected bodies

4   A text with subtitles

Performing ethnicity

> ... what is 'performed' works to conceal, if not disavow, what remains opaque, unconscious, unperformable.
>
> (Butler 1993: 234)

The positioning of minority cultures is symptomatic of the paradox at the heart of national cultures. Do they 'belong' in terms of assimilation and appropriation or do they constitute the exclusionary framework of 'foreign bodies' which both encloses and defines a national culture? In *Bodies That Matter* Judith Butler speaks of the abject in spatial terms as 'those "unlivable" and "uninhabitable" zones of social life which are nevertheless densely populated by those who do not enjoy the status of the subject, but whose living under the sign of the "unlivable" is required to circumscribe the domain of the subject . . . against which – and by virtue of which – the domain of the subject will circumscribe its own claim to autonomy and to life' (Butler 1993: 3). In the settler colony of Australia, the issue of minority literatures, for the most part, continues to function as irritant to those who maintain a particular version of the institution of Australian literature. After all, this cultural formation was really only consolidated in the 1970s by those left-wing intellectuals who managed to place class and, to some degree, gender at the centre of these definitions. Thus Australian literature emerges in the latter part of the twentieth century as respectably adorned with working-class and women writers. There was, however, little acknowledgment of the impact of post-Second World War immigration which redefined, in retrospect, the 'always/ already' diverse character of Australia. As has been argued in the earlier chapters, it has been difficult to gain any serious recognition for writers from those sixty or more groups who wrote both in English and other languages but whose writings were, until recently, neither systematically nor comprehensively collected or studied as a significant part of the Australian literary heritage (Gunew 1994a). The difficulties have continued to perplex critics in the field who have had to deal not so much with any version of 'backlash' as with an entrenched refusal to take minority cultures seriously. Indeed, the small gains that have been made, for example within the ambiguous orbit of 'multiculturalism' in both its state and 'community' manifestations, have provoked consistent 'backlash' reactions to attempts to introduce concepts of cultural and racialized difference, or efforts to illustrate the hybridized nature of all cultural productions (Gunew 1993c). A major literary controversy in Australia during the 90s highlights some of the complexities involved in these debates.

In September 1995, *Meanjin*, one of the oldest cultural journals in Australia, published a short story called 'Pieces of the Puzzle' by Helen Demidenko (1995a). Ostensibly there was nothing remarkable here, merely that in this journal, too, 'ethnic minority authors' were finally appearing as a matter of course. For those alert to such symptoms, here might be another tiny register that things were changing in the institutional networks which comprise any national literary formation. As part of setting the context for the story, the first-person narrator states the following:

> It is 1988 and my boyfriend is Croatian. . . . I grow up Ukrainian-Australian. No one has ever heard of my country, much less the enforced famine that killed seven million of its citizens. I do not write this at school. I carry it around in my head. This history is my cultural baggage.
>
> (Demidenko 1995a: 433)

Later in the story an archetypal Australian barbecue is the setting for an encounter between the narrator's uncle, Pavel Hryniuk, and an Australian neighbour, Keith McGuire:

> 'I am vairy bat person. Waffen-SS'.
> 'Look mate, I don't give a shit what uniform you wore, as long as it wasn't bloody Japanese!'
>
> (Demidenko 1995a: 434)

The story culminates in a fight between Pavel's son Vik and a school-fellow, Solomon Blatsky:

> People take sides. The halfdozen skips in the crowd look bewildered. Miryana stands behind Solomon. So do the rest of the Serbs. Vik looks wounded. Miryana was his girl until five minutes ago. . . . One of the skip girls yells and pleads. Her face is dusty and tears have left glistening snail trails on her cheeks. 'This is Australia, for fuck's sake. Stop it! Please stop!'
>
> (Demidenko 1995a: 436)

A footnote explains that 'skip' means the child of two Australian parents. The reader notes that the story divides its characters between 'Australians' who are 'skips' and other children who are identified as Ukrainian, Croatian, Jewish, although since they are growing up in Australia one could be forgiven for imagining that they too are Australian. While the story appears to suggest, through Keith's comment, that intolerance and racism are as rife amongst the 'skips' as the newcomers, the final section and the comment by the 'skip girl' seem to indicate otherwise, that these immigrant children are perpetuating hatreds which have no place in the new country.

In the same issue of *Meanjin*, and preceding this story, an essay by Morag Fraser (1995) titled 'The Begetting of Violence' describes the various types of international violence around events such as the O. J. Simpson trial, and suggests that Australians have 'a compensating advantage' in that they 'start off without a reflex recourse to vendetta' (Fraser 1995: 419). Fraser suggests that violence, according to US analysts, results from a mixture of the environmental and the biochemical (Fraser 1995: 420). Such triggers, she maintains, have been inadequately acknowledged and debated in the Australian public domain; hence the lack of understanding which greeted the publication of Helen Demidenko's novel *The Hand That Signed the Paper* (1994b). After a summary of the controversy she suggests that 'as it stands the voices from *outside the Ukrainian circle* are unconvincing. Demidenko herself admits to a failure there, a flatness, a retreat into stereotype. But it is not Jews alone who are schematized. So are Demidenko's Germans . . . ' (Fraser 1995: 425. My emphasis). Fraser ends her essay with the statement that 'the novel will prompt necessary questions about the cultural pathologies that spawn violence' (Fraser 1995: 429). At the back of this issue of *Meanjin* in the 'Notes on Contributors' there is a hasty and inexpertly interpolated note on Helen Demidenko stating that: 'About the time *Meanjin* went to press, she changed her name back to Helen Darville' (583). Clearly there were mysteries here which required further investigation, and Morag Fraser's suggestion that this novel gives an insight into 'cultural pathologies' relevant to Australia acquires, perhaps, a different meaning to the one suggested before the author 'Helen Demidenko' was found to be not quite the authentic 'ethnic spokesperson', fearlessly posing questions about 'cultural pathologies', she appeared to be.

The question of authenticity continues to haunt the reception of minority writings. In the struggle for minority rights and the battles over who controls representation there are those who take the position that only members of such minority groups have the authority, or at least moral right, to represent themselves. But who, institutionally speaking, decides the group membership and who interprets and legislates whether this authenticity has been achieved? Moreover, in a poststructuralist context of decentred subjectivity, one might argue that no one can fully represent anything. These days such questions are indicated by terms such as identity politics (where representation often means not so much 'depiction' as 'delegation' or 'speaking for') and in literary discussions by the 'appropriation of voice' issue aired in Canada some years ago.[1]

To summarize the controversy in question here: the first novel of what appeared to be the work of a young Australian-Ukrainian author, Helen Demidenko, won a major literary prize reserved for first novels – the Vogel award (1993). Her novel purported to be triggered by the war crimes trials that had surfaced in Australia as they had in other parts of the world. The novel's narrator, somewhat akin to the narrator in the short story described above, is a young Australian-Ukrainian woman, Fiona Kovalenko, whose uncle (and possibly father) is threatened with being tried for war crimes. She discovers some old photos implicating her uncle and father in the Holocaust. This in turn leads her to try and understand how people she had long loved and respected could have committed these deeds in the past. It leads her back to the 'evidence' in the pre-war Stalinist Soviet era where the Ukrainian famine is depicted in all its horrors. The implication throughout is that the 'Bolsheviks' who carried out these atrocities in the Ukraine at a local level were also 'Jews'. The terms 'Jews' and 'Bolsheviks' are consistently coupled throughout the book. In other words, the suggestion is that the hatred fuelled by the Stalinist measures, allegedly perpetrated by Jews, were the grounds for Ukrainian involvement in the Holocaust, seen here as a kind of reprisal. The implication is that these 'explained' the enthusiastic participation of figures such as 'Ivan the Terrible' at Treblinka.

Reception of the book was relatively muted until the author received the country's biggest literary prize, the Miles Franklin award, given for outstanding novels describing Australian life.[2] Meanwhile Demidenko had been gilding the 'ethnic' lily, appearing in 'ethnic' costume, signing her book with Ukrainian inscriptions and even performing Ukrainian songs and dances (Roberts and Makler 1995). When she received the Miles Franklin Award, the book came under more intensive scrutiny.

The first controversy generated around this text was that it was inherently anti-Semitic (Legge 1995; *Australian Book Review* #173). Readers appeared divided between saying that presenting or describing characters who were motivated by anti-Semitism was the same as condoning it and those who argued that this was an honest attempt by another generation to understand from within the twisted logic which led up to these horrors. This was Morag Fraser's line. Thus readers were split between calling this a very brave book which tackled difficult issues which needed to be aired in Australian debates and those who condemned it as perpetuating scurrilous myths. On the latter side historian Robert Manne (1995) wrote a long account in the national press detailing the various historical errors in the novel. He pointed out that Jews had been purged from the ranks once Stalin came to power; that the idea that Bolshevik and Jew were linked was in fact the cornerstone of Nazi propaganda and that anti-Semitism in the Ukraine and other parts of Eastern Europe did after all pre-date the era of the Second World War and so could not simply be 'explained' by the immediate pre-war events. These critiques were echoed by others (Christoff 1995; Henderson 1995a; 1995b; Indyk 1995a). Much of the argument rested on whether this text purported to be fact (or history) or whether it could claim the licence of fiction.

Helen Demidenko meanwhile defended herself by saying that the book was based on the oral evidence of her own family and indeed that members of her family had been killed by 'Jewish Bolsheviks', '. . . most of my father's family, including my grandfather, were killed by Jewish Communist Party officials in Vynnstia' (Demidenko 1995b). Thus she herself, at this stage, reached for a legitimation based on the 'facts' of history, albeit a history fashioned from the vagaries of personal memory.

The arguments to illustrate the novel's inherent anti-Semitism may be summarized in the following ways. There does seem to be little distance between the implied author (who focalizes much of the historical 'evidence') and the contemporary narrator 'Fiona'. Nor is there much guidance as to any moral condemnation this contemporary narrator might offer. Robert Manne (1995), for example, called it 'the coldest book I have ever read' and was echoed by many others. In an early defence of the technique, Demidenko argued that she deliberately attempted to be 'amoral' and not to provide a 'neat moral' (1995b), as though the two were synonymous. She also stated, in the same piece, that she regretted the two-dimensional characters she created, but offers this in connection with the German characters and not the Jewish ones and certainly not the Ukrainian ones. Reading through the text one notes that the term 'Jews and Communists' is a refrain constantly used in conjunction and that the link is never problematized (Demidenko 1994a: 9, 11, 15, 16, 28, 29, 32, 43, 45, 46, 65, 90, 96, 108, 117). If one were to argue that the book recirculates myths and a version of history which has a certain purchase in a range of ethnic groups in Australia, then this is, alas, quite probably true. However one would have to add the important rider that this anti-Semitic set of myths is retold across the spectrum of Australian ethnic groups, and that it includes Anglo-Celtic Australians who have a share in this exchange and indeed have their own idiosyncratic contributions to make to anti-Semitic propaganda.

As part of this debate, there were comments somewhat more direct than Morag Fraser's implication concerning 'cultural pathologies'. In other words, it elicited familiar murmurs among the ethnic majority groups that this book simply confirmed their fears regarding the pathologies residing in ethnic minorities, which were always threatening to break out into the larger body politic. Indeed the Miles Franklin judges' report stated that 'Helen Demidenko's first novel displays a powerful literary imagination coupled to a strong sense of history, and brings to light *a hitherto unspeakable aspect of Australian migrant experience*' (*Australian Book Review* #173: 19. My emphasis). It became increasingly clear that what was in the book was already less important than its reception and the ways in which this reception catalogued a number of the problems bedevilling the reading of minority literatures.

The controversy took a new twist when it was suddenly revealed that 'Helen Demidenko' was really Helen Darville, the daughter of two British immigrants who had no Ukrainian connections whatsoever (Roberts and Makler 1995). How did this affect the evaluation of the book? If it was solely regarded as fiction (as placed in binary opposition to the notional 'facts' of history) then it was, if anything, an even more significant imaginative creation than had hitherto been thought. If it was considered to be 'faction' (part fiction, part fact) then its legitimacy (the 'real' story of a 'hitherto unspeakable aspect of Australian history') was seriously undermined. One press commentator, Luke Slattery (1995), stated accurately enough that the 'Demidenko affair tells us rather a lot about ourselves' and then elaborated that 'we have been desperate for the authentic authorial voice of contemporary multiculturalism'.[3] David Marr (1995), one of 'Demidenko's' supporters in the controversy over the novel's anti-Semitism, wrote somewhat nostalgically in the face of the revelations, trying to recapture his earlier response, that 'I am moved by the *simplicity* of the figures on this Ukrainian landscape' (my emphasis). Helen Darville now maintained that she had encountered Ukrainian witnesses in her past and that their accounts had haunted her and that this had fuelled her treatment of events (Darville 1995). As tireless investigative reporters from her home town of Brisbane sifted the evidence, it was revealed that the author had a long history of 'passing' as an 'ethnic', although her specific allegiances had been all over the map, so to speak, ranging from Czechoslovakian to Hungarian, etc. (Bentley 1995; Dibben 1995). In the wake of the intense media coverage in Australia, the news was rather gleefully picked up by the international press.[4] She was also accused, at various stages, of plagiarism, but acquitted, although some of the cited evidence, including passages from Toni Morrison's work, would perhaps lead one to less charitable conclusions than those arrived at by the publisher's lawyers (Peel 1995). Increasingly, both author and book were perceived as a hoax and were discredited accordingly. Along the way various earlier supporters of the book within the literary establishment also had their reputations tarnished (Henderson 1995c). Others no doubt sighed with relief that they had not become involved. When the grounds of literary evaluations are examined by the predominantly anti-intellectual public eye, they are often perceived as absurd or at least as not having quite the absolute authority some might imagine. Certainly, the judges of the Miles Franklin award and those who had awarded her the prestigious Australian Literature Society gold medal were heavily criticized (Indyk 1995b; Daniel 1995; Wark 1995). In relation to this last award, a familiar refrain appeared in the judges' report: 'A text that positions itself within the wider questions posed by multiculturalism, it resists monolithic assumptions about culture and identity – assumptions that produced the horrors it so chillingly describes' (De Groen *et al.* 1995). Those who had previously argued that this was an anti-Semitic text would no doubt maintain that the text reinforced rather than resisted 'monolithic assumptions about culture and identity'.

In a recent and thought-provoking analysis of literary hoaxes Ken Ruthven contends that 'since what a society values will show up obliquely in what it rejects, reactions to literary forgeries illuminate perceptions of literariness' (Ruthven 2001: 3). A number of aspects make this story very interesting to those labouring in the field of ethnic minority literary criticism and their relationship to 'literariness'. Minority writers, as such, are invariably confined to the issue of their 'identity', even in a poststructuralist world of decentred subjectivity. They function as what Gayatri Spivak (1988) has termed the 'native informant', with an unproblematically coherent subjectivity projected upon them. They are constructed as 'insider' sources for 'information retrieval' rather than being deemed capable of postmodernist writing. In short, their ability to produce 'textuality' or to play textual games is rarely countenanced. As well they are legitimated in large part by their 'eye-witness' accounts of certain minority histories which also confine them to realist genres and, as I have argued in the past, they are read more for sociological evidence than for literary merit (Gunew 1994a). This is not to devalue the important testimonies (based on oral material) which have been recorded by minority writers but simply to suggest that this should not be the only interpretative lens applied to them. However, what the Demidenko/Darville case seems to illustrate is that we are concerned here with authenticity in terms of the performance of 'ethnicity'.

A number of models of performance in recent theoretical debates are available to us for understanding this bizarre episode in Australian literary history. Marjorie Garber sees cross-dressing and 'passing' as contributing to the deconstruction of gender through its excesses or over-determinations, 'Gender here exists only in representation – or performance. This is the scandal of transvestism – that transvestism tells the truth about gender' (Garber 1992: 250). When one looks at her analysis of David Hwang's play *M. Butterfly* and the notorious case on which it is based, there are some interesting parallels with the Demidenko performance. In the playwright's own words, the play is based on the following incident: 'A friend asked, had I heard about the French diplomat who'd fallen in love with a Chinese actress, who had subsequently turned out to be not only a spy, but a man?' (Hwang 1988a). Demidenko/Darville too could be described as a spy who 'cross-dresses' to infiltrate 'ethnic' circles and to bring back dispatches to the Anglo-Celtic majority who are not, of course, labeled as ethnic.[5] We note, for example, the comments by Slattery and Marr above. But there is also something more profound about this performance than merely putting on a costume in the superficial sense. Helen Darville, as has been pointed out, had a history of 'ethnic' cross-dressing and, as Garber speculates, in many of the studies of transvestism no one really looked closely at the figure of the transvestite in terms of 'the fact of transvestism as both a personal and a political, as well as an aesthetic and theoretical, mode of self-construction' (Garber 1992: 236). But what was the nature of the 'personal and political' investment here? Clues are found in the latter part of Garber's chapter. For example there is a moment in *M. Butterfly* when Song Liling (the transvestite) states that 'only a man knows how a woman should act' (Hwang 1988a: 63). It is interesting to substitute 'ethnic' here, implying that only those who are the 'non-ethnic' audience for the spectacle of ethnicity know how an 'ethnic' should act in order to produce that spectacle, that theatrical display, 'authentically'. This parallels the motif, suggested in the play, that Song Liling also performs the role of the perfect or idealised 'Oriental woman' and that Gallimard is ignorant, for example, of the genre within which he first encounters Song Liling, namely the

Peking Opera. His profound colonialist ignorance of a particular cultural tradition, within which men traditionally perform the female roles, provides the necessary conditions for the existence of the idealization of the conflated Oriental women.[6] In like fashion one might suggest that lack of knowledge of any of the details of ethnic differences (languages, history, etc.) provides the very conditions for the acceptable construction of ethnicity in the framework of official or state multiculturalism as a system of surveillance and control in the Foucaultian sense. Garber also quotes Hwang in an interview as stating that: 'A real woman can only be herself, but a man, because he is presenting an idealization, can aspire to the idea of the perfect woman' (Garber 1992: 246). Precisely, and so it is with ethnicity and its idealizations. Thus we could of course substitute ethnicity for Garber's earlier quotation (Garber 1992: 250) so that it reads: 'Ethnicity here exists only in representation – or performance. This is the scandal of transvestism – that transvestism tells the truth about ethnicity'. As a connoisseur of ethnicity, Helen Darville merely wished to perform the idealized or perfect 'ethnic'.

But let us now examine some other material evidence. The cover of Darville/Demidenko's book presents a hint of Cyrillic script in the font but is general enough to incorporate as well the whiff of German Gothic script. The muted background of a wheat field connotes both history (the sepia tone) and signals that wheat links the histories of Australia and the Ukraine through postwar immigration. The iconic author-goddess (pale-skinned with long white-blonde hair) appears in numerous newspaper photos in 'ethnic' dress (not just any Ukrainian blouse but one from Kiev)[7] and performs Ukrainian dances as well as sending cards and inscribing books in Ukrainian. Inside the book as part of the prefatory pages there is a Ukrainian glossary, as there is for the story quoted earlier. This is indeed a text with subtitles. 'Helen Demidenko' gave the Australian public everything it wanted, including the parade of pathologies – anti-Semitism and those festering wounds (old rivalries) that all right-thinking Australians know lie behind the costumes and the cooking which continue to be the acceptable face of multiculturalism.[8]

The props by now are well-established for ventriloquizing 'ethnicity'. What counts as 'ethnic' are: the foreign name; the 'un-Australian' history; the first-person narrator delivering an authentic story, the alleged eye-witness accounts underpinning and mediating the foreign. The history is suitably simplified into binary oppositions in which the characters remain two-dimensional because this is, of course, not where the complexities of 'real life' are played out. The sense of a wider community is also absent because this would complicate the essential(ist) frame of reference. By now these spectacles have been rehearsed so many times that many of those designated 'ethnics' in the prevailing paradigm have internalized them. After all, this is the only space available to them in the staging of Australian culture. It may be a small space and the genre is embarrassingly outmoded, but one takes what one can get. The Australian-Ukrainian community were also, it seems, unwittingly complicit players in the debacle.[9]

One way of situating these debates around 'cultural ventriloquism' is as an 'appropriation of voice' issue. This was a major point of contention in Canada some years ago and dealt in the main with debates over what was seen as the appropriation of First Nations Canadian voices by non-native writers such as W. P. Kinsella and Anne Cameron who wrote texts set amongst these communities purporting to incorporate these viewpoints.[10] In other words even relatively benign representations of minority groups contribute to stereotyping. Calling it ventriloquism accentuates the power relations involved and certainly raises questions about whose voices we are hearing and who the 'we' are. Whose voice did Australian readers, 'inside' and 'outside' ethnicity, believe they were hearing? Who, for that matter, is the implied reader inside the text? The narrator is a first-person one and traditionally there is not much of a gap between such a narrator and an implied reader. As 'Demidenko' stated in an early interview, 'A lot of Ukrainian families don't want to own up to their pasts' (Demidenko 1994b), and the moral dimension she ventriloquized was of course taken up by the Miles Franklin judges in their comments that she bravely represented the 'unspeakable aspect of Australian migrant experience'.

If anything, the controversy reiterated the fact that ethnic minority writings are read in a two-dimensional way in Australia for their authentic, and preferably 'simple', representation of the migrant experience (Marr 1995). In other words, those folk who came to Australia carried with them a certain foreign and exotic history which Australian readers could access as a bargain cultural tourism event. If a name signals a non-'skip' background (to borrow from the idiomatic speech reported in 'Demidenko's' short story), it is read for its authentic insights about being a migrant – nothing else. In other words this reading position is a way of reducing and trivializing a creative text into a piece of sociological data. Less benignly, there is the sense that ethnic minority writers are read to reconfirm views on inherited and imported pathologies, thus ensuring that the nation remains morally 'clean', or, in Fraser's terms, continues not to be animated by a 'reflex recourse to vendettas'. Consequently there is the anxiety and the confidence that the 'ethnic ghettos' both harbour but also serve to contain social pathologies. In her influential study *Imperial Leather*, Ann McClintock proposes what she designates as 'abject zones': 'Certain threshold zones become abject zones and are policed with vigour: the Arab casbah, the Jewish ghetto, the Irish slum, the Victorian garret and kitchen, the squatter camp, the mental asylum, the red-light district, and the bedroom' (McClintock 1995: 72). The ethnic ghettos constructed in the Demidenko/Darville case history functioned precisely as those abject zones which helped define the 'clean and proper' constituency of 'authentic' Australia.

Ever aware of their precarious and liminal positioning, spokespeople from the so-called 'ethnic' groups felt that although this seemed to be a fictional text it should none the less get its history right, particularly in the first stage of the affair (*Australian Book Review* #173). Here, too, there was a perception that the writer's function was a representative one (in the sense of delegation or speaking for) and therefore the minority view had to be 'correctly' represented. This kind of censorship (anxiety around representation of the minority) has bedevilled a number of writers who have seen their own communities (often self-appointed) turn against them.[11]

It is instructive to turn once more to Judith Butler and her distinction between performance and the performative. Butler (1993) defines the performative in the following way:

> Performative acts are forms of authoritative speech . . . statements that, in the uttering, also perform a certain action and exercise a binding power . . . performatives tend to include legal sentences, baptisms, inaugurations, declarations of ownership, statements which not only perform an action, but confer a binding power on the action performed.
>
> (Butler 1993: 225)

In this case it is not a subject who acts (or 'represents' herself in the traditional humanist sense) but the discursive and reiterated performance which conveys power to a subject: 'I can only say "I" to the extent that I have first been addressed, and that address has mobilized my place in speech . . . recognition is not conferred on a subject, but forms that subject' (Butler 1993: 225–6). Butler also distinguishes sharply between performance (in Garber's sense) and performativity:

> . . . performance as bounded 'act' is distinguished from performativity insofar as the latter consists in a reiteration of norms which precede, constrain, and exceed the performer . . . what is 'performed' works to conceal, if not disavow, what remains opaque, unconscious, unperformable.
>
> (Butler 1993: 234)

Canonical, national literary traditions might also be described as the constitution of cultural norms which pre-exist individual texts and authors. The 'Helen Demidenko Show' and its gratifying pathologies illustrate that ethnicity, conceived as minority or apprentice national subject-in-process, is always a performance and, significantly, that this performance is framed by a decades-long (in Australia, longer elsewhere) reception of such 'multicultural' texts and subjectivities. This gave 'Demidenko' the authority of not just a credible performance but of performativity.[12]

Reinforcing her point concerning the link between the performative and speech acts which reinscribe 'the law', Judith Butler refers in her study to the famous cartoon of a nurse holding up a baby to its proud parents with the comment, 'It's a lesbian!' (Butler 1993: 232). The 'joke' incorporates a number of elements: that this could be the first question asked about a child; that the information given in this case, concerning sexual preferences, is assigned the same importance as the sex of the child; that one can 'tell' merely by looking that a child contains the seeds of one sexual preference rather than another; that the doxa which blames mothers for the 'pathology' of lesbianism is suspended; and, perhaps most importantly, that the public expression or endorsement by someone invested with this authority decrees a certain kind of identity. The performative is confirmed in its authority by the iterability of the performance. 'It's a boy/girl' confirms the law; 'It's a lesbian/gay' may well disrupt the law, but can only do so as performance, as a joke. One cannot merely don the accoutrements of ethnicity, though this too has its place in these debates, but must, more pervasively, act out doxa, received wisdom as articulated in discourse and rendered prescriptive there. Althusser's notion of interpellation in which a subject (effect) is hailed into being by certain discourses or institutions is analogous here, and Butler draws upon this earlier work. Thus 'speaking as' can only be heard as 'authentically representative' in certain circumstances. In Australia, what is recognized as 'authentic' has in a sense been reduced to an 'identikit' of markers that we have been taught to recognize as 'ethnicity'.

The obligatory performances, in the more usual sense, which attend the promotion of a book carry a further charge of the performative. The author is paraded as part of the context of the text (Oakley 1995). 'It's an ethnic!' is elaborated as a mirror-doubling of author and text. Adherents of New Criticism in the debate tried to maintain that it was only the text they were dealing with, not the biographical context of the author, nor the historical context of the Second World War or of contemporary Australia. At the same time, the judges who had awarded the novel the Miles Franklin award had justified their decision in part with the words that it represented a 'first-hand' account of immigrant history. So among other things, Helen Demidenko/ Darville proved herself to be an extremely adroit reader of the general literary public's consumer habits. She gave them what they wanted and there is no doubt that in terms of market forces her book was a runaway bestseller, something harder to achieve in Australia, with its far more limited publishing industry, than elsewhere.[13]

But what are the further implications? For minority writers, including indigenous writers (Ruthven 2001: 30–1), it has eroded even further any chance to be published (and to be published in their variety) in the immediate future. Any hint of 'ethnicity' will now be drowned in the raucous laughter which has already long attended attempts to legitimate other than the familiar British and Irish-derived versions of Australian writing.[14] In Australian vernacular 'doing a demidenko' has entered the vocabulary.[15] The Australian cultural critic Mackenzie Wark (1995), noted for his abrasive lambasting of traditional cultural pundits and genres, argued that one of the lessons learned from the affair was that the traditional literary establishment should be overhauled. Amongst the more bizarre responses, for example, was the suggestion that the blame could be laid at the doors of English departments for their irresponsible teaching of postmodernist ideas (Daniel 1995).[16]

What might be a response to all this by those trying to argue a case for taking minority writing seriously and being alert to the importance of 'representation' both as depiction and delegation? One solution is not to suppress 'ethnic' histories or to ghettoize them as the foreign or the parasitic but to encourage more informed discussion, to proliferate the information concerning a more comprehensive history of migration. In relation to the question of representation as delegation, while no writer either wishes to be or can be described as being contained by a community, there is a sense that the communities, however broadly defined, carry information about their members and what they are creatively generating. If funding bodies were to attempt to implement specific funding quotas as a way to encourage a wider range of artistic activities, it would make sense to ensure representatives from those diverse groups. From media reports one gathers that such potential conduits of 'ethnic' information did not participate in the judging panels. The judges assumed, in the usual way, that they were knowledgeable enough to evaluate the 'migrant experience' and of course, in the vulgar sense, they were. There are also implications in relation to incorporating minority writings within the teaching of Australian literature so that they are read as complex texts and not exclusively as authentic histories of personal identity or of pathologized group identity, much less as surrogate cultural tours of exotic and foreign places outside the borders of the nation.

To return then to the Butler epigraph at the beginning of this chapter, Helen Darville/Demidenko might be perceived as akin to Butler's heterosexual melancholic, grieving for the loss of, or foreclosure on, the homosexual. Within questions of ethnicity, the unperformable or opaque element which 'Helen Demidenko' performs in Butler's sense of the performative could be construed as the dominant group's own disavowal, precisely, of ethnicity, for ethnicity, as we know, is *not* usually ascribed to those who come to Australia from either Britain or Ireland.[17]

5 Acoustic transgressions and identity politics

A translated performance

I wanted to know Helen's body so well I could climb in and zip up her skin around me.

(Lau 1995: 184)

The notion that we can somehow trust the visible remains a privileged register. The title of the lead article in a relatively recent and controversial issue of the lifestyle magazine *Vancouver* was 'Greetings from Asia Town'; the accompanying visual consisted of a collage of women's faces, both 'Caucasian' and 'Asian', with some dissolving into each other.[1] The accompanying article (North 1996) suggested that Vancouver's population would be half 'Asian' in the next century and that the resultant mix would precipitate either a new 'tribalism' (with its suggestion of gangs and serial conflict) or the kind of 'morphed' assimilation illustrated by the collage. Although the latter might be perceived as the more benign alternative, it could also be read as conjuring the spectre of miscegenation, the blurring of differences as the direct result of genealogical contaminations. Indeed, the visibility of 'difference' is itself registered via these markers of normative racialization. The visible body itself, what the viewer sees in terms of its surface corporeal inscriptions, functions as heuristic device to supposedly 'explain' these differences which in turn evoke both the incommensurabilities of postcolonial theory (the untranslateabilities of cultural difference) and the 'lifestyle incompatibilities' of 'culturalism' or cultural racism. The latter is at the core of what Etienne Balibar has dubbed (rather alarmingly) academic racism, 'theories of academic racism mimic scientific discursivity by basing themselves upon "visible evidence" (whence the essential importance of the stigmata of race and in particular of bodily stigmata) . . . they mimic the way in which scientific discursivity articulates "visible facts" to "hidden causes" . . . a violent *desire for* immediate *knowledge* of social relations' (Balibar 1991: 19). Balibar goes on to elaborate this nexus between racism and the visible as leading to a further convergence of racism and the politics of cultural difference:[2]

Ideologically, current racism, which in France centres upon the immigration complex, fits into a framework of 'racism without races' . . . It is a racism whose dominant theme is not biological heredity but the insurmountability of cultural differences, a racism which, at first sight, does not postulate the superiority of certain groups or peoples in relation to others but 'only' the harmfulness of abolishing frontiers, the incompatibility of life-styles and traditions; in short . . . a differentialist racism.

(Balibar 1991:21)

In an attempt to uncouple the visible from the mechanisms of naturalized racism (as described above) I wanted to find a way to take into consideration another of the senses, that of hearing. As noted, the register of the visible permeates much current theory but the aural dimension, including the category of voice and, for example, accent, has remained somewhat under-theorized. This train of thought suggested that classical western opera might represent a particularly fertile field as well as the genre of the conference presentation itself, where these speculations were first aired. In an exploratory effort to investigate these fields, I 'staged' a performance piece dealing with the first novel of Canadian poet Evelyn Lau.[3] Clearly the attempt to separate the visual from the aural functions more clumsily in print and is symptomatic as well of the intractable elements of translation at the heart of all cross-cultural and, for that matter, cross-disciplinary work. On the other hand, an alertness to ways in which translation is intrinsic to many of these debates is also signalled by the sometimes awkward transitions between the 'here' of the conference performance and its other temporalities when translated to the conference publication (which traditionally expunges any reference to the original context and delivery). I will therefore try to evoke the interpretive strategy for this endeavour while at the same time attempting to foreground its limitations.[4]

Working against the usual aural expectations set up by a conference delivery, the introductory *mise-en-scène* (an obligatory exercise when minority or non-canonical writers are being used) deliberately excluded my reading voice when, for the first fifteen minutes, a series of overhead transparencies were projected which began with extracts from Lau's novel (Lau 1995: 184; 189–90), from one short story (Lau 1993: 50), followed by the cover of her second collection of poems *Oedipal Dreams* (Lau 1992) with its iconic portrait of the artist. The fourth transparency commenting, amongst other things, on this cover was from a piece by Canadian critic Misao Dean:

Evelyn Lau's picture on the cover of *Oedipal Dreams* is a stark white mask, heavily marked with eyeliner and lipstick in order to evoke the classic female face of Chinese opera. Sold under the sign of the 'oriental girl', who is stereotypically both the mincing and modest virgin and the mysterious and sexually skilled courtesan, Lau's books are marketed in a way that evokes both racist and sexist stereotypes.

Lau disclaims responsibility for this public image . . . 'I like the fact that the photographs don't look like me as a person, because I wouldn't want to be walking down the street and be instantly recognizable. So there's definitely an element of disguise there too'.

(Dean 1995: 24–5)

The fifth transparency was from an interview with the Canadian journalist Jan Wong:

> Evelyn Lau is wearing a baggy oatmeal sweater. So it's not immediately apparent she is one of the few surgically unassisted Chinese women in the world to require a DD-cup bra. . . .
>
> But back to Lau's past. Now, I left my comfortable Montreal home at 19 to voluntarily haul pig manure in China during the Cultural Revolution. But I have trouble understanding why someone so smart would drop out of school and run away from home at 14 and end up as a junkie-whore. Yes, it's hard to be the dutiful daughter of immigrants from China and Hong Kong, the kind who consider friends a frivolity and an 89 per cent exam mark a failure . . . But I'm a parent now. Millions of Canadians have overcome such traumas, if that is the word, without self-indulgent melt-downs.

(Wong 1997: A11)

The final transparency was accompanied by the first moment of sound in the presentation consisting of an extract from the soundtrack of the film, *The Diary of Evelyn Lau*, made of Lau's first text, the autobiographically-based *Runaway: Diary of a Street Kid* (Lau 1989). The extract chosen dealt with a heuristic moment in the film when the protagonist experiences an apparent epiphany in the consulting room of her analyst:

Evelyn:	It's like all the stuff about how great you are. It gets to me you know, with Larry, with all of them. And when they come it's like I've done something right for once. Right from the beginning I felt that, that I'm good for something, that I belong.
Dr Hightower:	Go on.
Evelyn:	In prostitution, I mean, I can fulfill someone. Here, right now! Which I could never do with my parents.
Dr Hightower:	Yes.
Evelyn:	I could never . . . I could never do with my parents. Does it matter if it's only a john? I mean it's somebody. I mean, at home I could never please them. I could get 95 or do 6 hours of housework and never go out. Always hoping for something, you know. Some sign of love. But nothing was ever good enough. Dad left me and she, she would have a ruler, or her hand, or her mouth. I never had a mouth. She called me lazy,

                    fat, ugly, stupid slut . . . every day. And I swallowed it in. And
                    hated myself. O.K., O.K. maybe they do treat me like a piece
                    of meat on the street but at least I'm appreciated there. Oth-
                    erwise I'm nobody.
Dr Hightower: You're not nobody Evelyn. That's what they taught you but
                    it's not true . . . No!
Evelyn: No. I just wish they could have liked me for who I am. . .Yeah.
                    Yes . . . Thanks.

                                                                (Gunnarsson 1993)

At this point my own voice was introduced in a series of questions: What
happens when the visual intervenes, in print or the mind's eye of the reader,
when we join the voice to a body, have the voice issue from what has been
coded as a 'visible minority' face? How might one circumvent the 'disguise' of
the stereotype (to echo Lau), the 'orientalist' camouflage Lau's public persona
apparently adopts so that her private self will not be recognized in the streets?
One way to arrive at an answer is to consider what we as readers or audience
desire from the so-called minority writer who becomes constructed as part of
the contemporary quest for 'cultural difference' and who is often covertly
racialized (or sexualized) as 'deviant'. The term 'desire' and its link with
'differential racism' (as described above) suggests the field of psychoanalysis
for, as Ali Rattansi, following Bhabha, has pointed out: 'The ambivalence of
racism . . . is particularly open to psychoanalytic interpretation for it is in
psychoanalysis that the notion has its strongest roots. . . . [it] does not reduce
all racisms merely to supposedly eternal and universal psychic mechanisms'
(Rattansi 1995: 272–3).[5] Pursuing this train further, the question of desire in
psychoanalysis is posed, for example, by Slavoj Zizek: 'The original question
of desire is not directly "What do I want?" but "What do others want from me?
What do they see in me? What am I for others?"' (Zizek 1996: 117). How, in
other words, can we as readers *not* project the expectation that Lau should
'inform' us about what would, in Canada, be termed her visible minority
status, acknowledge it in some way and, if not, how do we avoid constructing
her in terms of a refusal or denial? These are the familiar burdens imposed on
the minority writer (Gunew 1994a).

   Canadian poet and short story writer Evelyn Lau represents an enigma in a
Canadian and North American west coast context where Asian-American and
Asian Canadian ethnic or diasporic canons are being institutionalized with a
great deal of relish, given the demographic changes along the west coast over
the past decade (Cheung 1997; Karpinski and Lea 1993; Lee and Wong-Chu
1991; Lim and Ling 1992; Okihiro *et al.* 1995; Palumbo-Liu 1995; 1999; Silvera
1994; Wong 1993; Wu and Song 2000). The semi-autobiographical work which
shot her to precocious fame at the age of 18, *Runaway: Diary of a Street Kid*,
dealt with a protagonist preferring a life on the street to the constrictions
of family expectations projected upon her. That the family were Chinese
immigrants was represented as deliberately incidental, in the written text at

least. The expectations concerning the Chinese as 'model immigrants' in terms of their abilities to assimilate are succinctly outlined in the extract quoted earlier by journalist Jan Wong.[6] In the film made of Lau's book it was another matter, for the demands of the visual medium meant that the ethnic identity of the protagonist and her family inevitably registered a certain kind of coded presence. Following this first text, Lau's poetry and short stories have subsequently explored an overtly heterosexual underworld of sadomasochism, prostitution and drug addiction and have been seen as deliberately avoiding any hint of a racialized perspective, in relation to which she supposedly has an 'insider's' knowledge (Dean 1995; Kamboureli 1997: 534). It may be, however, that an emerging group of Chinese Canadian critics interpret the insider/outsider dynamics differently. For example, in the words of Elaine K. Chang: 'Throughout *Runaway*, Lau identifies herself as Chinese only when her ethnicity signifies a measure of difference, and not sameness or "belonging"' (Chang 1994: 114). Lien Chao, author of the first full-length study of Chinese-Canadian writing in English perceives Lau's highly self-conscious individualism as being at odds with the supposedly 'collective' impetus of other Chinese-Canadian writers who are at pains to write their community into Canadian culture and history (Chao 1997: 156–84). Chao also perceives Lau's subject matter as restrictive and stereotypical. Thus from many directions Lau is perceived as flouting or refusing the so-called 'empowering' categories with which critics are eager to provide her, rarely appearing in anthologies of Asian-Canadian writing and, by her own account, refusing to participate in 'multicultural' events (Lau 1994b).

Her apparent refusal invites one to revisit theories around the question of how to situate the authority to speak and write for those designated minority cultural players and how to set up interpretive strategies which move beyond the thematization of cultural difference, a thematization which in turn functions to reinforce difference as a mechanism leading to marginalization since difference is always posited in relation to an implicit (and invisible) hegemonic norm. The dominant reference points for minoritarian questioning of the hegemonic are a mixture of postcolonial histories with their legacies of scepticism towards totalizing theoretical frameworks, invocations of anti-racism (often in opposition to the perceived wimpy liberalism of multiculturalism) and the perceived essentialisms of identity positionings. The slick invocation of terms such as tribalism, ethnic absolutism and ethnic cleansing are competing with principled attempts to constitute local pedagogies which incorporate an ethics of non-appropriation and recognition in relation to minorities. In the necessary tension between global diasporas, with their networks and coalitions, and localized manifestations and negotiations, how might one locate or construct intellectual and pedagogical interventions that avoid the compromised categories of 'ethnic community' and of the general reductionism often attached to identity politics?

The debates around identity politics have a particular resonance within global feminism although their detailed meanings are often dependent on local contexts. The phenomenon itself was seen as arising out of the 'consciousness-raising' tactics which are historically credited with the birth of second-wave feminism and led from the articulation of women's differences to the definition of other group differences. But, increasingly, these differences have congealed into imprisoning essentialisms which are often perceived as obscuring more than they illuminate, of occluding intra-group differences and 'intersectional identities' (Crenshaw 1995: 333). In the United Kingdom critics such as Nira Yuval-Davis warn that an identity politics which couples women with ethnicity within the political framework of multiculturalism obscures the political (rather than simply cultural) nature of ethnicity and can lead to the kinds of fundamentalism currently on the rise all over the world. Indeed, as she contends, 'political ethnicity uses cultural resources to promote its specific purposes in the name of the self-enclosed ethnic community in which women rarely are permitted to play a progressive role' (Yuval-Davis 1994: 411). In the United States Martha Minow argues that identity politics 'may freeze people in pain and also fuel their dependence on their own victim status as a source of meaning' (Minow 1997: 54). She goes on to state that: 'Identity politics tends to locate the problem in the identity group rather than the social relations that produce identity groupings' (Minow 1997: 56). In *Solidarity of Strangers: Feminisms After Identity Politics*, Jodi Dean states that: 'The articulation of particular identities has led to the rigidification of these very identities. At the legislative level, this rigidification appears as the reinforcement of minority status with its negative connotations of inferiority' (Dean 1996: 5). She continues her elucidation in the following manner:

> But framing the debate as an opposition between solidarity and reflection prevents us from acknowledging the ideals shared by both sides. Supporters of identity politics are united by the ideals of inclusion and community. They struggle against exclusions enacted in the name of universality. They endeavor to establish a space of belonging, a community that strengthens its members . . . Similarly, detractors and critics of identity politics also struggle against exclusion, this time that exclusion effected by the very sign of identity . . . They want to ensure that those aspects of the self that elude the boundaries established by any identity category will not remain silenced or neglected but will be allowed to appear and develop in all their differences and particularity.
>
> (Dean 1996: 6)

The solution however, as argued by Analouise Keating in the context of the struggle by 'women of colour' to assert their own politics of difference, is 'not to abandon all references to personal experiences but rather to take experientially based knowledge claims even further by redefining identity' (Keating 1998: 36). Keating draws on Chela Sandoval's concept of 'differential consciousness' (Sandoval 1991) and, like Rattansi, on Homi Bhabha's notion of 'ambivalent identification' as a way to move to such new definitions of identity. This is why Lau's case seems such an exemplary and compelling one. Do we see her as a minority writer who refuses the 'ethical responsibility' of representing her community and of choosing the deliberate individualism often associated with the subjectivity of late capitalism (Elam 1997) or do we use her example as a way to move beyond the constraints of identity categories as figuring the 'new racism', like Rattansi, or the limits identified by the feminist critics cited above? The following discussion comprises some sketchy notes towards a possible interpretative strategy for approaching such texts. Having attempted to set the scene and to explain how a project to establish the anti-universalist focus on cultural difference has been appropriated by a 'new racism' organized around an economy of visibility and, in particular, an emphasis on the visibly-racialized body, I will now link the question of the visible to the acoustic: voice and sound, the aural dimension residing within these questions.

In marked contradiction to film, one of the cultural domains where there is conventional acceptance of the disjunction between visible bodies and audible voices is opera. Western opera demands a suspension of disbelief not only with respect to the 'fat tenor/soprano' and the nubile characters they are asked to represent but, as well, in relation to the gender-crossings and 'colour-blind' casting that have always been present in this medium. What the audience 'sees' does not get in the way of what they are asked to imagine. Until recently, for example, few of the *non*-European roles in the standard canonical reper-toire were actually sung by those from the requisite categories but there have, however, been flurries of controversy around cases where leading roles were sung by non-European singers.[7] A systematic study of the chequered history of race and opera has still to be written.[8] Generally speaking, opera audiences are accustomed to hearing the voice and imaginatively substituting a very different body from the one which they see on the stage. What kind of interpretation would an 'operatic' reading produce of Lau's work in relation to the question of desire as posed by Zizek?[9]

In the reviews heralding the reception of *Other Women*, critics wondered whether Lau would, or could, ever move beyond a somewhat romantic adolescent rebelliousness suggested by the prevailing obsession with the underworld of sadomasochism and prostitution (Gunning 1995; Kornreich 1996; Chao 1997). My argument is that, in a sense, Lau's work invites a more allegorical reading, allegory being the supreme modality where what you see is *not* what you get and opera, in its splitting of the visible and the audible, helps us recognize this.

Indicative of soap opera rather than classical opera, the novel's title, *Other Women,* suggests that the women referred to are those who disrupt the dyad of the heterosexual couple. Instead the text is narrated from the point of view of the traditional 'mistress' so that the other woman is actually the 'wife'. Thus the whole text, and much of Lau's prose work, can be interpreted as celebrating a nostalgia for the 'normal' via the concept of symbolic identification. One needs to be reminded that within psychoanalysis the operations of identification are not with actual people but with possible 'types' or, more precisely and following Lacan, with positions in language where language constitutes a dominant manifestation of the symbolic order. Slavoj Zizek delineates the following distinction here between imaginary and symbolic identification:

> Imaginary identification is identification with the image in which we appear likeable to ourselves, with the image representing 'what we would like to be', and symbolic identification, identification with the very place *from where* we are being observed, *from where* we look at ourselves so that we appear to ourselves likeable, worthy of love.
>
> (Zizek 1989: 105)[10]

This site is the place of the Other (the symbolic order) from whence the gaze and the interrogation proceed and thus is identified with social doxa, the hegemonic codes of the social world. As constituted in Lau's work it becomes the location of social heteronormativity. The symbolic identification of the adulterous woman is with the position of the wife insofar as she connotes the heterosexual couple. She/they is/are in the place from which they observe her and where she wants to be. Consider the following extracts (which constituted the first transparency shown at the conference presentation):

> My fantasies of your wife grew increasingly intimate and violent. I wanted to strip Helen naked, to familiarize myself with her body, her responses; I wanted to put my face against her chest and listen to her heart-beat climb towards orgasm, and then the slowing of her breath and pulse. I wanted to examine between her thighs with the probing interest of a physician, to explore the inches of her skin for marks, moles, wrinkles, to measure the proportion of muscle to fat, the density and porosity of her skeleton.
>   I wanted to know Helen's body so well I could climb in and zip up her skin around me.
>
> (Lau 1995: 184)

> In the months that followed the end of the affair, I thought I saw you, or your wife, everywhere. Your face reflected back at me from the faces of men passing me on the vibrant street at lunch hour. Their eyes flashed like mica, their faces were similarly shaped, and I thought for the first time that in many respects you must be absolutely ordinary, otherwise how could so many strangers bear your resemblance? Yet none of them survived a second look. And so it went for your wife as well.
>
> (Lau 1995: 189–90)

What is described here are not imaginary identifications with an ideal self but attempts to gesture towards a place from which the 'normality' of these figures might be registered, atomized and desired. These sections from the novel, as well as the supposedly 'heuristic moment' in the film script (when everything is 'explained'), all point to the identification of a referential moralistic voice echoed as well in the extract from Jan Wong's prescriptive evaluation. There are certain societal standards, designated by invisible or spectral scripts, against which the protagonist transgresses – visibly and stereotypically. Paradoxically, the excesses of sexual perversion and addiction serve to confirm such social standards since the norm as measure is always there as a point of nostalgic invocation, as demonstrated by the closing pages of *Other Women* from which these quotations were taken. What is at one level a text dealing with obsessive emotional addiction is at another level the reconfirmation of the bourgeois heterosexual couple as constitutive norm for sexual-social relations. The fact that the chapters alternate between first-person and third-person intimate functions as a reminder of the mirror image, the to and fro, mutually constitutive relationship of the adulterous woman and the wife. That is one kind of reading.[11]

But that is not the whole story and there are other excesses at work beyond this. If we return to western opera, there are moments when the point of the music, or aria, functions to exceed meaning – as signifying the very disruption of meaning. In the words of Wayne Kostenbaum: 'When heterosexuality unveils itself as *sumptuous* and *delusional*, the libretto shatters, and shadow-knowledges speak . . . by loving Butterfly's entrance more than her death . . . by never outgrowing this entrance phrase, I can speak another Butterfly' (Kostenbaum 1993: 200). And Michel Poizat in *The Angel's Cry*: 'But when Callas sings, when she's going to kill herself, maybe it's idiotic, but I snap . . . it's hearing the voice, the music, I fall on my knees' (Poizat 1992: 26). The music leaks beyond the container of meaning provided by the libretto, the narrative, and thus permits multiple identifications, including queer ones (Abel 1996: 32–4). This exhilaration permits precisely the kinds of disruptive and paradoxical identifications which opera in a sense personifies by imbuing a visible and living body with the suggestion of ventriloquism. The instability of corporeality indicated by the imaginative possibilities of opera means that it is a genre where, historically at least and unlike film, the tyranny of the visible has been unseated by the precedence of the aural as organizing economy. We are reminded that in Zizek's formulation any manifestation of voice is always to some extent ventriloquized and exceeds the explanatory parameters of the body it ostensibly occupies. In an essay aptly titled, '"I Hear You with My Eyes": or, The Invisible Master', Zizek traces what he calls the homologous mechanisms of gaze and voice in the following manner:

> . . . it is as if, when we're talking, whatever we say is an answer to a primordial address by the Other – we're always already addressed, but this address is blank, it cannot be pinpointed to a specific agent, but is a kind of empty a priori, the formal 'condition of the possibility' of our speaking . . .
> (Zizek 1996: 90)

Which brings us to opera and to *Madama Butterfly*,[12] the most obviously orientalist of operas. In the many recent attentions Puccini's opera has received, much has been made of the fact that Cho-Cho San functions as the traditional good woman who sacrifices herself in the name of maternity.[13] She has also notoriously figured as the paradigmatic orientalist fantasy of the ultimate victim and ultimate seductress, both child and *femme fatale*, a combination informing, for example, Misao Dean's essay quoted earlier. David Hwang's play *M. Butterfly* has explored one kind of gloss on the opera and David Cronenberg's film of the play, a slightly different variation. The sustaining fantasy in these two depictions is that 'Butterfly' really wants to be the cad Pinkerton and vice-versa, that Gallimard finally realizes he wants to *be* Butterfly rather than to possess her. But isn't this constant see-sawing or mechanism of vice-versa that which has always sustained such binary frameworks for decades and isn't this why one needs to find a way beyond such a paralysing impasse? Therefore we return to the delirium of the aria and of music in general as documented by Jacques Attali (1989) and now many others in the developing field of sound theory. Zizek again:

> Voice is that which, in the signifier, resists meaning, it stands for the opaque inertia that cannot be recuperated by meaning ... the moment at which the singing voice cuts loose from its anchoring in meaning and accelerates into a consuming self-enjoyment.
>
> (Zizek 1996: 103–4)

On the one hand we see on stage the stereotype of Butterfly; we see the stereotype of Lau's adulterous woman and invest it with the supposedly 'withheld orientalism' of the author (as suggested by the critics' demands for her to inform us about her 'ethnic insider's' knowledge). But perhaps it is possible to break this move by turning from the visual to the acoustic, by situating Lau's text not in the genre of 'dirty realism'[14] (suggested by the prevailing themes in her work) but the lyrical genre of opera and sound. This move might also be facilitated by including her poetry which has been identified as traditionally lyrical in style, a contrast perhaps with the confrontational social themes of her work (Wah 1997–8). Turning now to the work of Kaja Silvermann on the disembodiment of the female voice, her suggestion in relation to desire is that perhaps it is the mother whom the daughter wishes to seduce ('both to seduce the mother and be seduced by her', Silvermann 1988: 153) rather than the traditional Freudian heterosexual seduction scenario of the father and daughter. If we recall the film script extract quoted earlier, there is a classic psychoanalytic example of this scenario in the sublimated form of male analyst and female analysand; meanwhile the protagonist recounts her own family saga as one where the father is merely absent while the mother has a *mouth*. In *Other Women* the narrator, speaking of herself in the third-person, repeatedly states that: 'It seems incredible to her, that at last she is making a sound' (Lau 1995: 13) and 'she could open her mouth, and with just a few words, enter Helen's life' (Lau

1995: 8). The place of symbolic identification reinforces the norm; but by focussing on sound rather than sight, and the *disjuncture* between body and voice, we are also reminded that the heteronormative couple is itself sustained by the fantasy of its perverse double. What is undeniably all-powerful in Lau's text is the open mouth and speaking (singing) female voice[15] which appears to exceed the meanings of normativity we have been attaching to it. Where that delirium may lead in terms of finding other meanings to Lau's oeuvre remains to be seen and would necessarily include her poetry.

One could also consider the contemporary poor cousin of opera, karaoke,[16] and suggest that it too functions as a consummate example of mimicry and ventriloquism. Invoking the odd conjunction of operatic karaoke in relation to Lau's work is that it is clearly not operatic in the classic sense since its preoccupations, in *Other Women* at least, suggest an accent on accessories and lifestyles that we have come to associate with soap opera. Operatic karaoke takes bathroom singing to new soap-operatic heights.[17] It is both the ultimate accolade and parody of this western musical form, though not necessarily from a racialization-conscious or postcolonial perspective. Western opera has always exceeded and been constituted by its own parodic contradictions (what you hear governs what you see). In Lau's work the reader's imagined ventriloquisms of the authorial body are undone by the delirium of the textual voice which exceeds the very norms it ostensibly functions to sustain. It might be productive, therefore, to learn to listen for voice outside the traditional narratives of race as presently constituted, with their normative privileging of the supposed accoutrements of a visibly raced body. These are the possibilities for exceeding the claustrophobic paradigms of identity politics which can be constraining even when supposedly benignly situated in the realms of postcolonial and multicultural interrogations. Here might be a way for those 'intersectional identities' (Crenshaw 1995) and 'differential consciousnesses' (Keating 1998) which are part of the new ways for defining identity to be articulated. Questions of desire (What do others want from me? What do they see in me? What am I for others?) continue to be posed by those designated minority writers to their audiences or readers.[18]

Part III

(Un)civilized communities

6 Somatic choreographies

Public spaces; private belongings

Slowly the representatives that formerly symbolized families, groups, and orders disappear from the stage they dominated during the epoch of the name. We witness the advent of the number . . . a multitude of quantified heroes who lose names and faces as they become the ciphered river of the streets, a mobile language of computations and rationalities that belong to no one.

(de Certeau 1988, Epigraph)

A slow composition of myself as a body in the middle of the spatial and temporal world . . .

(Fanon, 1967 [1952]: 111)

What does it mean to talk about multiculturalism in a globalized context? Is it concerned with the many ways in which multiculturalism functions as discourse and practice within differing nation states? Does it mean juxtaposing discrete nationally-bounded cultures in a global framework? Might one, following Sara Ahmed, usefully invoke Marxist concepts of commodity fetishism in which cultural difference becomes commodified as 'stranger fetishism' 'where commodity is assumed to "contain" the difference that the Western consumer can "have"' (Ahmed 2000: 168)?[1] Those are certainly the ways it operates in terms of global tourism and to some extent these elements carry over into the consumption of cultural difference within the borders of the nation – thus a translation into artefacts of the traditional without contextualizing critical or theoretical analyses of histories of labour, migration, racialization, etc. If we take up the idea of the stranger and migrancy as interpreted by Julia Kristeva, Iain Chambers or Rosi Braidotti, it can function as a kind of swashbuckling refusal of national borders of the sort expressed in Canadian writer Shani Mootoo's poem 'Mantra for Migrants':

Always becoming, will never be
Always arriving, must never land

Between back home and home unfathonable is me –
By definition: immigrant.

(Mootoo 2001: 81)

But what are the implications in terms of belonging? And what perspectives can I offer now as a portable or travelling immigrant theorist?[2] The new theories and debates concerning redefinitions of space and place offered a useful starting point for a response to these questions.

After almost ten years, former colleagues had begun to realize that I no longer lived in Australia. Around the turn of the millenium I was in Sydney with a group of Canadian colleagues attending a comparative Australian–Canadian research workshop – dealing with the sociological issues surrounding cities rather than nations. On this occasion, something happened that began a train of speculation concerning what might be designated as a repertoire of corporeal and semaphoric choreographies of belonging and the reverse, unbelonging. At the end of the workshop an Australian colleague came up to me at the farewell lunch and said: 'I don't know whether women do this, but it used to be the case that when I walked down the street and passed another bloke we would sort of wink at each other (and he demonstrated). Do you know what I mean? Young people don't do that anymore.' I think I responded that yes, I thought I knew what he meant, but cannot recall the details. What that anecdote might mean, though, has continued to haunt me and has been tested on a variety of people, in numerous national contexts. Their interpretations included the awareness that it demonstrated a palpable nostalgia – a mourning for a sense of community that had passed away. But whose community exactly? Some said that they could pinpoint this gesture more specifically as being on the Celtic side of Anglo-Celtic and that it was not only profoundly gendered but an indication of class as well. In other words, that it pointed to an identification with an Irish working-class background, and possibly small town or rural at that (though this last might be considered tautological in the sense that this version of an 'Irish' past generally comprises all those characteristics). I recalled as well Drusilla Modjeska's reference to Robert Drewe's memoir *Shark Net* in a two-part essay she wrote for the *Australian Review of Books* on the subject of memoirs and life-writing. Modjeska singles out a moment when the cadet reporter Drewe attends a trial and cannot refrain from returning the wink of the murderer in the dock because in suburban Perth he knows both the murderer and his victim (Modjeska 2000: 7). What does belonging and mateship signify here?

I came away, in turn, with the following questions: was it a matter of gender and did women give each other this kind of non-verbal public recognition: then or now? I also pondered the fact that the kind of history I had experienced growing up in Australia profoundly did *not* include these particular signals or, if so, if I happened to observe them, they placed me firmly as an outsider to that semaphoric repertoire. I was reminded of this when reading yet another recent survey in the national newspaper, post-9/11, of what multiculturalism meant in terms of everyday experience in Australia. A Lebanese teen was quoted in the following terms: 'Multiculturalism is something you just tell yourselves. Youse don't treat us like you treat other Aussies' (Toohey 2002:

23). What finally did that wink (even if rueful) mean in terms of an entitlement to a space and temporality in the sense of an accompanying history?

Homi Bhabha, drawing on Freud's famous essay 'The Uncanny', speaks of one of its translations as the 'unhomely', as that 'ambivalent structure of the civil State as it draws its rather paradoxical boundary between the private and the public spheres . . . The unhomely moment relates the traumatic ambivalences of a personal, psychic history to the wider disjunctions of political existence' (Bhabha 1994: 10). Did my various questions relating to the junctures of unhomeliness find a kind of answer in Canadian philosopher Charles Taylor's influential concept of the politics of recognition? Would the new theories on spatialization produced over the last decade be of help here? For example, did Judith Butler's work on abjected subjectivities indicate an alternative, or perhaps complementary, framework to Michel de Certeau's attempts to rehabilitate the importance of the 'common man'?[3] Butler speaks of the abject as 'those "unlivable" and "uninhabitable" zones of social life which are nevertheless densely populated by those who do not enjoy the status of the subject, but whose living under the sign of the "unlivable" is required to circumscribe the domain of the subject . . . against which – and by virtue of which – the domain of the subject will circumscribe its own claim to autonomy and to life' (Butler 1993: 3). Anne McClintock has mapped some of those abjected spaces in the South African context and colleagues in Vancouver have analysed the so-called 'Third world in the First world' in the downtown eastside of the city. There was also my realization that the sense of being at home included the audible or acoustic as well as the visual, and that the issue of language itself or the variously accented englishes was also of significance. And finally, there was a pervasive curiosity concerning the ways in which a body might be at ease, provisionally at least, in that dance of somatic gestures which, like tribal markings, indicated precisely this – a language of belonging to a wider community.

Bodied language

Let us consider a different kind of somatic or corporeal register of belonging from the one I attempted to sketch with the workshop anecdote and its converse, un-belonging; entertaining other scenarios of the body at home (or not) in other spaces; contemplating the ways in which bodies are recognized as particular kinds of bodies and are classified accordingly in terms of kinships and affiliations (or not). In *The Practice of Everyday Life*, Michel de Certeau distinguishes between 'strategies' and 'tactics' and designates the former as belonging to the 'proper' whereas: 'The Place of the tactic belongs to the other' (de Certeau 1988: xix). In a further elaboration, he describes the proper as encompassing a 'mastery of places through sight' (36) and tactics as 'guileful ruses' and a type of 'making do' which leaves traces of effects rather than visible or quantifiable trails – a kind of guerilla activity engendered by 'the absence of a proper locus' (de Certeau 1988: 37). In other words, tactics are produced by those who have a tenuous relation to the proper, who must improvise provisional rights to a particular place for a brief period. In the second volume (which appeared posthumously), in the chapter titled 'Ghosts in the City', de Certeau and Luce Giard speak about a new urban aesthetics organized according to the predominant terms of gestures and narratives:

> As gestural 'idiolects,' the practice of inhabitants creates, on the same urban space, a multitude of possible combinations between ancient places (the secrets of which childhoods or which deaths?) and new situations. They turn the city into an immense memory where many poetics proliferate.
>
> (de Certeau *et al.* 1998: 141)

In Vancouver, where I have now lived for eight years, amidst the many panhandlers who are a part of the life of most North American cities, there exists a curiously enigmatic figure. In the summer months in particular one can hear quite regularly the strains of classic opera sung in Italian wafting through the air. The voice, moving across a considerable spatial range, is not at all bad, and is attached to a body in motion. This perambulating pedestrian does indeed produce a gestural as well as an acoustic idiolect. In de Certeau's work acknowledgement of the specificity and ineradicability of the auditory is captured in the following: 'All the modalities sing a part in this chorus . . . These enunciatory operations are of unlimited diversity. They therefore cannot be reduced to their graphic detail' (de Certeau 1988: 99). The notion of 'gestural idiolect', mentioned in the previous extract, refers to the concept Certeau explores in his first volume – the 'modalities of pedestrian enunciation'. Investigating further this modality of the acoustic, curiosity drove me on a quest for the visual dimension, nonetheless, and I discovered that it emanated from a slight young man, perhaps in his mid-thirties, dressed very casually but neatly in the kind of attire that might well place him among the street people. However he never begs. He strides the streets purposefully, not making eye contact, singing his heart out. I have to confess that I have been totally cowed by the sonic space he creates around himself with his music, as though indeed this performance somehow translated the itinerant streetscape into a formal theatrical space. Even when I have passed him by as he pauses between arias, I have felt unable to approach him. The last time I saw him he was walking the seawall, a favourite Vancouver promenade. A group of sub-teens on bicycles decided to heckle him. He fell silent.

Like de Certeau's notion of pedestrian enunciations or speech acts, here was a reminder that language itself, spoken, written and heard, is one of those elements which fundamentally structures our sense of belonging, to the extent that it becomes invisible or transparent as a medium of interaction. In fact when it is *most* invisible (on signs or billboards) or inaudible, it registers most emphatically the fact that we are at home. The Italian he communicated would not be understood by many in this city and might well be a projection beyond himself of the profound foreignness within which he moves. The urban singer represents one of those moments when language usage becomes highly audible. It is linked in turn to those more formal narratives of community, city, nation which compel one to identify who remains outside those stories, outside those gestures of belonging. But cogitating further on the Vancouver artist, why did I assume the singer to be a stranger asserting a provisional acoustic entitlement? Why could he not be a member of the urban community, an operatic flâneur, who was in fact exercising entitlement by queering or transforming the acoustic space, rendering a public space strange in ways comparable to the private resonances of the bathroom and singing in the shower?[4] What I was hearing as an example of the ubiquitously exilic was quite possibly projected by my own nostalgia for those privateering moments of ontological migrancy. Perhaps the notion of spatial entitlement might yield interpretive tools for analysing this event.

Spatial entitlement

What does spatial entitlement entail? At a very local level, within the academic essays of my students at the University of British Columbia, within the highly structured genres of the literary critical essay, the uncanny moments and gestures of 'un-belonging' constantly erupt. Here is an example by a graduate student, Doritta Fong:[5]

> A lovely evening in early September, 1994. It is pleasantly warm, with blue skies, a languid breeze, and a vivid sunset lingering; my brother, mother and I are wandering along Victoria Drive, heading toward supper in a nearby restaurant. We are all wearing comfortable scruffy shoes, blue jeans, nondescript sweatshirts. At 44th Ave, Mum and Julian crossed the street on a red light, since there was no traffic. I waited until the light turned green, having listened attentively in elementary school. I trotted to catch up to them, and they had reduced to a shuffle. "Slow down," they said, and gestured to a young man, case of beer on his left shoulder, standing in front of a drug store window. He was standing still, so we approached him eventually.
>
> When we got quite close to him, (young white man, short brownish-blonde hair, blue eyes, regular features, clean cut, about twenty-five to thirty years old, not ruffianish), he called out, 'Hello Asian People!'
>
> I thought, 'What the hell? Are we babies or dogs or starlings?'
>
> So I trilled, in a chirpily cheery tone, similar to his, 'Hello White People!' as we continued walking.
>
> Flushing hot pink, he exploded, 'Don't you dare call me white people. My ancestors are from England, Ireland, Scotland, Germany, Italy, and the Ukraine. Don't you fucking well call me white people. You're in Canada now, you fucking Chinks . . .'

> We moved past him, I expecting a knife at my back, imagining a beer bottle hitting my head.
>
> (Fong 2000)

This essay by no means delineates an artless expression of a racist ambush and its effects are carefully crafted. However there is a force which propels it beyond the generic space of the academic essay and this 'excess' is presumably akin to those moments where a personal history is propelled into a cultural public space. Indeed it is the anger at not being included as a participant in that public space, as a matter of course which, one can assume, forms part of the motivation here.

In his compelling study, *White Nation,* of belonging, multiculturalism, and citizenship, Ghassan Hage has rather devastatingly linked his analysis of Australia to the growing literature in North America on white supremacism. Hage uses the term 'white' in a somewhat general way and predominantly distinguishes what he calls 'white' groups (those with white privilege) from what he terms 'Third World-looking' groups. The stories I have been organizing around gesture may be linked to one that is embedded in Hage's text and mined by him for all its ambiguities. Speaking of racist incidents that occurred in Australia during the Gulf War, Hage focuses in particular on those where Muslim women had their veils torn off:

> In the wake of the press coverage given to the incidents of tearing Muslim women's scarves, a film studies colleague and a group of his students produced a video with an anti-racist intent. The video featured a Muslim girl in an Australian school being harassed by a group of boys who eventually pull down her scarf. The girl passively retreats until a White girl comes forward picks up her scarf, gives it back to her while putting her arm around her (rap music in the background).
>
> I could not help focusing on the movement of the White girl's arm. Protective though it was, it kept reminding me of the very movement of the hand that it was negating – the hand that pulled down the scarf. Like it, it was a hand that had a sense of its spatial power and, also like it, it has moved onto something/someone perceived as a passive object.
>
> (Hage 1998: 96)

Hage's point throughout is that this sense of spatial control and legislative entitlement is at the heart of a much-vaunted Australian 'tolerance' which, as he points out repeatedly, always carries with it, indeed is defined by, its opposite – intolerance. The central (begged) question is always: who is permitted to exercise this tolerance? In Doritta Fong's story of a family moving in the street there was that same displacement from a sense of entitlement by someone who felt he had a right to legislate the language and gestures of particular groups on the street. Fortunately the bottle in her story was not actually flung; but symbolically it had been.

Charles Taylor's work on multiculturalism has been influential across North America and is also mentioned in Hage's study. Taylor's concept of the politics of recognition, whereby he meant a 'perfectly balanced reciprocity' (Taylor 1994: 48) amongst equals, takes as its starting point the understanding that there is now, within modernity, an inextricable link between identity and recognition. We construct our very own 'authentic' identity by having our selves partially reflected back through the eyes of others. The absence of that reflection can cause all kinds of fissures within identity. To quote Taylor:

> The thesis is that our identity is partly shaped by recognition or its absence, often by misrecognition of others, and so a person or group of people can suffer real damage, real distortion, if the people or society around them mirror back to them a confining or demeaning or contempt-ible picture of themselves. Nonrecognition or misrecognition can inflict harm, can be a form of oppression, imprisoning someone in a false, distorted, and reduced mode of being.
>
> (Taylor 1994: 25)

Taylor goes on to chart a series of apparent contradictions between the liberal proponents of universal rights and those who espouse 'difference', meaning that people are entitled within a framework of overarching universal rights to assert their own differences. The problem is that the one is often seen as contradicting the other. Taylor attempts to negotiate this difficulty by generating the concept of mutual recognition underpinned by respect. His critics have drawn attention to further problems not unrelated to Hage's point concerning the logic of tolerance. For example, Anthony Appiah suggests that ultimately this process functions to lock people into essentialist categories; that the notion of setting up such categories as a basis for recognition would confine people to structuring their identities according to rather prescriptive characteristics, in his own case, ways of being both black and gay in America. Ghassan Hage sees Taylor as ultimately exemplifying the 'white multi-culturalism' he traces in his study, in other words, that it positions a certain group (white, liberal) as being able to offer recognition or tolerance, and of using the cultures and values of others to 'enrich' their own, thus maintaining their centrist and legislative positionality rather than dissolving this exclusive 'we' into a more inclusive and multicultural entity (Hage 1998: 138–9).[6]

It might be useful at this point to recall one of the paradigmatic moments that help define the concept of the unhomely or abjected body that occurs in Fanon's *Black Skin, White Masks*, the moment when the narrator is inter-pellated in the streets with a child's cry: 'Look, a Negro!' (Fanon 1967 [1952]: 111). The child pointing out to its mother the intrusion of a black body encapsulates for Fanon the turmoil of unhomeliness and unbelonging for certain bodies in certain spaces. 'My body was given back to me sprawled out, distorted, recolored, clad in mourning in that white winter day. The Negro is an animal, the Negro is bad ... the nigger's going to eat me up' (Fanon 1967

[1952]: 114–15).[7] Recent theorization of public and private spaces has been particularly interested in cities as abstract spaces in which bodies exist at best as generic types rather than being differentiated or individualized to any extent (Gregory 1994). David Harvey points out that the body, like Habermas's depiction of modernity, is an unfinished project and proposes a porous body in relational flux instead of the body as closed system of an earlier era (Harvey 1998). With the advent of feminist geographers, we have questions being raised concerning the ways in which women remain unseen, particularly as they traverse public spaces. Gillian Rose (1999) suggests that, like Harvey's body, space too is relational and that rather than being pre-existent it is created through performance (in Judith Butler's sense of that term). Choice becomes a relative term here. One cannot determine how one's body is perceived. At best one may choose from a repertoire of gestures which may undermine the smooth functioning of those insidious designations. The Vancouver singer chose one such approach, which also represented a type of ironic mockery of the commercialization of an activity that elsewhere and hitherto had been part of everyday life.[8] Singing by anyone and anywhere is something of which we remain aware; but music generally has been com-modified in ways that make it less possible, demanding a kind of courage, for amateurs to pursue in public places.

Walls of darkness

Literature provides a number of poignant examples of the dance of the body as it weaves filaments of entitlement in public spaces. In David Malouf's *12 Edmonstone Street*, a series of linked autobiographical stories, there is one section, 'A Foot in the Stream', where the authorial persona writes of visiting India, and in this example of visiting a mosaic workshop in Agra:

> One of the boys (he might have been fifteen), using a pair of tweezers and a live coal, was engaged in setting the stones in a white paste. Suddenly, as the factory owner turned away a moment, he gave us a wild look and held up four fingers in some sort of appeal. Another demand for rupees? It looked like more than that. In a more melodramatic situation it would quite clearly have been a sign that he was being held against his will, a desperate cry for rescue.
>
> Nothing explained itself, we passed on. But I see that wordless gesture, four tense upthrust fingers and an open mouth as an image of what I have failed to understand here, a message I am deaf to and have not received, an uncomfortable reminder of the million tiny events I have been present at that escaped my attention and which added together would make a wall of darkness in which what I have seen is the merest flash of chips in a mosaic, an eye, a hand, the fragment of a broken arch, the passage of a kingfisher's, a bluejay's wing.

(Malouf 1986: 122)

That 'wall of darkness' indicates a failure to communicate, the fragility of communication itself, traditionally perceived as the sign of our common humanity, something supposedly distinguishing us from other species. The accompanying images evoked by Malouf's narrator at the end add up to the glitter of exotica as much as they reflect back the narrator's own lack: his inability to gaze back with understanding interrupts the formation of identity; a profound moment of non-recognition takes place. The momentum to recognize a common humanity is indeed what is at stake in these attempts to instigate a register of belonging.

In Canadian poet Roy Kiyooka's posthumously published book *Mothertalk* there is a succinct description of another such failure, this time not at an individual but at a massive state level. The reference is to the internment of Canadians of Japanese background (sometimes many generations ago) after the bombing of Pearl Harbor. Kiyooka was taken out of school, his formal education abruptly terminated.

> In and through all the ideological strife we avidly attended via the local paper and the radio a small 'I' felt as if a punitive fist kept clenching and unclenching behind my back but each time I turned to catch it flexing it would disappear into the unlit corners of the small log house.
>
> (Kiyooka 1997: 188)

The gesture recalls the one in Doritta Fong's essay. Kiyooka was haunted for the rest of his life, as were many others, by that sudden suspension of civic rights and the assumptions concerning belonging which accompanied them. The renowned ecologist David Suzuki is another example. The next generation who had to deal with that traumatic history is represented here by the Calgary writer Hiromi Goto whose first novel *Chorus of Mushrooms* deals with three generations of women caught up in the legacy generated by the internment experience. While not engaging directly with memories of that event, her book catalogues the effects of internalizing the shame of being designated an outsider. The mother reinvents herself as an Anglo-Canadian whose deracination eventually leads to utter paralysis when her own mother chooses to exile herself from the family home. The feisty grandmother, who speaks no English but functions as an alter ego of the narrator, takes to the road and ends up as the Purple Mask rodeo rider at the Calgary Stampede. The mother, who occupies that difficult middle position which is too close to become the stuff of mythological escapades, becomes unable to deal with any aspects of everyday life, including even the basic task of eating to keep herself alive. Her daughter nurtures her back to functional life by learning to cook the homely Japanese dishes that had hitherto been banned from the family's cuisine. The father, meanwhile, registers his own dysfunctional state by a sudden muteness with respect to his own mother tongue. He can still read Japanese but is unable to speak it any longer (Goto 1994: 205). The book is filled with such eloquent moments testifying to the struggle with the effects of the non-recognition of some individuals by a wider society. However I would like to quote a short self-contained passage told through the eyes of the novel's protagonist Muriel/Murasaki:

> I met this guy at the airport in the departures area. Where are you going, he said. Japan, I said. Back to the ole homeland, huh, he said. I just shrugged and smiled a bit. You know, he said, you're pretty cute for a Nip. He said. Most Nips are pretty damn ugly. All that inbreeding. Even now. He said. Well, have a good one. He said. And boarded his plane. And I felt really funny inside, him saying Nip and everything. Because he was one too.
>
> (Goto 1994: 53)

That passage could, like my opening anecdote, generate many interpretations, partly influenced by the logic which allows racist remarks to convey one kind of meaning if spoken by an 'insider' but offer a very different meaning if an 'outsider' utters them. In other words, the appropriation of racist terms by those who are intended to be its targets can paradoxically function to establish a sense of kinship and therefore potential agency.

'Hyphenated transpicuities'

Fred Wah is a well-established poet who has recently begun to explore his own Scandinavian, English and Chinese legacies, particularly in his latest book *Diamond Grill*, his first collection of linked prose poems examining the nature of what it means to live the everyday realities of 'mixed race' in small-town Canada. The title refers to the cafe run by the family in Nelson, British Columbia. One of the earlier pieces in the collection sets up the image of the door between the kitchen and front part of the cafe as a kind of hyphen which becomes a signifier for the state of in-betweenness embodied by the son who provides the narrative voice for most of the poems.

> . . . between the Occident and Orient to break the hush of the whole cafe before first light the rolling gait with which I ride this silence that is a hyphen and the hyphen is the door.
>
> (Wah 1996: 16)

The hyphen sets up the binaries of East and West which the narrator feels he is forced constantly to negotiate, not only during his own lifetime but through all the generations of his increasingly extended and 'muddled' family.

UNTIL MARY McNUTTER
CALLS ME A CHINK I'M
not one. That's in elementary school. Later, I don't have to be because I don't look like one. But just then, I'm stunned. I've never thought about it.

After that I start to listen, and watch. Some people are different. You can see it. Or hear it.

The old Chinamen have always been friends of my dad's. They give us kids candy. I go fishing down by the boat-houses with one of them. He's a nice man, shiny brown knuckles, baits my hook, shows me how to catch mudsuckers, shows me how to row a boat. We're walking back up the hill with our catch of suckers and some kids start chinky, chinky Chinaman and I figure I'd better not be caught with him anymore.

I become as white as I can, which, considering I'm mostly Scandinavian, is pretty easy for me. Not for my dad and some of my cousins though. They're stuck, I think, with how they look. I only have the name to contend with. And I not only hear my friends put down the Chinks (and the Japs, and the Wops, and the Spiks, and the Douks) but comic books and movies confirm that the Chinese are yellow (meaning cowardly), not-to-be-trusted, heathens, devils, slant-eyed, dirty, and talk incomprehensible gobblydee-gook.

(Wah 1996: 98)

Like Goto's character at the airport, the narrator feels trapped within those binaries and participates in the camouflage of racism as a way of building a precarious foothold in the dominant group. On the other hand, the binaries are increasingly seen to be inappropriate and the occasion of a family reunion, for example, gives rise to a satire on ethnic purity:

I'M JUST A BABY, MAYBE
SIX MONTHS (.5%)
old. One of my aunts is holding me on her knee. Sitting on the ground in front of us are her two daughters, 50% Scottish. Another aunt, the one who grew up in China with my father, sits on the step with her first two children around her. They are 75% Chinese. There is another little 75% girl cousin, the daughter of another 50% aunt who married a 100% full-blooded Chinaman (full-blooded, from China even). At the back of the black-and-white photograph is my oldest boy cousin; he's 25% Chinese. His mother married a Scot from North Battleford and his sisters married Italians from Trail. So there, spread out on the stoop of a house in Swift Current, Saskatchewan, we have our own little western Canadian multi-cultural stock exchange.

We all grew up together, in Swift Current, Calgary, Trail, Nelson and Vancouver (27% of John A's nation) and only get together now every three years (33%) for a family reunion, to which between 70% and 80% of us show up. Out of fifteen cousins only one (6.6%) married a 100% pure Chinese.

(Wah 1996: 83)

One of the ways of 'selling' immigration and the resultant cultural mix has always been in terms of the economic benefits to a country and in this way Canada does not differ from Australia. In another poem Wah's narrator encounters a 'paper son' (someone sent out from China using false papers); but unlike the example from Malouf quoted earlier, a kind of communication *does* take place:

> A couple of days later I have to go to the basement for some more paper napkins and I say hi to Wing Bo as I walk past. His eyes light up and he starts to say something in Chinese. I just say sorry I can only speak English. He looks lonely. When he realizes we're not going to be able to talk he just holds up a cleanly peeled spud and laughs. I tell him what a great job he's doing by sticking my thumb in the air. We both sputter meaningless phrases and get on with our work.
>
> (Wah 1996: 118)

The narrator points out in a number of poems that the binaries work both ways in that this 'mixed-race' family is rejected as much by the Chinese community as by the 'white' one. In a compelling image used in another poem the narrator dissects that burden of 'mixed race' in relation to himself as that of being 'stained by genealogy': 'Physically, I'm racially transpicuous and I've come to prefer that mode . . .' (Wah 1996: 136–8). It leads finally to an impatience with the essentialism of the prescriptive categories of recognition and identification mentioned earlier by Appiah in his critique of Taylor. In an essay 'Half-Bred Poetics' included in his recent collection *Faking It: Poets and Hybridity* (2000) Wah speaks of his own conceptualization of the hyphen:

> The Hyphen, even when it is notated, is often silent and transparent. I'd like to make the noise surrounding it more audible, the pigment of its skin more visible . . . My own interest in the site and sign of the hyphen is essentially from a blood quantum point of view, that is, as a 'mixed blood.' Others occupy the site as immigrant, or as visible minorities, or as political allies.
>
> (Wah 2000: 74–5)

Fred Wah, like Charles Taylor, is a writer and thinker who is exploring, along with many others in Canada, what it means to confound the binaries of Canada conceived as an English–French settler colony as well as the discrete ethnicities convened under the totalizing gestures of state multiculturalism. In pondering some Australian examples of 'in-betweenness' to juxtapose with Wah's work, I recalled the film *Head On* directed by Anna Kokkinos based on the novel *Loaded* by Christos Tsiolkas. I saw it on that same visit to Sydney (described above) and was haunted (once more) by the use of corporeal gestures in the film, this time much more formally choreographed in various dance sequences. One of the stunning achievements of the film is that it walks the tightrope of taking visual stereotypes and reworking them. After all, we expect Greek dancing in a film about Greek Australians, since ethnic essentialism still rules. But in this film dance is not simply a superficial ethnic accessory, it is used to build and weave the nuances of character, for example, within the protagonist Ari's family to show the various implications of their emotional investments. The son and daughter dance with the mother in a kind of dreamy solidarity to retro pop music before the father-patriarch enters and changes the music to the 'real' Greek stuff so that he can reinstate that same 'ethnic purity' which causes so much tension throughout the film because it is the only way he knows how to maintain the fortress of the family in a semi-hostile environment. The sequence ends with Ari in effect demonstrating to his father that he can perform all the moves in the authentic stuff too. The father grudgingly acknowledges that Ari is 'almost' as good a dancer as he is. Later we have the subversive moment when Toula the transvestite dances in the Greek club and is subsequently beaten up by the Greek-Australian cop for her impersonation of, among other things, 'ethnicity as family'. By her very existence Toula is excluded from embodying such belonging because she challenges the boundaries of the heterosexual family, functioning as an ethnic 'out-law' rather than 'in-law'. The film ends with Ari having, like Wah's narrator, questioned and violently rejected all the ethnic (and several other) categories of identity formation, none the less executing a Greek dance on the beach – repeating the movements he had performed for his father. If there is recognition here it comes from the deadbeats, the other outsiders, barely conscious and barely present. The dance is rather more reminiscent of being performed in front of those mirrors which professional dancers use to hone their skills, a calculated way of 'making strange' rather than signifying simple narcissism.[9]

All these examples suggest that we are now increasingly enmeshed in a further step in those multi-multiculturalisms where a kind of basic set of differences is now so accepted that we can afford to confound it further with complexities well beyond binaries or their attendant deadening essentialisms. What multiculturalism may look like set against these palimpsests, these texts overwritten with other texts, globally connected, locally defined, we can only wait and see. And what does the comparison between Australia and Canada in this instance convey? Certainly, for all kinds of unfortunate reasons, there is not the same level of support for publishing of any kind in Australia, and to me what does get published continues to be more culturally homogeneous than what is coming out of either Canada or the United States for that matter. A Canadian colleague informs me that English-speaking Canada has roughly the same population as Australia but the level of English-language publication of all kinds (including academic) there is nowhere comparable to Canada. Nor is there the same support for outreach research work related to Australia that the Canadian Government is able to offer. Thus Canadian Studies Centres proliferate across the world (hence the robustness of the International Council for Canadian Studies) much more than do Australian ones.

To return to the wink with which I began, one aspect I like about this anecdote (and perhaps this addresses the 'Anglo Celtic anxiety' a number of people, such as Meaghan Morris, Jon Stratton and (in a different mode) Miriam Dixson believe they perceive in Australia at the moment) is that (belatedly, perhaps for the first time) it illustrates overt recognition of a group rather than assuming an invisibly positioned 'we' that is not answerable nor accountable to anyone in terms of identifying a specificity of gender or culture, etc. The understanding that this group's identity is predicated on acknowledgement by others of its *own* kind means, by default, an understanding that there are other others who are indeed *not* recognizing this group's traditionally conceived identity, reflecting back unexpected elements. For the first time in 200 years, perhaps, a space is opened up for alternative gestures of recognition and a consequent identity. One hopes that the accumulated affect of these moments and these spaces and the bodies which move through them will ultimately constitute a permanent impediment to the smooth workings of nationalism.

In all these spaces which echo the discursive effects of 'multiculturalism' there remains the need to disrupt dominant categories and identities without at the same time containing the non-dominant within the same classificatory logic. It has always been a fine line to tread. There is the unquestionable need to critique and even disclaim multiculturalism as state discourse and practice at the same time that one needs to find ways to create the spatial entitlement within and among individuals and institutions caught up in that rhetoric.

7   Can ghosts emigrate?

Diaspora, exile and community

But isn't any autobiography, even if it doesn't involve 'us', a desire to make a collective public image exist, for 'you', for 'us'?

(Kristeva 1984: 220)

. . . it's only by our lack of ghosts
we're haunted.

(Birney 1990, 'Can. Lit.')

In the concluding chapter of this analysis of multicultural nations haunted by their colonial histories, I dwell on the notion of diaspora as an endless process of travelling and change rather than simply being framed by leaving and arriving, with mourning or nostalgia as its dominant markers. This chapter considers the ways in which a variety of genres ranging from literary histories to autobiographies and memoirs function to construct models of belonging, the tactics employed in a diasporic context by minority subjects whose cultural survival is constantly in danger of being overwhelmed by the master narratives of nationalism, globalization and assimilationist versions of state multi-culturalism. The chapter singles out the somewhat modernist figure of the poet-pedagogue, those individuals who, for whatever reason, have projected onto them the burden of formulating and expressing a minority's cultural representations, metaphors and distinctiveness, for a variety of readers in the world at large. In his 'Defence of Poetry', the English poet Percy Shelley described poets as the 'unacknowledged legislators of the world', and was referring to an imagined golden era in the Greek *polis* when poet-pedagogues such as Plato were popularly believed to represent political life; in other words, that there was seamless continuity between politics, culture and an ethical existence. Years later, William Butler Yeats, poet turned politician, invoked Shelley's phrase as a way of attempting to represent and give legitimacy to his role in the Irish nationalist movement at the end of the nineteenth and beginning of the twentieth century. In this latter example in particular critics have traced a clear continuity between such sentiments and a public and very interested version of nationalism (not to mention patriarchy). While cultural representations have in recent times often been analysed as compromised culturalisms, functioning to camouflage dubious national (and increasingly global) political agendas, it might be time to rethink the question of how poet-pedagogues, a version of the public intellectual, function within conditions of diaspora.[1] The reason for raising such an issue is that minority writers (poets and others) are often burdened with being seen as the spokes-people for their group, in other words, that they have the double yoke of representation as delegation (in the political sense) and depiction (in the cultural sense).

Diasporic studies have now become a hugely complicated field which overlaps with postcolonial and multicultural studies and, more recently, with attempts to theorize globalization and transnationalism. As Iain Chambers puts it, 'The chronicles of diasporas – those of the black Atlantic, of metropolitan Jewry, of mass rural displacement – constitute the groundswell of modernity' (Chambers 1994: 16). But how does one avoid the pitfalls of the diasporic condition, as articulated by Radhakrishnan: 'The diasporan hunger for knowledge about and intimacy with the home country should not turn into a transhistorical and mystic quest for origins' (Radhakrishnan 1996: 212), for it is precisely such quests for 'mystic origins' which fuel the kinds of ethnic absolutism explored in Chapters 1 and 4? However, before we become too attached to terms like 'diaspora', there is a useful distinction drawn by Shirley Geok-lin Lim between 'diaspora' and the 'transnational'. The comment is embedded in a special issue of the *Women's Review of Books* dealing with 'Women Writing in the Asian Diaspora' and is part of a group interview with two other writers brought together under the rubric 'Singaporean diaspora'. Lim states the following: '"Diaspora" was appropriate at a time in human history when, if populations left a location of origin, it was difficult for them to return . . . I think some of us prefer the notion of transnationality as opposed to diaspora, a sense of continuing relationships with the location of origin' (Lim *et al.* 2002: 25). Lim then encourages the other two writers, Lydia Kwa (in Vancouver) and Fiona Cheong (in the United States), to return to Singapore to give readings and establish an audience there, as she has done herself over many years. This sense of responsibility to one's serial homes and the various communities of which one was once a part is a tangible element in all of Lim's writing, both poetic and critical, and it is a model which has gained new impetus in the current era when we have suddenly been made acutely aware of the ways in which we are part of global networks, at once disparate and all too connected. That sense of still being attached, and therefore of having to analyse and comment on, or having to bring the locality of one's previous communities into one's current work, certainly animates my own work and this book.

This chapter examines a number of different texts ranging from literary histories to memoirs and includes revisiting Shirley Geok-lin Lim's memoirs discussed already in Chapter 3. As well it considers Garrett Hongo's *Volcano: A Memoir of Hawai'i*. Both Lim and Hongo have been key figures in the academic institutionalization of the field of Asian-American literature and both have been embroiled in the gender tensions involved.[2] The chapter also examines Roy Kiyooka's *Mothertalk*, Lien Chao's pioneering history of Chinese-Canadian literature, and a number of accounts dealing with the Italo-Canadian diaspora. The overarching question is how these writers constitute belonging in the tensions between individualized lives and the necessity for community in diaspora – that will to belong which survives, it seems, every attempt to dismantle or undermine it. One of the historical threads connecting these disparate accounts is the internment of Japanese Americans and Canadians as well as Italian Canadians as 'enemy aliens' during the Second World War. How do these writers assemble appropriate tactics for a localized response to this dilemma? How does the individual writer develop the formal devices to bear witness to cultural dispersion and dissolution that precede the establishment of other forms of legitimacy in a new cultural aggregation? How does gender structure these representations? Moreover, what does a pedagogical imperative add to these questions?[3]

To convey more concretely these abstract speculations, there is a fleeting moment in Shirley Geok-lin Lim's memoir which captures the poignancy of diaspora constructed as that which may be lost beyond recall, the dispersed seed which fails to take root:

> I fretted over a strand of bright orange butterfly weed that had sprung up by Route 100 . . . just below our white-and-green colonial home. It was too exotic, an endangered wildflower, in plain view, with the red-winged blackbirds flashing among the sumac bushes. Sure enough in a few days the butterfly weed blossoms . . . were gone. Some passing human had picked them, robbing the seeds that would have borne more orange wings for the year after.
>
> (Lim 1996a: 196)

While diasporic studies have in the past tended to focus on what is culturally retained or carried over in the sense of custom, religion, histories (always anachronistic) and languages, it may be time to consider the role of the writer as inventor of community where community is conceived not in the sense of the nostalgic return to the past and a lost place but as the impulse forward, the potential carried by the seeding of diaspora in hybridity, the reality of a process more easily recognized here and now as hegemonic groups within the nation are forced to accommodate the third- and fourth-generation descendants of major migrations. The attempt here is to analyse the components and strategies of a kind of belonging that has not yet been established which, like Lim's butterfly weed, is assembled precariously out of the shards of individual lives and their 'imagined relations' to genealogies (private histories) and public events, that is, global or national histories. This phrase gestures of course to Benedict Anderson's (1983/91) well-known thesis that nations are formed in their imagined communities through the dissemination and ubiquity of print. Whereas Anderson explored the novel and newspapers, in this chapter one generic consideration is the memoir produced by poet-pedagogues. In other words, there is a certain preoccupation with the texture of language and the memoir defined as the licence (in the sense of a cultural contract with an imagined readership) to produce one's own interpretation of a personal history which is inevitably located within a public one.[4] At the same time, the last thing I want to reinstate here with the notion of poet-pedagogue is a simple reconstitution of the humanist subject. Rather, I am using these figures more as clusters or points of convergence in a discursive economy, perhaps a thickening of discursive effects around fluid subjects whose presence functions to destabilize cultural certainties around dominant communities, nations, etc. The image I have is of those ectoplasms who stalk the nineteenth century, precursors to virtual realities, kin to those various ghosts who haunt the pages of this book.

Both Hongo and Lim have an uneasy and at the same time acutely self-conscious relationship to the English language as always involving a translation and therefore being always a compromise invoking a mechanism of both suppression and apprenticeship. Both texts are haunted by the shadowy presence of multiple languages as signifying, among other things, an attachment to the specific histories attached to those languages. In Lim's text we return to the statement (quoted earlier) that: 'Depriving us of Chinese or Malay or Hindi, British teachers reminded us nonetheless that English was only on loan, a borrowed tongue which we could only garble' (Lim 1996a: 121).

As discussed in Chapter 3, Lim's text is a kind of *Künstlerroman* dealing with the formation of the artist as a young woman and is permeated by the effects of British colonialism on pedagogy, ranging from the kinds of institutions (mirroring the British public school and its unselfconscious elitism) to the curriculum, where in postcolonial writing all over the ex-empire there is a depiction of canonical narratives structuring taste, culture and belonging, as imposed from another place – the evocation of an imaginary landscape of daffodils and snow in places which had never seen them.[5] This disciplinary regime involved training the imagination in a semiotics or system of representation constructed out of the building blocks or signs of another literature, another tradition of representation. For example, the narrator describes learning the song of 'The Jolly Miller' who cared for nobody, etc.

> The miller working alone had no analogue in the Malayan world. In Malacca everyone was surrounded by everyone else . . . Caring was not a concept that signified . . . Caring denoted a field of choice, of individual voluntary action, that was foreign to family, the place of compulsory relations.
>
> (Lim 1996a: 64)

There is also a haunting in terms of another subjugated tongue – not so much the expected Chinese Hokkien dialect of the father, as the Malay of her mother, the mother who is depicted as having 'abandoned' the family and her only daughter. Within the narrator's extended family Hokkien represents the paternal legacy and is an alienating factor testifying to the fragmentation of the narrator's immediate family (after bankruptcy) and its envelopment in the warren of the grandfather's patriarchal house where the narrator and her immediate siblings were fed only leftovers due to their lowly position in the family hierarchy.[6] In the larger national context, however, Chinese-ness is depicted as being at odds with, first, British colonialism and then the Malay drive for independence. The accessories of Chinese-ness include the language constituted as an internalized and self-alienating force:

> I heard Hokkien as an infant and resisted it, because my mother did not speak it to me . . . calling into question the notion of a mother tongue tied to a racial origin. As a child of a Hokkien community, I should have felt that propulsive abrasive dialect in my genes. Instead, when I speak Hokkien, it is at the level of a five-year-old . . . It remains at a more powerful level a language of exclusion, the speech act which disowns me in the very place of birth.
>
> (Lim 1996: 11)

Later, after migration to the United States, the narrator encounters the scepticism with which her English is greeted when delivered through her 'visible minority' body.[7] As graduate student and then as teacher in two community colleges she increasingly doubts the value of teaching standard English composition to, in the first example, predominantly Puerto Rican students, and in the second to conservative working-class students who inhabit a bizarre mid-western Raymond Carver world. There are never any doubts, though, from childhood onwards, that acquiring an education in the dominant language, English, remains the key to a future displaced as far as possible from poverty.

Garrett Hongo's text, in turn, depicts an opposition between the pidgin of Hawai'i and the standard English he encounters in the United States. The narrator feels ambivalent because in the search for community and identity traced by this text, pidgin signifies establishing community whereas his guides and mentors on the road to becoming a poet write in (or have been translated into) English. The Prologue describes the rituals of having the mother tongue reshaped by a mother ambitious for her son to succeed according to the hegemonic dictates of the new culture:

> She teaches me to flatten the melody of my speaking, taking the lilt of Portuguese from my sentences, the singsong of Canton Chinese. I extract the hard, clipped vowel-oriented syllables of Hawaiian, saying poor, not pu'a. I have to soften my tongue to shape it around the new way of saying words, to make it shape itself in my mouth more quickly so that I can make more sounds, smaller sounds, faster sounds in a sentence that has to flutter the way a mullet swims . . .
>
> (Hongo 1995: x)

In the journey back to Hawai'i and the search for a genealogy connected to community, pidgin becomes a key factor. Although the narrator bears the name of his grandfather's well-known grocery store in the town of Volcano, it is not until he lapses into pidgin that the locals acknowledge his right to this genealogy and its associated communal histories and, indeed, it is only then that they are prepared to offer stories which contribute to the density and texture of those histories. Weaving through these engagements with the hybrid pidgin, akin to Lim's *Peranakan* hybrid ancestry (Lim 1996: 4), is the narrator's access to Japanese, a knowledge he hides strategically when he encounters the ghosts/*ugetsu* from his family's past, particularly the women. As in Lim's text, here too there is another set of stories that purport to be transparently about female betrayal and abandonment. The narrator hides his knowledge of Japanese from the step-grandmother who supposedly cheated his father of his inheritance and from the grandmother herself, a professional dancer who, like Lim's mother, was perceived to have 'abandoned' her children. However, the term 'abandon' is highly ambiguous and who abandons whom is often not addressed as a valid question. The edifice of the family, of the culture, remains paramount and within it women have their tight fit. The fact that they may be forced to leave an oppressive structure then becomes re-coded as 'abandonment'. Clearly though, women must at times 'abandon' the family, a particular genealogy, if they are to retain any sense of themselves outside the 'glue' of family (Lim 1996a: 92).[8] Hongo's narrator hides his knowledge of Japanese so that he can ambush these grandmothers into a confession that will explain their supposed 'crimes' and in this recognition of their 'guilt' reconstitute tidy and masculinist genealogies. But for readers informed by feminism it doesn't quite work in such a seamless way.

It is interesting to note in passing that the framework for this memoir is the classic one of the detective or crime novel in which the autobiographical narrator seeks the hidden clues to his or her genealogy. The model may be traced to Sophocles' *Oedipus* and, like that drama, links the individual's destiny to larger societal responsibilities. There is a certain monomaniacal solepsism at work here in which the world, the state, the community are personified as the self, *tout court*. On the other hand, taking on the responsi-bility of bearing witness necessarily underpins this self-centred version of subjectivity, as does the genre of the memoir. In Lim's text the narrator states: 'Meaning radiated from me.' But this is a child's position, a type of primary oral-sadistic viewpoint before separations of various kind take place.[9]

Hongo's text, more so than Lim's, tries to uncover the crimes against self-as-community, whether they be of female forebears or of the US government's wartime policy of internment of Japanese Americans. In complex ways these actions function to produce simultaneously a 'unique' individual history which also signifies as a typical one (in the sense of a typology). It points as well to the pedagogical component in the autobiography-as-detective-yarn where the scales fall progressively from the narrator's eyes until, like Oedipus, his paradoxical blindness, or castration (read as cultural subjugation) in the

Freudian model, may be read as symptomatic of his knowledge of a higher truth of self in relation to community. As with Oedipus the riddle of origins is intimately tied to the female-as-betrayer, whether it be Jocasta, or the Sphinx or the Oracle at Delphi. Hongo's grandmothers are connected with the other *ugetsu* he pursues in the text. In the attempt to 'replant' himself in the island he conjures a vision of Pele, the goddess of Hawai'i, and notes in himself the desire to step on the body of woman which characterizes his exploration of the flora and geology of the island. His rootedness, or attempts to construct autochthony (a classic move in the quest Radhakrishnan identifies for mystic origins), is charged with heteronormativity, and the encounter with the female principle often involves betrayals, more often than not his own, in that it betrays him into revealing his own perceived inadequacy, or lack of inner resources. This admission of vulnerability is not unlike Lim's narrator when she feels that she is sustained by only 'thin stories' once she has left her family behind (Lim 1996a: 161). The problem is that while genealogy is usually analysed as supporting traditional patriarchal rights to property, the loss of a family tree may also deprive one of any place in the world at all. The individual, as in certain classic landscape paintings, serves as a kind of measure or scale in and of the landscape, primarily for another human viewer who recognizes the appropriate codes.

Hongo's struggle with language is traced as well in the desire to be a poet through numerous creative writing classes and through the rather Bloomian anxiety (of influence)[10] he traces an affiliation with mostly male (and white) poets who haunt his own poetic education – Yeats, Dante, Rilke and his own paternal grandfather whose lost death ode is recreated, or ghosted, through him by the grandfather. On the other hand, it is his maternal grandfather's injunction to write, to bear witness to the history of Japanese internment, that gives him the legitimation to seek (as well as invent) community as both poet and pedagogue.[11]

This brings us to the further stages of how the wrestling with language leads to the legitimation of the poet as both inspired proponent of language and the poet in her and his most ancient sense as the chronicler of community, the local.[12] In one of the appendices to *Mothertalk*, Roy Kiyooka refers to 'the pulse of an English . . . not my mother tongue' (1997a: 181), thus conjuring the spectacle of someone caught between two languages, adrift from the fundamental bedrock of a culture. Indeed, this text exudes an almost unbearable poignancy. Paradoxically perhaps, its mediated nature heightens rather than dilutes this effect. In the first instance *Mothertalk* evokes the relatively traditional memoir of a parent by a child but in this case the parent in fact, as we learn in the preface, outlives the child and the text is in turn edited by a former companion, Daphne Marlatt, well known for her own nuanced writings on relations among women, including those between mothers and daughters. Her graceful execution of the task of ordering this monologue also represents, in its own right, her homage to her late friend, Roy Kiyooka. Thus in its very form the text is both a very particularized excursion into a communal and individual life as well as being visibly linked to a wider national history and culture. In some respects and implicitly, Marlatt inserts Kiyooka's life within the mother's text, both in the structuring of these memoirs and by means of the inclusion of the introduction and appendices, the latter comprising a brief interview with Kiyooka's father and a talk and letter by Kiyooka himself by way of autobiographically contextualizing the familial relationships.

As this book demonstrates, Kiyooka's mother represented his access to an imagined ethnicity, that of being Japanese as well as Japanese Canadian at a certain fraught historical juncture which culminated in the internment of Japanese Canadians. 'She and she alone reminds me of my Japanese self by talking to me before I even had thought of learning anything . . . So that it is that I find myself going home to keep in touch with my mother's tongue and, it must be, the ghost of my father's silences' (Kiyooka 1997a:182). In fact, fathers figure prominently in this text. Mary Kiyooka's strongest affiliations, as presented here, are, arguably, to her own father, that last scion of an impoverished samurai family who educated his daughter in the particular form of kendo swordsmanship (*Iai*) of which he was the last acknowledged master. The other dominant note is Mary's own nostalgia, not for some diffused 'Japan' but for a very specific place – Tosa, conjured up in all its idiosyncrasies through the cast of characters which populated her early life. While the stringencies of an arranged marriage and life in Canada are luminously presented as well – enhanced by their fragmented nature because it allows the reader's imagination to enter the text – the defining focus remains Tosa and Mary's overwhelming desire to return there.

Kiyooka's own life touched many people (O'Brian *et al.* 2002) and testified to a particular cultural period in Canadian Modernism which, amongst other elements, illustrated a country coming to terms with its own diversity and hybridity. Kiyooka was a Canadian whose formal education ended with the bombing of Pearl Harbor (Kiyooka 1997c). The sense of interlocking communities is illustrated in this text as well as in Kiyooka's classic *Transcanada Letters* (Kiyooka 1975) which threads the country together in affectionate delight at its bewildering variety. With the posthumous publication of Kiyooka's collected poems, edited by Roy Miki, himself a tireless advocate of Japanese Canadian culture and history (particularly with respect to the Japanese Redress movement), Kiyooka is established as a substantial figure illustrating the art of this group, this history, which is at the same time a unique and individualistic artistic achievement. The sense of belonging in his poems (Kiyooka 1997a) alternates with that feeling of internal exile partially captured by a loss of language (as documented in *Mothertalk*) and conveyed in such moments in the poems as the meditations which bridge a visit to Hiroshima and the internment of Canadians of Japanese descent. 'I never saw the "yellow peril" in myself (Mackenzie King did)' (Kiyooka 1997a: 170).[13]

Here we encounter the familiar tension of the global and local: that the local signals its own disavowal in the global where the local tends to be defined solely by global interests. The driving imperative of these texts is that there is a right to write and be read no matter what one's position in a larger geopolitical entity. The never-ending proliferation of the local (Hall 1996a; Wilson and Dissanayake 1996) necessarily rewrites a national narrative of belonging and its obverse, unbelonging, the unhomely, as analysed by Bhabha and others, for example in the work of Toni Morrison and Salman Rushdie (Bhabha 1994). Such 'local' perspectives also rewrite global lines of power and significance. As Lim's narrator states, somewhat sardonically, 'I listened to the chatter of Americans caught up in the great adventure of their culture . . . The United States and I were too provincial for each other. I felt the intensity of our self-absorption' (Lim 1996a: 159).[14]

The idea of what constitutes community has been a contentious and compelling one for some time in multicultural debates because it has foreclosed on as much as it has facilitated modes of belonging (Cohen *et al.* 1999). As national and global boundaries change, as ethnic absolutism regains a footing, the concept of community is constantly redefined. A revealing evocation of a stable community, harking back to a classic pastoral model, occurs in the Australian writer David Malouf's description of a Tuscan village where the sense of community is represented by the fact that 'all the dead are still living here' both in the stories told about them in the small tapestry of the village's history as well as in the alternate village of the dead, the lovingly tended cemetery (Malouf 1986: 76). The image is in stark contrast to the lines from Canadian poet Earle Birney quoted at the beginning of this chapter. There are many senses of community evoked by these texts. In Lim's memoirs they range from the extended family whose influence is often felt as a constricting one to the provisional alliances formed, for example, by the block group in her Brooklyn street:

> In the Malaysia of my childhood, stratified by race, religion, and long-standing familial bonds, historically existing communal identities so dominated political action that new formations of civic identity were difficult if not impossible. In contrast, the necessity for political action in the United States . . . could create community where none existed before, thus contributing to the continuous fresh construction of civic identities. But the community offered by such block associations is as transient and unstable as its members.
>
> (Lim 1996: 177)

More prolonged satisfaction comes from the extended community of sisterhood she gradually forges through the women's movement.[15] In Hongo's text the sense of community of any kind is elusive until he begins to gather its fragments together in the town of Volcano. Before then he is haunted by his family's sense of detachment and fragmentation.[16] All three poets, however, find their most sustained consolations in the writerly communities differently forged by each.

A way of measuring whether this community does indeed exist is signalled in each text by the right to criticize cultural politics from within, where critique does not lead to denial of belonging. Lim's narrator is constantly punished for her inability to stifle this questioning and often this punishment is aggravated by the fact that she is doubly displaced as a racialized woman. Hongo traces the implications of the denial of this right on a whole community. In the formalized generational groupings characteristic of Japanese-American society he observes how the Issei and Nisei (first and second generation) were unable to deal with the betrayal constituted by the internment experience. Their silence and apparent amnesia were a way of rejecting a 'defiled' history.[17] It was the only way to go on living, but the costs of this were manifold (and here there are numerous traces of the pedagogical cautionary tale). On the one hand it resulted in the tribalism of the schoolyard, where the narrator is beaten up by his Japanese-American schoolmates because he dates someone outside the group:

> All spring and summer, I'd been immune, unaware of the enmity of the crowd. I hadn't realized that, in society, humiliation is a force more powerful than love. Love does not exist within society, but only between two, or among family ... The Japanese American community understood their public disgrace and lived modestly, with deep prohibitions. I was acting outside of this history ... I was not yet initiated into the knowledge that we Japanese were *not* like anyone else, that we lived in a community of violent shame ... I can still taste the blood ... and feel the depth of anger that must have been *historical*, *tribal*, arising from fears of dissolution and diaspora.
>
> (Hongo 1995a: 220–1)

There is also the more oblique example of his father's funeral where, 'though all of a genuine grief and honoring was there, there were only these little and ragged ways of finding symbols and completed processes, and the sadness had no way of entering my mind as anything more than the sincere white noise of modern loss, a consolational fumbling toward ceremony in diaspora' (Hongo 1995a: 290).[18] To balance this cultural vacuum, the narrator attempts to create new rituals rooted in the body, from learning to walk in 'Japanese' fashion on the slippery pathway to the outside shower, to preparing meals. Ritualized corporeal action steadies the mind, a kind of meditation, and privileged among such communally shared rituals is the public performance of poetry. Unlike Lim's depiction, Hongo's experience of poetry is consistently transmitted in the context of performance: the poetry reading or the workshop which transforms poetry into a communal experience, an ordering of the public sphere along certain celebratory and consensual lines. Indeed a public reading in Hawai'i begins the journey which will take him back to Volcano and the family history.

But, as stated earlier, perhaps the most nuanced sense of belonging is signified by the right to criticize. In the preface to his collection of Asian-

American writers, Hongo discusses the factional struggles within the Asian-American community, arguing both that these have to be treated with more tolerance and that, indeed, they need to take place. 'There is a profound difference', he argues, 'between the idea that any group has an exclusive right to engage in authorized acts of cultural representation and the idea that cultural representations are not open to criticism, whether by a group or an individual critic' (Hongo 1995a: 30). In other words, whereas no one has the right to monopolize or exclusively represent certain groups or histories, whether these be mainstream or minority, by the same token any writer can be criticized for his or her representations.

In Lim's text the search for sociality leading to the active manufacture of community is rather differently presented. Community is defined as existing outside the restrictions of the family (restrictions which are exacerbated for women) and as a way out of these constraints. Lim traces her relationship to various communities as a way of demonstrating both the narrator's isolation and the power hierarchies (and their abuse) by which these communities are often structured. They range from the convent school and its mandate to construct the administrative 'mimic men' (both writers refer to Naipaul), or intermediaries of British colonialism, to the new national agenda which has overtaken Malaysia and the *Bumiputra* programme of 'Malaysianization'. The female principle as enigma at the centre in this case is not so much the abandoning woman as the abandonment *of* women. In other words, there is the increasing recognition by the narrator that these structures exclude women by their very constitution or, at the very least, divide women along racialized lines in terms of privilege (as in the case of the nuns at the convent school or her faculty colleagues later on in the college hierarchy).

Consistently the narrator succeeds in jumping through the institutional hoops. She gains a first at the University of Malaya and subsequent fellowships to the United States, yet none of these are 'pure' triumphs. There is always the sense of having had to violently contort or suppress aspects of herself, or that the achievement is devalued by the very fact of her having acquired it (a familiar spectre in feminist memoirs). These achievements are also linked to male mentors who are mostly abusive, beginning with her father and then progressing through a series of lovers including, devastatingly, an academic supervisor. The one thing she can never silence is her anarchic and questioning voice which always lands her in trouble or, one might say with equal truth, saves her.

The entry to the United States is a lesson in patronization – from the Canadian nudists who are her first landlords to the department head who accuses her of trying to intimidate him because she seeks clarification regarding his criteria for giving promotions. Even the attempts to forge solidarity in a Brooklyn neighbourhood with the renters who impinge on her as house-owner are fraught with compromise and a recognition of painfully internalized class contradictions.[19]

Throughout these encounters it is the assumed role of poet-pedagogue which helps her to survive. There are the frustrations of recognizing that the Puerto Rican students in the community college are only too reminiscent of her own fight against systemic racism and resulting poverty in Malaysia:

> Over and over again I wondered if my hours of intense teaching were helping or actively harming my students . . . Were we setting up obstacles to lengthen their social dependency and lowly economic status and to justify our salaries and professional rank? . . . Is all written English formulaic, and is teaching English the teaching of a series of formulae . . . Is an educated person a writing person? What does it mean to be a writing person? . . . We exhorted our tough ghetto students to express their feelings, but only in acceptable grammar. The contradictions were unbearable.
>
> (Lim 1996: 180–1)

While the processes described are the by now familiar contradictions traced in much colonial education, the answer to these bleak questions is, to some degree, provided by her own return visits to Malaysia and her growing reputation there as a poet. Her assumption of the role of poet-chronicler is combined with research establishing the academic credibility of the literature of the South-East Asian region (Lim 1993; 1994). The ironies provided by colonialism and diaspora are collapsed in the curious example where, during a visit to Malaysia to copy-edit a brother's thesis (for correct English style, one assumes), an Australian professor fluent in Bahasa Malaysian, as she is not, asks her to check his translation of an Indonesian text set in America for American idiomatic usage (Lim 1996a: 174). It is one of the few moments she experiences of being interpellated as 'American'.

The eventual awareness of these accidents of history as constituting her private strengths are confirmed by finally being hired by a university (rather than community college) to inspire other students of the Asian diaspora. Through it all weaves the personalized quest founded on the grim desire to have her son accepted in the United States. As she puts it, 'there are many ways in which America tells you you don't belong' (Lim 1996a: 199). The right to criticize from within is seized here also. By reaching this position, or legitimation, and in a return journey to family, though differently constituted, she re-establishes a sense of community. The growing legitimacy she and others are able to give South-East Asian writing in its various sites in Malaysia, Singapore and the Philippines, in turn helps her establish the importance of Asian-American writing and enables her finally to create a reciprocal relationship with a growing body of students attracted to this field, either because of personal histories or because of a growing recognition that America cannot afford to remain exclusively a Western civilization (Lim 1996a: 230). The memoir ends on the following note: 'Everywhere I have lived in the United States . . . I have felt an absence of place, myself absent in America' (Lim 1996a: 232).[20] Inspiration is drawn from the fluid mutability of the sea and the refrain in her text that 'the sea is my mother'. It represents a kind of accommodation with the mother without resorting to a glib resolution.

Meanwhile Hongo's text concludes on a less tranquil note in its summation of and responses to the amnesia cultivated by his forebears in America:

> And I grew up *detached* too – from a family history, from a feeling of a kind of *personal* and a kind of *tribal* stake in the world . . . I merely feel worthless. Or lost. Dispirited. . . . I realize I am without that governing story of a familial past . . . I am detached from all legitimacy . . . I am here on *sufferance*. A token . . . vaporous and far from home, removed from earth and the volcano . . . If my grandmother the dancer, left any legacy behind, it is one of detachment, of abandonment, of things let go . . . the long ceremony of detachment . . . it is as if my identity did not exist before I came to Volcano, before I stuck to *one* place in my mind and heart and tried to build an identity from there.
>
> (Hongo 1995a: 334–8)

While I have dealt with the memoirs of Lim and Hongo, both writers are at least as well known for their critical and pedagogical work in creating profiles for Asian-American writing. In other words, that they have changed the literary and cultural history of the United States. This is also true of the example of Roy Kiyooka in Canada, although his legacy is only posthumously being established (O'Brian *et al.* 2002; Egan and Helms 1999). As Roy Miki traces it, Kiyooka attempted to learn the idiom of aesthetic belonging, particularly during his period as a painter, but as he grew older he was drawn increasingly toward an attempt to recreate and identify with what he perceived as a lost Japanese heritage (Miki 2002: 80–1). This symbolic identification (as described in Chapter 5) allowed him to evaluate in retrospect the cultural specificity of those supposedly neutral aesthetic categories.

In her pioneering study of Chinese-Canadian literature Lien Chao assesses individual writers as subservient to the requirements of the larger community. The argument permeating Lien Chao's book is that Chinese Canadian writing is primarily (and perhaps exclusively) to be viewed as a representation of community. This approach in some respects throws one back to assumptions contained in the kind of Marxist literary criticism which suggests that cultural productions are to be seen predominantly as the expression of the social, particularly in the case of the novel.[21]

The literary historical plot produced by Chao is a familiar one to students concerned with the analysis of ethnic writings. The community spends the first generation struggling to survive so that cultural production is kept to a minimum and appears to be most authentically captured by oral life-stories. To some extent these tales are rendered all the more poignant by their seeming artlessness. The tension in these accounts is that individuals, as well as the group, are pitted against a cultural norm, a way of being in the world with which they are at odds, through language, through skin colour, or some of the other markers of difference which are to some extent always arbitrary and all the more painful for being that. There is no logic in the racism precipitated by cultural differences. Indeed to call them cultural differences is, after the work of Balibar and others, to some extent to invite the charge of indulging in a form of racism itself since difference is being invoked via the cultural, that is, a 'racism without races'.

Chao delineates the Canadian historical contexts of the Chinese exclusion legislation which meant that Chinese immigrants were forced to live in all-male communities since their wives and children were not permitted to join them. Their resulting lives of loneliness and isolation in turn fuelled the racist myths which functioned to keep this ethnic group on the margins of Canadian society. In the midst of these survival struggles the attempts to tell stories and to release those stories as a way to cement the community internally, in the first instance, are documented. 'As most of the Chinese-Canadian writers are also community activists and archivists, the need to reclaim the community history preceded their literary endeavours' (Chao 1997: 27). Myths and folklore are the homeland glue binding the generations together, closely followed by theatre as the first attempts to represent that communal experience.[22] Stories are kept in circulation to conjure up reminders of the imagined motherland. Eventually, according to Chao, anthologies mark the first steps that bind the group to the larger community of the nation. These attempts to attain cultural franchise are part of the freight of the slender anthologies launched into the world. Only three at this stage (Powell Street *et al.* 1979; Lee and Wong-Chu 1991; Quan and Wong-Chu 1999) though, more recently, there has been the added ballast of individual writers whose productions are drawing the attention of a wider community of readers.[23]

Chao describes this journey as a progress from silence to voice and notes, among other analytical insights, the trope of bone-gathering in many of these texts as one which stands figuratively for the production of a community archive of ancestral voices and presences. This interpretive lens is used relatively effectively with some texts but runs into difficulties when dealing with a 'bad girl' writer such as Evelyn Lau,[24] who, she concedes, may indeed represent the possibility of new forms and new aesthetic directions (Chao 1997: 172–3) but who is, at greater length, castigated for not being a proper activist (Chao 1997: 162). Chao is more comfortable with documentary accounts such as Denise Chong's *The Concubine's Children* and the more complex works of fiction such as Sky Lee's *Disappearing Moon Café* and Wayson Choy's *Jade Peony*. Chinese Canadian history and its specific perspectives are the result of yoking the general Canadian legacy of representation to the mediated and muted traditions emanating from an imagined China, a China which needs to be recovered and partially invented by the generations not born there.[25] Given the difficult history of Chinese migration in Canada, the specific community histories are shrouded in secrecy, thus making the project of recovery particularly difficult. The spectre of officialdom or surveillance lurks in the background of these family stories.

It is useful to compare these accounts of the rise of Asian-American and Asian-Canadian writing over the last decade to an older tradition in Canada, that of the Italo-Canadian community. In 1990 there appeared the proceedings of the first national conference of Italian-Canadian writers which had taken place in 1986 (Minni 1990). More than a decade later the conference of Italian-Canadian writers held in October 1998 in Vancouver was appropriately dominated by a celebration of the publishing house Guernica's twentieth anniversary. The struggles of this publisher are documented in the collection of essays *In Italics* by its founder Antonio D'Alfonso, described at the meeting as a 'renaissance man' who was a writer himself as well as a public intellectual and promoter of other people's work – another example of those poet-pedagogues this chapter has been analysing. At the meeting, tables were arrayed with a selection from Guernica and among them a catalogue as artfully produced as any of the other texts there. In its small way it illustrated an attention to detail and the fact that this venture remains more a labour of love than a commercial enterprise – an oddity in a publishing world where the dominant stories concern mega-bookstore chains and the serial takeover of well-known publishers by transnational corporations. This perilous durability is substantiated by the history delineated in D'Alfonso's essays. The story of Guernica is also intimately entwined with the recent history of Montréal, where the venture began but where it no longer persists.

In the eyes of D'Alfonso and other Italian Canadians the group represents an alternative mediating perspective that could, if used properly, represent a kind of resolution to the protracted oppositional struggle between franco-phone and anglophone Canada. As a group which is trilingual rather than bilingual, Italian Canadians may lay claim to European modernity in ways comparable to the founding cultures but are not, in their own eyes, as confined within an intransigent history of conflict (Salvatore 1991; Linteau 1992). In D'Alfonso's analysis they function as a conduit for the respectful inclusion of all the ethnic minorities encompassed by Canada and this inclusion is predicated in terms of a pragmatic access to production (D'Alfonso 1996: 17). In other words, without documentation, through the publishing of these texts, the community's presence in the cultural landscape is too easily rendered invisible (Salvatore 1998: 12).

D'Alfonso draws a parallel with another dissident group in Montréal, the Jews, most identified perhaps with a writer like Mordecai Richler who is more aligned with an anglophone dispensation. In ways akin to Kiyooka's work, these essays too are fraught with pain and a sense of lost opportunities, a mourning for a city and for what has become of francophone culture and, in its wake, of Canadian culture: 'The main questions that Quebec must ask itself are: Can it (and will it) allow all the voices to speak about the culture of this province? Or does it still have the power to decide which voice belongs and which voice does not belong to Quebecois culture?' (D'Alfonso 1996: 99). Given the bitter legacy of the October 1995 referendum on Quebec sovereignty narrowly lost by the sovereignists allegedly because of the 'ethnic vote' (Kostash 2000: 89–99), the delegates at the conference generally interpreted this to be a coded reference to the Italian Canadian community. Indeed, the subsequent publication of Fulvio Caccia's *Republic Denied: The Loss of Canada* (Caccia 2002) confirms this perception.[26]

Translation and the question of which language dominates is a motif which weaves its way through D'Alfonso's book. As in the case of Chao's history, and more obviously in Kiyooka's volumes, the ghosts of other languages haunt the Canadian cultural landscape. In this case D'Alfonso asks why the issue of translation is not rendered more central to Canada's unique national culture, for example, why translations emanating from within Canada are judged to be less commercially desirable than those produced in France? Or why the Canada Council (the national funding body for the Arts) refuses to consider books written in Italian to be Canadian texts (D'Alfonso 1996: 81, 225)? These concerns have animated D'Alfonso's work for many years. In a novel written a decade ago he has his protagonist voice the following:

> The city I call my native city was called *Monreale*. It had no accent on the *e* nor a *t* for the cross on Mount Royal, yet the term gained a glorious *e* at the end which acted as a constant reminder of my origins.
>
> Monreale confers on me the privilege of being three persons in one. Being a strange combination of three cultures, I was able to converge my three views of this city and form a completely unique triangular (*tripartite*) worldview which was not always appreciated by either the francophones or the anglophones who forced me to take sides in their strife for power . . . My Monreale is a city of many visions. . . .
>
> (D'Alfonso 1995: 212)

Interestingly, and in contrast to Chao's history, the focus on a particular group strenuously avoids any appeal to an essential identity. Such dilemmas are always an issue in the critiques of multiculturalism, particularly insofar as these emanate from so-called ethnic writers themselves, that is, from within multiculturalism rather than by conservative opinions which find the very recognition of cultural difference to be divisive. According to D'Alfonso, to see these texts as communal texts means that one would read them simply for content alone (D'Alfonso 1996: 68), avoiding their formal and aesthetic dimensions. This point of view is further developed in Pasquale Verdicchio's collection of essays where he refers to multiculturalism as 'institutionalised ethnicism' (Verdicchio 1997: 15).[27] Another refrain in his and D'Alfonso's texts is that diaspora is not simply a matter of separation and exile but that it involves a new formation because the various communities connect across the global terrain retaining their individual indiosyncracies as well as forming broader constituencies. Verdicchio argues for the need to consider the North American Italian diasporic histories within the grid of racialization in order not to naturalize 'pigmentation' or 'whiteness' and other 'favoured somatic markers' (Verdicchio 1997: 45). 'Whiteness is salvaged as the only safe category for all good citizens, no matter what their background. White is in fact a color-blind category; one does not have to be white (as in Caucasian) to be white, for this is an aesthetics, an ideology of cultural absorption and erasure rather than an ethnic category' (Verdicchio 1997: 75). He argues further that it is preferable to speak of an Italian continuum rather than to continue to single out 'decontextualized subalterns' whose experiences were 'truncated by immigration itself' (Verdicchio 1997: 146).

While Filippe Salvatore's controversial study deals primarily with fascism amongst the Italians in Montréal, his book also demonstrates the history of a community which was 'the cradle of Italian settlement in Canada from the beginning of the nineteenth century' (Salvatore 1998: 12). The fascism he documents within this community was as much a manifestation of diasporic nostalgia, an identification with 'the notion of *italianitá*' (Salvatore 1998: 19), as anything more overtly political in the classic sense. In 1940 many members of the community were arrested as 'enemy aliens', their assets confiscated, and some were imprisoned for many years (Salvatore 1998: 32ff). For those who considered themselves as the 'third solitude' within Canada, this was quite a blow to their collective sense of belonging.[28] After the Quebecois politics of the 60s many of the community defected from Montréal to Toronto, a move which was also a linguistic one from francophone to anglophone orientation. It is precisely this move, and the many losses it entails, which is at the centre of D'Alfonso's text.

All these texts offer eloquent testimony to hybridity in diaspora as figured in the hauntings of language, family and the representative interpellations (in the Althusserian sense) of diaspora. Recalling Malouf's image, within language too there needs to be the recognition of the presence of those ghosts, those forgers of idiolects, who take up room in a particular language and change it by their presence as they progress from being tenants, to citizens, to the historical continuity of community provided by the living dead.

Conclusion

Transcultural improvisations

Pedagogy, the performative, and abjection tied to a reconsideration of bodies and spaces are concerns which haunt this book. In recent months I have been trying to articulate a theory of stammering pedagogy, drawing on Deleuze's work, and attempting to find ways of expressing the alertness to differences within which my teaching has functioned over the last three decades. A stammering and unsettling pedagogy may well be the only ethical possibility for a serial immigrant critic and teacher such as myself. I have over the decades attempted to locate a home within language (which language and within it what kind of register?), a language which is not one's first language complicated further by having to fashion it into a pedagogical tool and having to do this in a displaced context, that is, one in which one did not 'grow up' like a tendril or vine clinging to the certainties of particular social and physical structures. Yet in a different sense, language remains the most portable of accessories, one which has carved out a corporeal space; and when there are several languages the body sometimes transits from one to the other less than gracefully.[1] None the less languages, with their inflections and rhythms, as much as their overt signification, invariably function to remind one of home in palpable ways. It is the meanings we first encounter in a specific language that structure our later lives psychically and physically and at the same time provide a prophylactic against the universalist claims of other linguistic meaning structures. Displaced from home, we are thus unable to feel at home because we are too aware of the alternative and parallel worlds we could be inhabiting equally well.

But what more can one say about this stammer? Kristeva notes that for classical Greek culture the barbarians are the ones identified by their clumsy and improper speech (Kristeva 1991: 51). In a relatively recent essay, Gilles Deleuze conceptualizes the stammer or stutter in ways reminiscent of the better-known concept of deterritorialisation, also linked to Deleuze and Guattari's early work on Kafka and minority languages (Deleuze and Guattari 1986). The stutter in language is carefully differentiated from the stutter in speech. In the former, language itself begins to 'vibrate and stutter' (Deleuze 1997: 108) and the writer 'makes the language as such stutter: an affective and intensive language, and no longer an affectation of the one who speaks'

(Deleuze 1997: 107). As in the Kafka essay, Deleuze describes the process as inventing a '*minor* use of the major language' (Deleuze 1997: 109) as 'minorizing' the major language. In sum, it renders the native language foreign or discovers the foreignness within it, 'he carves out a nonpreexistent foreign language *within* his own language' (Deleuze 1997: 110). The further result is to conjure the limits of language and to situate it primarily in relation to silence.

Attempting to turn the stammer into a pedagogical model, as I am trying to do, means that one reveals to North American students, for example, both the 'foreignness' of another culture at the same time that one destabilizes their own cultural assumptions and certainties in producing meaning. At this moment in history it appears to be a worthwhile exercise.

Hauntologies[2]

> . . . it obliges us to ponder if the end of history is but the end of a certain concept of history.
>
> (Derrida 1994: 15)

But the notion of performative pedagogies which runs through this book may also be approached in other ways. I am of course using the notion of performance both in the commonplace way of staging a theatrical event in which all kinds of 'acts' and 'acting' take place and in the sense that it circulates in relation to Judith Butler's work where it is embedded in concepts of iterated citational practices, that is, that all performances take place within speech acts and within regimes of discourse whose authority is underwritten by their repetition. The latter meaning creates problems when one attempts to argue for a certain kind of agency which, in Butler's frameworks, is much more difficult to achieve since, generally speaking, she does not permit agency or volition (or rebellion) outside discursive regimes, at least not in the ways agency is conceived in many sociological discussions. In the first chapter of *Excitable Speech* Butler states the following:

> Could language injure us if we were not, in some sense, linguistic beings, beings who require language in order to be? . . . If we are formed in language, then that formative power precedes and conditions any decision we might make about it . . . To be called a name is one of the first forms of linguistic injury that one learns. But not all name calling is injurious. Being called a name is also one of the conditions by which a subject is constituted in language . . .
>
> (Butler 1997: 1–2)

Language as site and symptom of trauma is a theme winding its way through this book. Fulvio Caccia, part of that group of Italo-Canadians who mourned their exile from Montréal, traces the loss of a utopian republic which Canada might have become in the various linguistic shifts that were emebedded in its history. Like a number of us, he identifies 'transculturalism' as the latest term in a continuum to which multiculturalism belongs; a continuing quest to capture the hybrid realities of diaspora and globalisation. Locating the genealogy of 'tranculturalism' in the work of Latin American critics like Fernando Ortiz, he also finds it in recent developments in psychoanalysis where it is used to name 'disjunctive behaviour': 'Thus in sociological circles, transculture is a positive way of perceiving the future; in medicine it designates a trauma' (Caccia 2002: 69).

The theme of hauntings wound its way through a symposium on 'Trans-culturalisms: Métissage' which I co-ordinated in February 2002.[3] Françoise Lionnet discussed Maryse Condé's rewriting of Emily Brontë's *Wuthering Heights* as *Windward Heights*, resetting it in Guadeloupe. In other words, a canonical text of British literature is rewritten by someone from the margins of an adjacent postcolonial world haunted by memories of slavery and a complex system of classifications of 'race'. Roy Miki spoke eloquently of his experiences of the Canadian Japanese Redress movement which continues to haunt Canadian (and in a kindred version US) history. Monika Kin Gagnon spoke of trying to find a way to locate her position as a Canadian 'multicultural' critic when analysing the increasingly spiritual work of First Nations film-maker Dana Claxton. This attempt to position oneself ethically as a non-indigenous critic when engaging with indigenous cultures and artists was also grappled with in the third session by Ann Kaplan, in an analysis of films and visual work by Australian Aboriginal women, and by Elspeth Probyn, who triangulated her relationship to the Australian Aboriginal Reconciliation movement with a poem written by her own grandmother in which she spoke from the position of a First Nations woman in Canada. These days it would be difficult to conceive of such an act, but within the ideologies of that era it carried the pathos of someone trying to position herself in another cultural milieu. Rosalyn Ing's account of the Canadian residential schools, part of her PhD. thesis, formed a stark reminder of the contemporary implications of this still too-hidden history.

Other presentations could also be seen in terms of hauntings. But I'd like to focus on the final session in which Simon Harel spoke of the tormented analyses of a psychoanalytical precursor in Montréal, Julien Bigras. Here is his abstract:

Trauma and 'métissage': the American journey of Julien Bigras.

Julien Bigras, psychiatrist, psychoanalyst and writer, is an important figure in the literature of Quebec and of the francophone world. He was trained in France in the sixties by Conrad Stein, a colleague of Jacques Lacan. His life was dedicated to the study of borderline states like psychosis and incest. His highly original work can be situated between autobiography and self-fiction (autofiction); it deals with the psychoanalyst's suffering

and with his place in the psychoanalytic process. In *Ma vie, ma folie* and
L'Enfant dans le grenier, the narrative 'métissage' inscribes genealogic
insanity as a major motive in America's territorial foundation. In *Ma vie,
ma folie*, Julien Bigras interrogates the ambivalent place of métissage in
the heart of the colonial psyche, the tragic dimension of this in-between
which gives rise to a history traumatized by the origin's impurity.

(Harel 2002)

Harel referred to Bigras' life and work as, in turn, haunting him. Bigras' work
took the strange shape of counter-transference where he identified with a First
Nations 'Iroquois' patient, Marie, who, in a sense, takes him over. Harel spoke
of this in the context of indigeneity as a kind of ghostly presence, a haunting in
the ways that we have come to associate with the work of Toni Morrison, for
example. Sitting next to him in that session, was Drew Hayden Taylor, an
Ojibway Canadian writer who grew up on a reserve very close to the space
Bigras/Harel was discussing. And there was nothing ghostly about Drew.[4] His
funny and perceptive comments on the history of First Nations Theatre in
Canada, focusing on his own work and that of Tomson Highway, provided a
robust and very material counterpoint to Simon Harel's analysis. Here is an
unforgettable moment of cross-cultural translation from his talk:

. . . I got a call one day from a man saying he would like to produce that
play [a comedy] and I went, "Oh, cool, go ahead. More power to you. Send
me the check." And he says, "But, yes, first I would like to get your
permission to translate it into Italian." I said, "Pardon? Where are you
calling from?" And he says, "Venice." So, he was the chair of the
University of Venice Theatre Department and he wanted to produce an
aboriginal comedy in downtown Venice. And, we started doing this whole
translation thing back and forth, again, and it was even worse this time.
There's a line in the play where one of the characters says, "Yeah,
whatever turns your crank." And he emails me and says, "What is crank?
Is that a reference to drugs?" And, I make a reference to . . . AIM, the
American Indian Movement, which was a political movement in the late
1960s and 1970s and it's still around today – and, in terms of the context of
the play, they had no idea what it meant. They just decided to use it. The
line was "I used to be a member of AIM." They translated it as "I used to
aim real good." So, they sent me the videotape of this production and I'm
watching this play, this aboriginal comedy, taking place at a Canadian
powwow with a group of Italian actors, who have probably never been to
Canada, let alone a powwow, wearing costumes by a costume designer
who had probably never been to Canada, let alone seen a powwow, on a
set designed by someone who had probably never been to Canada, or seen
a powwow, and they're just running back and forth in big pig-tails, like
Indian pig-tails with a headband, going "Il powwow!".[5]

(Taylor 2002)

Hybridity indeed! Thus the performative nature of the event occurred at a number of levels and brings to mind Peggy Phelan's analysis, 'transformative becoming is the almost always elegiac function of performance theory and writing, if not performance itself' (Phelan 1998: 11). The session was followed by a very lively discussion about the nature of ghosts in relation to indigeneity. Some of this was performed in incommensurable or untranslateable ways in that the body of theory upon which Harel was drawing, the distinction Freud made between mourning and melancholia (taken up as well in the work of Abraham and Torok 1994), tried to pose a separation between mourning (a healthy acknowledgment of loss) and melancholia, where the lost object remains buried or encrypted within the mourner who is never able to deal with this loss and wills it (in the sense of inheritance) to his/her descendants. In other words the loss is denied in all kinds of ways.[6]

The idea of such ghosting as a way of dealing with the attempted genocides and associated atrocities of colonialism has, understandably, cropped up all over the place. In the United States, for example, Avery Gordon's *Ghostly Matters* examines the phenomenon of cultural 'haunting' in sociology:

> Haunting is a constituent element of social life. It is neither premodern superstition nor individual psychosis; it is a generalizable social pheno-menon of great import. . . . The ghost is not simply a dead or missing person, but a social figure, and investigating it can lead to that dense site where history and subjectivity make social life. . . . Being haunted draws us affectively, sometimes against our will and always a bit magically, into the structure of feeling of a reality we come to experience, not as cold knowledge, but as transformative recognition.
>
> (Gordon 1997: 7–8)

For a tangible example, Australian Aboriginal film-maker Tracey Moffatt's *Night Cries: A Rural Tragedy* is a useful one. The film depicts an Aboriginal woman administering to the final days of her aged white mother, presumably her mother by adoption. Here is Ann Kaplan on the final sequence in the film:

> The mother's death frees the daughter into mourning for her loss. Movingly, the film shows the daughter curled up in the fetal position besides her mother's corpse. We first see the couple at eye level, but on the soundtrack we hear now only the baby's soulful cry. The angle then moves to an overview shot so that the daughter appears in a fetal position – as if returned to the position within the womb. Can we say that the daughter has moved through her trauma to find her unexpressed love for her pathetically aged mother – a love that seemed impossible before? . . . [a] performative working through [not] in the sense of 'cure' or healing but in that of mourning.
>
> (Kaplan 2001: 114)

Kaplan productively links her analysis to her continuing work on trauma and witnessing and in this spirit my own question is at a tangent to hers, informed by Derrida's quotation cited above: if the daughter is mourning her mother where does that leave the *white* mother, the whiteness of this other mother? The womb of this white mother was indeed never part of her history, but the tragedy resides in the promises it offered while at the same time eclipsing another history and other futures. As mentioned in earlier chapters, like the residential schools in Canada, in Australia as well, Aboriginal children were taken from their families to missions and mission schools and to adoption by white families. This led to terrible tragedies, some of which, as mentioned in Chapter 2, are captured in the long report called *Bringing Them Home* (Wilson 1997).

These abductions of so-called 'light-skinned' children, in order to force them to assimilate, are not so far removed from the traumatic history of slavery. Thus what are the ways in which the daughter is haunted by whiteness itself? There have, of course, been many studies which have dealt with the manner (as in the case of Bigras) in which the descendants of white colonizers have mourned or fallen prey to the complexities of melancholia in relation to indigeneity.[7] However, this continues to locate indigenous survivors (like Drew Hayden Taylor) as occluded by a ghostly indigeneity, at best, and always in the past, more or less moribund. If the mourning/melancholia of the indigenous peoples themselves are mentioned at all, it is usually in relation to the cultures they have lost and their own attempts to recover something from the ruins and traces which remain.

In a number of ways, *Night Cries* evokes the genre of the horror film and the influential work on the 'monstrous feminine' by Barbara Creed (1993) in which she suggests that the mother's participation in the symbolic needs to be re-evaluated. Creed explores the concept of the castrating (rather than castrated and abjected) maternal and traces its manifestations in the horror film, using it to explain the unsettling nature of the genre. It is possible to see the white mother, death-in-life, in the film as akin to Creed's castrating mother linked with the petrifying gaze of the Medusa. In one of the film's flashbacks the daughter, as little girl playing with two Aboriginal boys by the seashore, appears to be strangled by seaweed while her mother is absent or uncannily invisible. It is possible to link the seaweed to the Medusan icon and to perceive a metonymic sequence to the white mother who prevents the little girl from benign interaction with these emissaries from her other cultural world. At the end, one could also interpret the figure of the daughter reduced to child as being in fact castrated, as effectively prevented from ever living out the potential of other cultural selves. In Rosalyn Ing's painful account of the Canadian residential schools, one of the most poignant details on which she focused was the fact that children were prevented from learning parenting skills so that they found it difficult to become parents themselves. While there are moments of tenderness between the daughter and white mother in the film, it is pervaded as well by the daughter's barely controlled frustrated attempts to escape from this claustrophobic world – a dyadic unit whose destructive effects are analysed in various modalities by Creed.

For a different recovery of the maternal and a somewhat ironic statement on origins we turn to a work by urban Aboriginal artist Fiona Foley. Foley's installation was part of the 1996 exhibition *Colonial Post Colonial*, and is titled 'Native Blood'. Foley's ancestral homeland of Fraser Island was named after a white woman 'captured' by Aborigines.[8] In this piece, Foley replaces this charged colonial figure with an untitled photograph of her Aboriginal ancestress whom she states she recognizes through a similarity in the shape of their breasts (Losche 1996: 34). Foley provides this explanation:

> . . . to recast the heroine a perverse re-enactment takes place. The black heroine of yore. The heroine in this instance is Badtjala. The only way I could come close to her was to recast her in my image. The skirt I wear in the photograph titled *Native blood* is from Maningrida. Like the shell and the reed necklaces, these objects were made by Aboriginal women coming from a remote Australian community. The red, black and yellow hand-painted shoes symbolising the Aboriginal land rights flag. . . .
>
> (Foley qtd. in Losche 1996: 34–5)

This statement functions as a succinct example of the colonized subject wrenching indigeneity out of the paralysis effected by the petrifying colonialist gaze and reinserting it within the mobile and changing modalities of modernity – another concept of history, as Derrida's hauntology suggests, and a performative act at many levels.

In a recent and characteristically illuminating manner, Rey Chow has revisited the relationship between ethnic writing, narcissism and freedom. Chow's comments on the field of Asian-American studies in relation to abjection and narcissism and what she terms the 'difference revolution' are a fitting reference point for these concluding comments. Tracing a tradition of contradictions, she comments that:

> there is a certain rift between the laudable theorization of difference, on the one hand, and the numerous sociocultural and/or geopolitical situations in which difference has led not so much to emancipation as it has to oppression, on the other. This rift – this incommensurability between . . . equally compelling arguments about difference – is the key problem for any ethically responsible discussion of the politics of ethnicity today, and one ought not to think that a solution can be had simply by choosing one over the other. It would be more instructive to let the rift stand as a reminder of the ineluctable, overdetermined complexities at hand.
>
> (Chow 2002: 135)

The 'rift' to which she refers is that of 'a distinctive affective dissonance between theoretical writing, on the one hand, and fictional and autobiographical writing on the other' (Chow 2002: 135). The declarative abstractions of the theorists flatten and to some degree homogenize the many and varied experiences of the creative writers. In part this is due to a different relation to the temporal, according to Chow, that is, the orientation toward the future of the theorist as distinct from a preoccupation with the past of the auto-biographical writer. I suppose that by bringing together the two concerns through the 'discursive economy' of the 'poet-pedagogue' I could indeed stand accused of attempting to reconcile the rift rather than simply acknowledge it. On reflection, my pedagogical enterprise of the stammering immigrant critic/ artist attempts to recognize, and indeed emphasize, coexistent contradictions and destabilizations. If there is a utopian element in these pedagogies or these claims they are modest ones, constantly haunted by the unexpected borders of abjection – those dotted lines where meaning suddenly collapses or is blurred by melancholic presence. Whether this may be attributed to either the poet or the pedagogue is a matter of expediency. We live in a moment, once again, where there are too many answers and allegiance is demanded to a range of suspect truth-claims. Dwelling on the pedagogical processes of uncertainty, or, in Chow's terms, the wounded narcissism that may be linked to both an individual and group articulation (Chow 2002: 138–52) allows one to consider the ways in which theoretical writings are disturbed in their privileged claims to represent discursive rationalism. After all, theory too, as this book illustrates in many ways, may be permeated by the autobiographical impulse.

Just as these hauntologies offer different histories, so the notion of a stammering pedagogy does not offer grandiose claims. It is an attempt to suggest a model for teaching that does not claim to have absolute answers, indeed, is sceptical of the discourse of answers, the position of 'those who know'. Such a pedagogy is attuned to the ghostly dimension of other meanings in any pursuit of a definitive meaning. It is tuned in to the stammering, the dislocations which seethe beneath surfaces, whether these be of globalization or nationalisms. Within this framework, and when used strategically and critically, those multi-multiculturalisms help sustain such a stammering pedagogy, allowing it to disrupt the gathering menace, once again, of mono-lithic models of knowledge.

Notes

Introduction

1 See also Ch. 9 'Situated Knowledges' in Haraway 1991.

2 Edward Said's collection *Reflections on Exile and Other Essays* (Said 2000) eloquently articulates this condition and reveals why his example continues to be an inspiration for my own work and those of many others.

3 Critical multiculturalism is a term used to distinguish the kinds of analyses of multiculturalism which arise out of the fact that multiculturalism resonates globally and, as one would expect, carries very localized meanings. It does not mean an uncritical allegiance to various versions of state multiculturalism around the world. Some of these issues are covered in the Chicago Cultural Studies Group, 'Critical Multiculturalism', in Goldberg 1994.

4 The Canadian English departments I have encountered hold to English literature in its canonical British form rather more than do comparable departments in Australia who seem to have metamorphosed into Cultural Studies departments with relative ease. Some of it has to do with the prevalent Canadian desire to maintain a difference from the US models across the border. Another factor is that all undergraduate students in Canada (and most of North America generally) have to take a first-year English course. This functions to make university teachers of English the 'guardians' of the English language in ways that differ from the Australian models.

5 My own sense of the term was guided by Bob Hodge and Vijay Mishra's influential and much cited paper 'What is Post(-)colonialism?'. Hodge and Mishra distinguish between what they term complicit and oppositional postcolonialisms. The distinction arises out of debates around whether or not settler colonies such as Australia, New Zealand and Canada are entitled to call themselves postcolonial. Mishra and Hodge argue that the term postcolonial in such cases should be reserved for the struggles of the indigenous peoples who continue internal battles against the descendants of the settler colonisers in those countries. See Mishra and Hodge 1993.

6 See Gunew and Longley 1992; Gunew *et al.* 1992; Gunew and Rizvi 1994; Gunew 1994a.

7 *A Bibliography of Australian Multicultural Writers* in its electronic form has been incorporated into the database of *Australia's Literary Heritage: A National Bibliographic Data Bank*. My warm thanks to Wenche Ommundsen (Deakin University) for keeping me apprised of these developments.

8 Some of this struggle is documented in Gunew 1994a.

9 See for example Kaplan and Looser 1997.

10 See Gunew 1994a and Gunew and Rizvi 1994 where some of this history is captured. See also Blonski 1992.

11 See Gunew 1993a.
12 See Gunew 1993c; Bannerji 2000; Kamboureli 2000.
13 See Gordon and Newfield 1996a. Having said this, there is the implementation of 'multicultural' requirements which the educational system imposes that is very locally organized (e.g. the power of the local school board) which has in some ways far more powerful ramifications than the generalized 'Multicultural Agenda' which for a while at least (for example during the existence of the 'Office for Multicultural Affairs' within the Prime Minister's Department) was regarded as permeating federal policy in Australia.
14 Critics of multiculturalism in these debates operated from a number of positions. Those from the Right saw it as undermining Western/American values including those of individual liberty and free speech. Even a cursory analysis reveals that the degree of dissidence supposedly represented by PC advocates had been much exaggerated and was scarcely impinging on 'business as usual' across American campuses (Bartlett 1992; Ehrenreich 1992; Mowatt 1992). Stanley Fish (1992) helpfully pointed out the anomalies inherent in trying to argue for 'free speech' in which free speech is only appropriate if speech is seen as contentless or as mere noise. In a related vein Richard Perry and Patricia Williams (1992) pondered the implications and effects of permitting 'freedom of hate speech'. The Right saw multiculturalism in those caricatured terms intrinsic to the binary approach which translates any questioning of power or positionality into rule by the other, that is, not the redefining of power structures but simply their inversion (Grosz 1994).

1 The terms of (multi)cultural difference

1 That Canada also participated in slavery is becoming more widely known. See Clarke 1997.
2 The Oka crisis, for example, was not seen as a Mohawk–Canada struggle, but as a demonstration of how Quebec could not manage the native issue (as a sovereign nation should). Thus the RCMP and Army had to rescue the Mohawk elders and women from the 'fascist' Sûreté de Québec and from 'racist' Quebecois. My thanks to Margery Fee for this information and for her many other helpful suggestions.
3 For a recent example of the persistence of these mechanisms see the vituperative and ill-informed review by Michael Duffy of Cope and Kalantzis's book *A Place in the Sun* (Duffy 2000).
4 King gives the following definition of 'Pakeha': 'simply a descriptive word applied to non-Polynesian people and things in New Zealand that derive originally from outside New Zealand – most often from Europe, and even more specifically, because of the nature of our history, from the United Kingdom' (King 1991: 16). Later he attempts to argue that Pakeha indicates a 'second indigenous New Zealand culture' (King 1991: 19).
5 This move is taken even further in Dixson 1999.
6 In an adjacent (and to some degree contradictory) argument, Tonkinson comments that she is perplexed by the fact that, unlike the relativist 'ethnic' mechanisms just described, much Aboriginal discourse of resistance and protest echoes the questionable essentialist terms and concepts of scientific racism (Graham 1994: 169), an element which is also deplored by Paul Gilroy in his statements on the new 'Africancentrism', an argument developed even further in his recent book (Gilroy 2000).
7 Consider the contrast of the introduction mentioned earlier where the Irish are designated honorary blacks.
8 The series then became a book. See Ignatieff 1994.
9 The chain of substitutions traced in this episode is indebted to Jennifer Sharpe's study of rape in the 'Indian Mutiny' (Sharpe 1993).

10 For more on this episode see Dabydeen 1994; and Miki 1994, 1998.

11 In a highly complex argument taking off in part from speech act theory, Butler suggests that sexual differences constitute the performing of gender and that the legitimacy of certain discursive interpellations ('It's a girl/boy!') is interrogated and undermined by the repetitive stagings of sexual difference as gender: 'recognition is not conferred on a subject but forms that subject' (Butler 1993: 226).

12 Note Lyotard's suggestion that 'post' means anterior, that which has been forgotten in the conditions enabling or governing the emergence of something new, in this case the relations between modernity and postmodernity (Lyotard 1986).

13 Note here Paul Gilroy's critique of the ignoring of blackness by theorists such as Zygmunt Bauman, or of modernity's ignoring of slavery (Gilroy 1993a: 213) cf. Bhabha's concept of varying temporalities in relation to modernity (Bhabha 1994) and the important collection on 'alternative modernities' (Gaonkar 2001).

2 Colonial hauntings: the colonial seeds of multiculturalism

1 As Arjun Appadurai puts it, 'the use of these words by political actors and their audiences may be subject to very different sets of contextual conventions that mediate their translation into public politics' (Appadurai 1996: 36).

2 The acronym 'NESB' is peculiar to the Australian context and appears in most policy documents and analyses. That the term is revealing of certain structuring ideological assumptions will, I hope, become clear by the end of this chapter.

3 Note their interesting appearance in David Malouf's recent novel about the first colonial moments, *Remembering Babylon*. These old colonial histories (as distinct from the refrain in anti-multicultural discourse that ethnic groups import their feuds to the new country) are also played out in Canada and not only in relation to the question of Québec. See the essays in Driedger.

4 The report *Bringing Them Home* states: 'Nationally we can conclude with confidence that between one in three and one in ten Indigenous children were forcibly removed from their families and communities in the period from approximately 1910 until 1970. In certain regions and in certain periods the figure was undoubtedly much greater than one in ten. In that time not one Indigenous family has escaped the effects of forcible removal . . . Most families have been affected, in one or more generations, by the forcible removal of one or more children' (Wilson 1997: 36).

5 The term 'faction' means a combination of fact and fiction, a genre Helen Garner has made her own, although 'Helen Demidenko' also claimed the genre, as argued in Chapter 4.

6 There are interesting echoes of David Mamet's insinuations in the play *Oleanna* which deals with comparable issues: a fine man brought down by feminist harpies.

7 I have written elsewhere about this peculiarly tenacious usage in Australia with respect to anyone who is of non-Anglo-Celtic background. This term 'migrant' persists as a way of registering these differences even when third-generation Australians are being indicated. It complements my argument in this chapter. See Gunew 1994a.

8 See Masao Miyoshi 1993, Arif Dirlik 1994 and recent variants on such analyses such as those by Aihwa Ong with her notion of 'flexible citizenship' as being uncoupled from the old baggage of nostalgia for lost homeland or cultures (Ong 1999).

9 James Clifford provides a useful summary of diaspora studies in his collection of essays. See Clifford 1997. But see the critique in Ang 2001.

10 In her important study of the emergent field of Asian-American studies, Sau-ling Cynthia Wong argues that Chinese Americans were historically blocked from participating in the consent model (Wong 1993: 75).

11 See for example Canada's national newspaper the *Globe & Mail*: Letters 15 March 1997, 22 March 1997, 26 March 1997. One needs to point out that in the United States there are of course many academic conferences on multiculturalism but there the term clearly signals racialized differences rather than naming a policy concerned with policing national identity formations.
12 For example, see Hall on Dirlik (Hall 1996a).
13 Interestingly, in the United States these arguments have also been advanced by neo-liberalists such as David Hollinger.
14 Andrew Milner (1991: 32) points out that Raymond Williams coined this term.
15 For discussion of the term 'visible minorities' see Bannerji (1993) and Carty and Brand (1993).
16 This is also very much the line taken by Himani Bannerji in her critique of Canadian multiculturalism, which she sees as a direct legacy of the colonial struggle between the English and French (Bannerji 2000).
17 The construction of ethnic communities as abject spaces is related to Ann McClintock's (1995) analysis of such sites in *Imperial Leather*.
18 No matter how much recent attempts to redefine multicultural rhetoric occur, e.g. the Minister for Immigration, Phil Ruddock's speech, arguing that the First Fleet was multicultural and that Australia has always already been multicultural, as though the simple citation of points of origin for a few individuals were equivalent to and interchangeable with the demographic changes brought about by postwar migrations.
19 See also Alistair Pennycook (1998), *English and the Discourses of Colonialism*, particularly the last chapter.
20 I would none the less maintain that there would historically have been a hierarchy of acceptable 'whiteness' in relation to different ethnic groups. For the workings of this dynamic in the United States, see Roedinger (2002).
21 The speech was available with the full report on August 27th 1999 at the following website: http://www.immi.gov.au/nmac/index.html.
22 In a subsequent issue of *Critical Inquiry* (where Povinelli's essay, now the introduction to her book, first appeared) John Frow and Meaghan Morris take her to task for 'two aspects of her critique . . . The first is the instrumentalism that she ascribes to multicultural policy' and the second 'to the state, understood as a singular, unified, and intelligent agent' (Frow and Morris 1999: 627). In contrast to my own analysis, their concern is with the second rather than the first. I would however endorse their statement that: 'Policies are the hybrid products of diverse political activities by many social agents . . . open to contestation, sudden abandonment, and unpredictable change' (Frow and Morris 1999: 629). Povinelli's response emphasized that she was dealing with the psychic limits and implications of national affects but there is no recognition in her statement that different citizens have different kinds of access to the public sphere where these anxieties concerning (in)tolerance are aired and addressed.
23 Compare this with Canada, e.g. Sky Lee's *Disappearing Moon Café*, where Chinese and First Nations relationships are represented. More recently these concerns are also being addressed in Australian material. See Australian Aboriginal writer Melissa Lucashenko's first novel *Steam Pigs*.
24 See, for example Terry O'Connor's interview with Mudrooroo (O'Connor 1998) and Oboe (2003).
25 Bobbi Sykes has come into the news again with the publication of three volumes of her autobiography. Sykes too has had to defend her genealogy in the national press. See K. Mead 1998 and R. Sykes 1998c.
26 But see Docker 1994.
27 In the Canadian case 'English' would include the Scots, though not the Irish, at least initially. See Driedger 1987.

28 These speculations permeate as well her account of travelling through Eastern
  Europe in the 80s before the fall of the Soviet Empire. Note in particular the
  section 'Where does Europe end?' (Kostash 1993: 72ff).
29 See note 2 in this chapter.
30 For the very different response of two writers to this debate see Drakulic (1996)
  and Hoffman (1999).
31 According to a personal email from Joseph Pivato (University of Athabasca and
  leading critic of Italian Canadian writing): 'The term mangiacakes originated in
  Ontario among Italian construction workers as a derogatory term for English
  Canadians. It literally means the cake-eaters and implies that English Canadian
  men were less manly that Italian men. It uses the food that we eat as symbolic of
  our character, and is a common practice among Italians. For example, the people
  of Vicenza, my home province in N. Italy, are identified in a nursery rhyme as
  "Vicentini mangiagatti" – the cat-eaters – an example of our poverty. I have been
  told that mangiacakes refers to the soft sliced breads in sandwiches that Canadians
  often eat and to the donuts and cakes that workers eat during breaks on the job. It
  is a sissy image. In contrast, Italian men ate big crusty buns, often, hot meats and
  raw vegetables. They often did not take coffee breaks but continued to work.The
  Italians cultivated the image of the better, stronger worker. This did not endear
  them to their English Canadian co-workers. So in answer to being called a "wop"
  or a "dago" an Italian could always answer back with mangiacakes. Now it seems to
  be applied to both men and women.'

3 Corporeal choreographies of transnational English

1 The character Hà in the play by Noëlle Janaczewska, *The History of Water*, 1995:
  37–8.
2 Hoffman 1998: 22.
3 Affect is defined as 'the emotional repercussions of an experience' (Laplanche
  and Pontalis 1973: 14). Affect has become a much discussed term in recent psychoanalytical and cultural debates. See, for example, Sedgwick and Frank 1995. It is
  invoked here because it is intertwined with the complexities of mechanisms of
  repression, something invariably associated with what happens to first languages
  in the colonial or diasporic state.
4 The distinction between (received standard) English and its variants as 'english' is
  a suggestion put forward in Ashcroft *et al.* (1989: 8).
5 As exemplified in a seminar and lecture Foucault gave at the University of
  Vermont in 1982 (Foucault 1988b) as well as the particular context he gives
  it in the third volume of his *History of Sexuality: The Care of the Self* (Foucault
  1988a).
6 One thinks here of the paradigmatic diasporic group, the Jews, in all their varieties,
  and more recently of Indian communities in Africa or of various groups of
  Chinese, for example, the history associated with Shirley Geok-lin Lim's memoirs
  discussed below. See also Ang 2001.
7 Cheah 1998: 36–7. In the same volume Cheah (291–303) takes issue with Clifford's
  notion of 'discrepant cosmopolitanism' and Clifford, in turn, provides a response
  (1997: 364–6).
8 In England itself, see Brooker and Humm 1989; Batsleer *et al.* 1985; Doyle 1989;
  Widdowson 1982. In Australia Dale 1997. In Canada, Fee 1993; Murray 1996, to
  name a few.
9 See Pratt 1992 as well as Sara Suleri's fascinating study of the amateur ethno-
  graphic productions of Anglo-Indian women who served to exemplify the colonial
  panic at not being able to institute proper boundaries around the colonial enterprise (Suleri 1992a: 82 ff).

10 One thinks as well of Fanon (1952/67) and the famous moment when the narrator confronts the white child analysed in Chapter 5 of *Black Skin, White Masks*.

11 Julia Kristeva's concept of the 'abject', as delineated in Kristeva 1982, remains a useful tool for analysing what happens to former languages in, for example, a diasporic or neocolonial situation. In addition now there is her *Strangers to Ourselves* (Kristeva 1991), which analyses the psychic consequences of migration and diaspora.

12 A character in Zimbabwean writer Tsitsi Dangarembga's (1988) novel *Nervous Conditions* attributes her society's implosion to the divisive and internally alienating effects of too much Englishness.

4 A text with subtitles: performing ethnicity

1 I attempted to canvas some of this debate in Gunew 1993a but it continues to be a highly complex and continuing issue as exemplified in the Canadian 'Writing Through Race' controversy (Miki 1994; 1998: 144–59; Dabydeen 1994). Interestingly enough, apart from Frederick Philip Grove (Spettigue 1969) most Canadian examples of literary transvestism are in relation to Europeans 'passing' as Native Canadians, e.g. the Englishman who became 'Grey Owl'.

2 There had been some controversy around the interpretation of 'Australian life' even before the Demidenko case. See *Australian Book Review* #173 and #174 (both 1995).

3 As one of the compilers of the first comprehensive bibliography of Australian multicultural writers (Gunew *et al.* 1992), I note such remarks with a degree of wry interest. Certainly such 'authentic' voices abound for those who wish to seek them out but this, as I've indicated in my opening comments, does not include the Australian media or even the literary establishment to any great degree. Studies in ethnic minority writings are far less advanced in Australia than they are in Canada or the United States.

4 See *Globe & Mail* 23 August 1995; London *Sunday Times* 27 August 1995; Manchester *Guardian Weekly* 27 August 1995; *New York Times International* 26 September 1995. The spate of media attention produced three volumes: Jost *et al.* 1996; Maune 1996; Prior 1996; Riemer 1996.

5 Reports by her boyfriend indicate that she had long been dissatisfied with the 'drabness' of her 'race' (Koutsoukis 1995).

6 Song Liling attacks Gallimard (and through him Western sensibilities) for not being able to tell the difference between Chinese and Japanese women and for having no knowledge of the historical enmity between the two nations.

7 See Oakley 1995. It is interesting that the gender of the author is more of an issue in the visual representations of her (photographs and, later, cartoons) than in the written reports and essays. Analysis of this visual material would require a separate essay and it can merely be raised here as another complex element in this case study.

8 See for example an early review by Susan Mitchell 1994.

9 This is in part based on private communications, but see also Marko Pavlyshyn 1995.

10 See Note 1 in this chapter.

11 One notes here the controversy which both Maxine Hong Kingston and Alice Walker have attracted in these terms. See Chin 1985; Lee 1991; Harris 1984; Walker 1988. See also Rey Chow's important analysis of 'ethnic ressentiment' (Chow 2002: 183–191).

12 It is useful to offer a reminder here of one of the most famous Australian 'migrant text', *They're a Weird Mob* purportedly written by an Italian migrant called 'Nino Culotta' (1957). This was standard issue to arriving immigrants. The book

culminates in a paean to Australian life as preferable to any other. It therefore functioned as effective paradigm for the limited interpretations permitted such 'outsider' texts, even now. The author was eventually revealed to be an Anglo-Celtic Australian journalist called John O'Grady.

13 One might compare this, for example, with the much more highly subsidized Canadian scene, for example, where small publishers abound and even academic writing, including cultural analyses, are supported by the aid to scholarly publications programme run by the Social Sciences and Humanities Research Council. In part this is fuelled by the perception that a distinct Canadian culture is always in danger of being swamped by the big neighbour to the south – the United States.

14 The charge that the judges in the various prizes were motivated by 'political correctness' rather than aesthetic criteria surfaced repeatedly in the press reports and a number of commentators alluded to the competitive edge which being 'ethnic' or female could give a writer (Wommersley 1995; Syson 1995; Castan 1995).

15 Witness the cartoon in the *Australian Book Review* #174: 5.

16 One should note here that the late Helen Daniel was at that time the editor of the *Australian Book Review*. The controversy around the book and author could arguably be said to have affected the structures which govern the public support for the arts in Australia. The much-vaunted principle of arm's length peer review always hides very specific political agendas. During the late 80s and early 90s funding bodies briefly attempted (albeit in very minor ways) to acknowledge the increasing diversity of Australian culture and such attempts were met with overwhelming criticism from the established arts community (Gunew and Rizvi 1994). Attempts to redress the balance (e.g. at one stage 7 per cent of Australia Council funding was tagged to go to 'multicultural arts' very broadly defined) were countered by stories concerning pernicious social engineering and arguments that claiming a minority 'ethnicity' will get you prizes or that funding bodies will give you preferential treatment (Legge 1995b). Such views are a familiar part of a rhetorical reversal pattern that characterizes the Political Correctness (PC) debates mentioned in Chapter 1 in which the mainstream cries victim and argues that those really discriminated against are white heterosexual males (Weir and Richer 1995).

17 A comparable trajectory could be traced in relation to 'becoming indigenous' as has been exemplified in the work of the Canadian critic Terry Goldie (1989) and around 'white aboriginality' by the Australian critic Ian McLean.

5 Acoustic transgressions and identity politics: a translated performance

1 The popular culture term for the manipulated faces would probably be that they were 'morphing' into each other. The resultant composite invokes the Science Fiction genre with its twin traditions of utopia and dystopia.

2 I am indebted to Mishra 1996 for leading me to Balibar's work. Note here Rattansi's critique that the 'new racism' is perhaps not so new since national and racist discourses have always been linked in the terms used to delineate 'cultural racism' (Rattansi 1995: 255).

3 The 'Transformations: Thinking Through Feminism' conference held at the University of Lancaster (July 1997).

4 Such limitations include the reinforcement of the general disparagement of 'performance' in relation to print that persistently haunts the academic endeavour. See the useful analysis in Sebesta (1999–2000). My thanks to Erin Hurley for this reference.

5 Rattansi's essay is particularly indebted to the work of Homi Bhabha who, following the pioneering work of Frantz Fanon, uses psychoanalytic theory as a

useful tool for analysing the hidden structures of colonialism and its aftermaths. See Bhabha 1994.

6 Wong is herself the author of two recent bestsellers *Red China Blues: My Long March from Mao to Now* (1996) and *Jan Wong's China: Notes from a not so Foreign Correspondent* (1999).

7 Dame Kiri Te Kanewa is a breakthrough case in point.

8 In their fascinating study, Linda and Michael Hutcheon (1996) deal with the many permutations of illness and opera (including AIDS) but don't deal extensively with race. Matters of race have been mentioned in, for example, Kostenbaum (1993), McClary (1991), and the pioneering work of Catherine Clément (1989), but a systematic study does not as yet, to my knowledge, exist.

9 The reason for invoking Zizek's work is that his current popularity is in part at least due to the fact that he is managing to bring together those ancient rivals: Marxism and Psychoanalysis. To put it another way, he consistently brings to bear psychoanalytic concepts and intepretive frameworks on questions of the social and the political. The questions of desire in its various manifestations is at the heart of his work as well as being at the centre of his wife, Renate Salecl's, increasingly influential research. See their recent collaborative text (Salecl and Zizek 1996).

10 The short quotation hardly does justice to this highly complex interaction and I recommend that interested readers seek out the fuller treatment in Chapter 3 of Zizek 1989 and pages 105–10 in particular. To amplify a little further, Zizek uses the example of 'hysterical theatre' in which the hysterical woman identifies with a particular model of the fragile feminine but does so from the vantage point (the place) of the paternal gaze 'to which she wants to appear likeable' (Zizek 1989: 106). The underlying question echoes the one quoted earlier: Who sees me in this kind of way?

11 Elaine Chang identifies a comparable move in *Runaway*, when she observes that 'Lau asserts her longing for the traditional home' (Chang 1994: 109).

12 The plot of Puccini's *Madama Butterfly* takes place during the American occupation of Japan at the turn of the century and concerns the exploits of Lt. Pinkerton who acquires (indeed marries in a Japanese ceremony) a young geisha (Cho-Cho San) as part of a rental package. Cho-Cho San, or Butterfly, makes the mistake of falling in love with Pinkerton who returns to his ship and country leaving her pregnant. In the latter part of the opera we observe Butterfly's longing for Pinkerton and pride in their son as expressed to her faithful female servant Suzuki. On being confronted with Pinkerton and his 'American' wife who desire to adopt her son, Butterfly kills herself in a ritual seppuku manner since an honourable death is preferable to life without honour.

13 Note that this scenario is repeated even in 'modern' versions of the tale such as the musical *Miss Saigon*. See Kondo 1997, Chapter 2 for a recent analysis of the 'orientalist' variations and significance of this story.

14 The genre of 'dirty realism' as exemplified by the work of Carver, Ford, Mamet, etc., appears to be the dominant interpretive framework for the little critical attention Lau's work has received. My thanks to Michael Zeitlin for information on this genre.

15 The all-powerful female mouth is also reminiscent, of course, of the castrating vagina dentata.

16 For the colonial history of karaoke as originating in Taiwan see Chen (1996). I am indebted to Rachel Lee for alerting me to this article. Casey Lum's study gives it a Japanese provenance (Lum 1996).

17 Casey Lum's pioneering study of the role of karaoke in identificatory community processes within three American-Chinese communities associates it with Cantonese opera for one of his groups (Lum 1996, Chapter 3 in particular). To my knowledge there is nothing to link Lau with Cantonese opera, though there is a

tradition within the Vancouver Chinese-Canadian community (Ho 1994). Lau has stated in an interview I have been unable to track down that she listened to *Madama Butterfly* while composing *Other Women*. In this regard it is also interesting to note Lau's poem 'My Tragic Opera' (Lau 1994) which evokes the scenario of an adulterous woman visiting her lover's house while his wife and children are absent. She insinuates herself into the domestic space, particularly the bathroom, as a way of appropriating the heterosexual family and its everyday life. The 'desiring' identificatory moves I have outlined in relation to the novel are clearly visible here as well.

18 At the end of the conference presentation I played the full film extract (starring the incomparable Sandra Oh, who happens to be Korean-Canadian, as Lau) from which the earlier soundtrack had been taken. The hope was that the audience would now see this 'ethnic' face as more than merely a 'native informant' on ethnicity.

6 Somatic choreographies: public spaces; private belongings

1 Commodity fetishism means the commodity exists in a vacuum which uncouples it from the specificities of its production.

2 While being challenged by Rey Chow's useful distinction between theoretical and autobiographical writing (Chow 2002), I consider that theoretical writing may also be read for autobiographical affect and have attempted to facilitate such a reading throughout this book.

3 See the passage quoted at the beginning of this chapter.

4 Opera has in recent years been associated with queer cultural theory, e.g. see Chapter 5.

5 My thanks to Doritta Fong for giving me permission to quote from her essay.

6 See also I. Young 1990.

7 There have been many analyses of this moment but in terms of the new geography see Pile 1996, p. 250ff. There is an interesting reverse moment of symbolic identification in Yu and MacKenzie 2000.

8 I am thinking here of the ways in which music has been changed into a commodity and process of ventriloquism, as pointed out by Jacques Attali and subsequent theorists. I am indebted here to Julie Smith for helping me explore these debates.

9 That there is nothing 'simple' about the linking of ethnicity and narcissism is explored by Rey Chow in her analysis of the workings of ethnic abjection in relation to narcissism (Chow 2002).

7 Can ghosts emigrate? Diaspora, exile and community

1 Probably the most influential recent theorizing about intellectuals are Edward Said's 1994 Reith lectures *Representations of the Intellectual*. See also Abdul JanMohammed's appraisal of Said as an influential intellectual in his own right (JanMohammed 1992). More recently, Ann Kaplan has worked with the notion of 'embodied translators', those figures who mediate between liminal and hegemonic communities (Kaplan 2003).

2 Shirley Geok-lin Lim, for example, edited the first anthology of Asian-American women's writing (Lim *et al.* 1989). In the introduction to his anthology *Under Western Eyes*, another pioneering landmark in the establishment of Asian-American writing, Garrett Hongo describes his own position in the controversial case which split the Asian-American writing community and involved the well-known writer Frank Chin's attack on Maxine Hong Kingston. For a selection of Shirley Geok-lin Lim's many contributions to critical work on Asian-American writing see Lim and Ling 1992, Cheung 1997. For a critique of her work in this field see Koshy 2000.

3 For more on diasporic studies see Appadurai 1996, 2001; Bhabha 1990, 1994; Brah 1996; Brah and Coombes 2000; Chang 1994a; Clifford 1997; Frankenberg and Mani 1996; Gilroy 1987, 1993, 2000; Grewal and Kaplan 1994; Hall and du Gay 1996; JanMohammed 1992; Kumar 1997; Lloyd 1994; Lowe 1996; Papastergiadis 1998; Radhakrishnan 1996; Shohat 1998; Shohat and Stam 1994.

4 There is an interesting discussion of these categories between Shirley Geok-lin Lim, Valerie Miner and Judith Barrington in a special issue on memoir in *The Women's Review of Books* (XIII, 10–11, July 1996, pp. 24–5).

5 See my further explorations of these tensions in Chapter 3.

6 Elsewhere I have traced the competitiveness between food and language as each other's doubles in the Kristevan framework of abjection. See Gunew 1999.

7 One thinks here of Avtar Brah's discussion of 'minoritization' as always involving hierarchies of power (Brah 1996).

8 In the case of the mother in Lim's text there are clear indications that she fled from physical abuse. None the less it is a tribute to the text's refusal to avoid ambiguities in favour of easy resolutions that Lim depicts in detail the contradictory tensions of the young narrator who does not know or fully perceive the mother's dilemma and hence also condemns her for leaving them, particularly when the early years are invoked.

9 See Melanie Klein's analysis of the child, language, orality and the mother in Ravel's opera 'L'Enfant et les sortilèges' in L. and R. Grinberg (1989), particularly Chapter 11, *Migration and Language*. My thanks to Anna Yeatman for drawing my attention to this text.

10 I am referring here to a pattern in poetic influence characterized by Harold Bloom as an oedipal struggle between fathers and sons. See Bloom (1973).

11 The notion of haunting has gained currency in many recent cultural studies, whether it be the Derridean concept of 'hauntology' (Derrida 1994) or Bhabha's references to 'living ghosts' (Bhabha 1996) or the influential concept of 'encrypt-ment' in the work of Abraham and Torok (1994). See also Gordon (1997).

12 I am referring here to the roots of history which were composed of genealogical chronicles. One thinks of 'Genesis' in the Old Testament in the Judaeo-Christian tradition.

13 Mackenzie King was Prime Minister of Canada during the Second World War.

14 The statement has an interesting echo in Homi Bhabha's comment on a relatively recent essay by Martha Nussbaum in the following manner: 'In her attempt to avoid nationalist or patriotic sovereignty, Nussabum embraces a "universalism" that is profoundly provincial' (Bhabha 1996: 200).

15 Having said this, my sense is that the kinds of coalitions which have often served as utopian reference points for contemporary feminist (and other postcolonial, multicultural, etc.) theorists (e.g. as traced by many of the essays in Shohat 1998) are contemplated rather bleakly in Lim's text. The narrator views such networks with a certain scepticism.

16 For another version of this 'diasporic condition' see Radhakrishnan (1996).

17 In this respect see Chow 2002, discussed again in the Conclusion.

18 For another version of the insidious consequences of such alienation see Mura (1996).

19 This constitutes an example where a potential solidarity forged along lines of racialisation becomes undermined by class differences.

20 One thinks here of Lisa Lowe's statement 'the Asian is always seen as an immigrant, as the "foreigner-within" . . . the Asian American, even as citizen, continues to be located outside the cultural and racial boundaries of the nation' (Lowe 1996: 5–6).

21 One thinks here, for example, of the work of Georg Lukács.

22 For an illuminating fictional account of the importance of theatre to the Chinese-American communities see Maxine Hong Kingston's novel *Tripmaster Monkey* (Kingston 1989).

23 Note as well the tireless efforts of cultural activists such as Jim Wong-Chu and his work in creating the Asian-Canadian Writers' Workshop whose journal *Rice Paper* is testament to a very lively cultural community.

24 For an analysis of Evelyn Lau as refusing the categories of the 'ethnic writer' see Chapter 5.

25 The notion that all such traditions are invented is a reference to the work of Hobsbawm and Ranger (1983), Benedict Anderson (1983/1991) and many more since.

26 The book was originally published in French as *La République Métis* (Caccia 1997); the English translation was published by Guernica, thus continuing the debate of the Italo-Canadians as the third alternative to which I have been referring.

27 Verdicchio recently moved to Bologna but was formerly based at the University of California San Diego and so had the advantage of looking at the Italian diaspora in a broader North American context.

28 The reference is to novelist Hugh MacLennan's famous novel *The Two Solitudes* which dealt with the foundational francophone–anglophone split in Canada. Interestingly, Salvatore begins his oral history with an interview with MacLennan.

Conclusion: transcultural improvisations

1 I look at some of the ways in which languages carve a corporeal space in Chapter 3.

2 The term derives from Derrida's *Spectres of Marx* where he coins it to convey both haunting and ontology in relation to the sense of endings: of man, of Marxism, of history, etc. (1994: 10; 14).

3 Both programme and many of the papers are posted on the website: http://transculturalisms.arts.ubc.ca. The Transculturalisms project is described on the website as well. In short, together with five others, I was asked by the International Council for Canadian Studies to co-ordinate an international team of scholars to examine the topic of cultural métissage and its impact on Canadian culture. We have a sister team based in South America, particularly Brazil, with whom we have been in dialogue for three years.

4 I hasten to add that Harel was using notions of 'haunting' in highly conceptual and abstract ways, deriving from psychoanalysis and I certainly don't wish to suggest that merely moving to material realities somehow undermines these concepts. None the less, there are also some issues with respect to signification which were raised in the 'dramatization' of the session and in the subsequent discussion and these may in turn suggest conceptual issues which help us deconstruct (in the Derridean sense of clarifying the nature of the constitutive contradictions) some of our assumptions.

5 Drew's text is on the website but see also Taylor 1996; 1999.

6 An argument I pursue in Chapter 4.

7 Grey Owl is an example. See also the discussions of white indigeneity/aboriginality in the work of Terrie Goldie (1989) in Canada and Ian McLean (1998) in Australia.

8 See Kay Schaffer's *In the Wake of First Contact: The Eliza Fraser Stories* (1995) which ends with an analysis of Foley's series on Eliza Fraser produced in the early 1990s.

Bibliography

Abel, S. (1996) *Opera in the Flesh: Sexuality in Operatic Performance*, Boulder, CO: Westview Press.

Abraham, N. and M. Torok (1994) *The Shell and the Kernel: Renewals of Psychoanalysis*, vol. 1. trans. Nicholas Rand, London: University of Chicago Press.

Ahmed, S. (2000) *Strange Encounters: Embodied Others in Postcolonialism*, London and New York: Routledge.

Ali, Y. (1992) 'Muslim Women and the Politics of Ethnicity and Culture in Northern England', in Gita Saghal and Nira Yuval-Davis (eds) *Refusing Holy Orders: Women and Fundamentalism in Britain*, London: Virago Press.

Anderson, B. (1983/91) *Imagined Communities: Reflections on the Origins and Spread of Nationalism*, London: Verso.

Ang, I. (2001) *On Not Speaking Chinese: Living Between Asia and the West*, London and New York: Routledge.

Ang, I. and J. Stratton (1998) 'Multiculturalism in Crisis: The New Politics of Race and National Identity in Australia', *Topia: Canadian Journal of Cultural Studies*, 2: 22–41.

Anthias, F. and N. Yuval-Davis (1992) *Racialized Boundaries: Race, Nation, Gender, Colour and Class and the Anti-Racist Struggle*, London: Routledge.

Appadurai, A. (1996) *Modernity at Large: Cultural Dimensions of Globalization*, Minneapolis: University of Minnesota Press.

Appadurai, A. (ed.) (2001) *Globalization*, Durham, NC and London: Duke University Press.

Appiah, A. K. (1994) 'Identity, Authenticity, Survival: Multicultural Societies and Social Reproduction', in Amy Gutman (ed.) *Multiculturalism: Examining the Politics of Recognition*, Princeton, NJ: Princeton University Press.

Asante, M. K. (1992) 'Multiculturalism: An Exchange', in P. Berman (ed.) *Debating P.C.: The Controversy over Political Correctness on College Campuses*, New York: Laurel.

Ashcroft, B., G. Griffith and H. Tiffin (eds) (1989) *The Empire Writes Back: Theory and Practice in Post-Colonial Literatures*, London: Methuen.

Attali, J. (1989) *Noise: The Political Economy of Music*, Minneapolis: University of Minnesota Press.

Aufderheide, P. (ed.) (1992) *Beyond P.C.: Toward a Politics of Understanding*, Minnesota, MN: Graywolf Press.

Australian Book Review #173 (1995) 'Forum on the Demidenko Controversy', August: 14–20.

Australian Book Review #174 (1995) 'Letters', September: 3–6.

Balibar, E. (1991) 'Is There a "Neo-racism?"', in E. Balibar and I. Wallerstein (eds) *Race, Nation, Class: Ambiguous Identities*, London: Verso.

Bannerji, H. (1990) Interview, in L. Hutcheon and M. Richmond (eds) *Other Solitudes: Canadian Multicultural Fictions*, Toronto: Oxford University Press.

Bannerji, H. (1993) 'Popular Images of South Asian Women', in H. Bannerji (ed.) *Returning the Gaze: Essays on Racism, Feminism and Politics*, Toronto: Sister Vision Press.

Bannerji, H. (2000) *The Dark Side of the Nation: Esays on Multiculturalism, Nationalism and Gender*, Toronto: Canadian Scholars' Press.

Bartlett, K. T. (1992) 'Surplus Visibility', in P. Aufderheide (ed.) *Beyond P.C.: Toward a Politics of Understanding*, Minnesota, MN: Graywolf Press.

Bartlett, R. H. (1993) *The Mabo Decision*, Sydney: Butterworths.

Batsleer, J., T. Davies, R. O'Rourke and C. Weedon (eds) (1985) *Rewriting English: Cultural Politics of Gender and Class*, London: Methuen.

Bentley, D. (1995) 'Questions Posed on Author's Life', *Courier-Mail* (Queensland), 19 August.

Berman, P. (ed.) (1992a) *Debating P.C.: The Controversy over Political Correctness on College Campuses*, New York: Laurel.

Berman, P. (1992b) 'Introduction: The Debate and Its Origins', in P. Berman (ed.) *Debating P.C.: The Controversy over Political Correctness on College Campuses*, New York: Laurel.

Bérubé, M. (1992) 'Public Image Limited: Political Correctness and the Media's Big Lie', in P. Berman (ed.) *Debating P.C.: The Controversy over Political Correctness on College Campuses*, New York: Laurel.

Bhabha, H. (1983) 'The Other Question – the Stereotype and Colonial Discourse', *Screen*, 24.6: 18–36.

Bhabha, H. (1990) 'DissemiNation: Time, Narrative, and the Margins of the Modern Nation', in H. Bhabha (ed.) *Nation and Narration*, London: Routledge.

Bhabha, H. (1993) 'Culture's In Between', *Artforum*, September: 167–214.

Bhabha, H. (1994) *The Location of Culture*, Routledge: London.

Bhabha, H. (1996) 'Unpacking My Library . . . Again', in I. Chambers and L. Curti (eds) *The Post-Colonial Question*, London: Routledge.

Bhabha, H. (1997) 'Editor's Introduction: Minority Maneuvers and Unsettled Negotiations', *Critical Inquiry*, 23.3 (Spring): 431–59.

Birney, E. (1990) 'Can. Lit.', in R. Brown, D. Bennett and N. Cooke (eds) *An Anthology of Canadian Literature in English*, Toronto: Oxford University Press, 296.

Blodgett, E. D. (1990) 'Ethnic Writing in Canadian Literature as Paratext', *Signature*, 3 (Summer): 13–26.

Blodgett, E. D. and A. G. Purdy (eds) (1988) *Problems of Literary Reception*, Edmonton: Research Institute for Comparative Studies, University of Alberta.

Blodgett, E. D. and A. G. Purdy (eds) (1990) *Prefaces and Literary Manifestoes*, Edmonton: Research Institute for Comparative Studies, University of Alberta.

Blonski, A. (1992) *Arts for a Multicultural Australia 1973–1991. An Account of Australia Council Policies*, Sydney: Australia Council.

Bloom, H. (1973) *The Anxiety of Influence: A Theory of Poetry*, London: Oxford University Press.

Books in Canada (1991) 'Whose Voice Is It, Anyway?', February: 11–17.

Bourdieu, P. (1986) 'The Forms of Capital', in J. G. Richardson (ed.) *Handbook of Theory and Research for the Sociology of Education*, New York: Greenwood Press.

Boyarin, D. and J. Boyarin (1995) 'Diaspora: Generation and the Ground of Jewish Identity', in K. A. Appiah and H. L. Gates Jr. (eds) *Identities*, Chicago, IL: University of Chicago Press.

Boyte, H. C. (1992) 'The Politics of Innocence', in P. Aufderheide (ed.) *Beyond P.C.: Toward a Politics of Understanding*, Minnesota, MN: Graywolf Press.

Brah, A. (1996) *Cartographies of Diaspora: Contesting Identities*, London: Routledge.

Brah, A. and A. E. Coombes (eds) (2000) *Hybridity and Its Discontents*, London and New York: Routledge.

Braidotti, R. (1994) *Nomadic: Embodiment and Sexual Difference in Contemporary Feminist Theory*, New York: Columbia University Press.

Braidotti, R. (1997) 'Remembering Fitzroy High', in J. Mead (ed.) *Bodyjamming: Sexual Harassment, Feminism and Public Life*, NSW, Australia: Random House.

Brand, D. (1990) Interview, in L. Hutcheon and M. Richmond (eds) *Other Solitudes: Canadian Multicultural Fictions*, Toronto: Oxford University Press.

Brand, D. (1994) *Bread Out of Stone*, Toronto: Coach House.

Brooker, P. and Peter Humm (eds) (1989) *Dialogue and Difference: English in the Nineties*, London: Methuen.

Butler, J. (1993) *Bodies that Matter: On the Discursive Limits of 'Sex'*, New York: Routledge.

Butler, J. (1997) *Excitable Speech: A Politics of the Performative*, New York: Routledge.

Caccia, F. (1997) *La République Métis*, Paris: Les Éditions Balzac.

Caccia, F. (2002) *Republic Denied: The Loss of Canada*, Toronto: Guernica.

Carby, H. (1992) 'The Multicultural Wars', in G. Dent (ed.) *Black Popular Culture*, Seattle, WA: Bay Press.

Carty, L. and D. Brand (1993) 'Visible Minority Women: A Creation of the Canadian State', in H. Bannerji (ed.) *Returning the Gaze: Essays on Racism, Feminism and Politics*, Toronto: Sister Vision Press.

Castan, C. (1995) 'Esteem "The Hand" as a Multicultural Gift', *Australian*, September: 8.

Castles, S. (1996) 'The Racisms of Globalisation', in E. Vasta and S. Castles (eds) *The Teeth are Smiling: The Persistence of Racism in Multicultural Australia*, Sydney: Allen & Unwin.

Castles, S. and E. Vasta (1996) 'Introduction: Multicultural or Multi-Racist Australia?', in E. Vasta and S. Castles (eds) *The Teeth are Smiling: The Persistence of Racism in Multicultural Australia*, Sydney: Allen & Unwin.

Certeau, M. de (1988) *The Practice of Everyday Life*, Berkeley: University of California Press.

Certeau, M. de, L. Giard and P. Mayol (1998) *The Practice of Everyday Life: Living and Cooking*, vol. 2, Minneapolis: University of Minnesota Press.

Chakrabarty, D. (2000) *Provincializing Europe: Postcolonial Thought and Historical Difference*, Princeton, NJ: Princeton University Press.

Chamberlin, E. (1993) *Come Back to Me My Language: Poetry and the West Indies*, Urbana: University of Illinois Press.

Chambers, I. (1994) *Migrancy, Culture, Identity*, London: Routledge.

Chang, E. K. (1994a) 'Where the "Street Kid" Meets the City', in P. Delany (ed.) *Vancouver: Representing the Postmodern City*, Vancouver: Arsenal Press.

Chang, E. K. (1994b) 'A Not-So-New Spelling of My Name: Notes Toward (and against) a Politics of Equivocation', in A. Bammer (ed.) *Displacements: Cultural Identities in Question*, Bloomington: Indiana University Press.

Chao, L. (1997) *Beyond Silence: Chinese Canadian Literature in English*, Toronto: Tsar.

Cheah, P. (1998) 'Introduction Part II: The Cosmopolitical – Today', in P. Cheah and B. Robbins (eds) *Cosmopolitics: Thinking Freely Beyond the Nation*, Minneapolis: University of Minnesota Press.

Chen, K.-H. (1996) 'Not Yet the Postcolonial Era: The (Super) Nation-State and Transnationalism of Cultural Studies: Response to Ang and Stratton', *Cultural Studies*, 10.1: 37–70.

Cheung, F., L. Kwa and S. G.-l. Lim (2002) 'Singapore on My Mind', *Women's Review of Books*, vol. xix, no. 10–11, July: 24–25.

Cheung, K.-K. (1993) *Articulate Silences*, Ithaca, NY: Cornell University Press.

Cheung, K.-K. (ed.) (1997) *An Interethnic Companion to Asian American Literature*, New York: Cambridge University Press.

Chicago Cultural Studies Group (1994) 'Critical Multiculturalism', in D. T. Goldberg (ed.) *Multiculturalism: A Critical Reader*, Oxford: Blackwell.

Chin, F. (1985) 'This Is Not an Autobiography', *Genre* 18.2: 109–30.

Chong, D. (1994) *The Concubine's Children: Portrait of a Family Divided*, Toronto: Viking Press.

Chow, Rey (1991) *Woman and Chinese Modernity: The Politics of Reading Between East and West*, Minneapolis: University of Minnesota Press.

Chow, Rey (1993) *Writing Diaspora: Tactics of Intervention in Contemporary Cultural Studies*, Bloomington: Indiana University Press.

Chow, Rey (1998) *Ethics After Idealism*, Bloomington: Indiana University Press.

Chow, Rey (2002) *The Protestant Ethnic and the Spirit of Capitalism*, New York: Columbia University Press.

Choy, W. (1995) *The Jade Peony: A Novel*, Vancouver and Toronto: Douglas & McIntyre.

Christoff, P. (1995) 'Assassins of Memory', *Arena Magazine*, August–September: 44–8.

Clarke, G. E. (ed.) (1997) *Eyeing the North Star: Directions in African-Canadian Literature*, Toronto: McLellan and Stewart.

Clément, C. (1989) *Opera, or the Undoing of Women*, trans. Betsy Wing, London: Virago.

Clifford, J. (1997) *Routes: Travel and Translation in the Late Twentieth Century*, Cambridge, MA: Harvard University Press.

Cohen, J., M. Howard and M. C. Nussbaum (eds) (1999) *Is Multiculturalism Bad for Women? Susan Moller Oikin and Respondents*, Princeton, NJ: Princeton University Press.

Colls, R. and P. Dodd (eds) (1987) *Englishness: Politics and Culture 1880–1920*, London: Croom Helm.

Corelli, R. (1991) 'The Silencers: "Politically Correct" Crusaders Are Stifling Expression and Behavior', *Maclean's*, 27 May: 40–50.

Creed, B. (1993) *The Monstrous-Feminine: Film, Feminism, Psychoanalysis*, London and New York: Routledge.

Creighton-Kelly, C. (1991) *Report on Racial Equality in the Arts at the Canada Council*, Ottawa: Canada Council.

Crenshaw, K. (1995) 'Mapping the Margins: Intersectionality, Identity Politics, and Violence Against Women of Color', in D. Danielsen and K. Engle (eds) *After Identity: A Reader in Law and Culture*, New York: Routledge.

Crosby, Marcia (1994) 'Construction of the Imaginary Indian', in W. Waring (ed.) *By, For and About: Feminist Cultural Politics*, Toronto: Women's Press.

'Culotta, Nino' (John O'Grady) (1957) *They're a Weird Mob*, Sydney: Ure Smith.

Curthoys, A. and S. Muecke (1993) 'Australia, for Example', in W. Hudson and D. Carter (eds) *The Republicanism Debate*, Sydney: New South Wales University Press.

Dabydeen, C. (1994) 'Celebrating Difference', *Books in Canada*, September: 23–5.

Dale, L. (1997) *The English Men: Professing Literature in Australian Universities*, Queensland: Association for the Study of Australian Literature (ASAL).

D'Alfonso, A. (1988) 'Roma–Montréal', in *The Other Shore*, Montréal: Guernica.

D'Alfonso, A. (1995) *Fabrizio's Passion: A Novel*, Toronto: Guernica.

D'Alfonso, A. (1996) *In Italics: In Defense of Ethnicity*, Toronto: Guernica.

D'Alfonso, A. (1997) *Guernica 20th Anniversary Book Catalog. A Complete List: 1978–1988*, Toronto: Guernica.

Dangarembga, T. (1988) *Nervous Conditions*, Seattle, WA: Seal Press.

Daniel, H. (1995) 'Double Cover', *Australian*, September: 16.

Darville, H. (1995) 'Helen Darville Apologises', *Sydney Morning Herald*, 26 August: 1.

Dasenbrock, R. W. (1992) 'The Multicultural West', in P. Aufderheide (ed.) *Beyond P.C.: Toward a Politics of Understanding*, Minnesota, MN: Graywolf Press.

Davidson, A. (1997) 'Multiculturalism and Citizenship: Silencing the Migrant Voice', *Journal of Intercultural Studies*, 18.2: 77–92.

De Groen, F., P. Kirkpatrick and K. Stewart (Judges ALS Medal) (1995) 'Letter', *Age (Higher Education)*, July: 26.

Dean, J. (1996) *Solidarity of Strangers: Feminism After Identity Politics*, Berkeley: University of California Press.

Dean, M. (1995) 'Reading Evelyn Right: The Literary Layers of Evelyn Lau', *Canadian Forum*, March: 22–6.

Deleuze, G. (1997) 'He Stuttered', in *Gilles Deleuze: Essays Critical and Clinical*, trans. D. W. Smith and M. A. Greco, Minneapolis: University of Minnesota Press.

Deleuze, G. and F. Guattari (1986) *Kafka: Toward a Minor Literature*, trans. Dana Polan, Minneapolis: University of Minnesota Press.

Demidenko, H. (1994a) 'Interview', *Australian Book Review* #165, October: 21.

Demidenko, H. (1994b) *The Hand That Signed the Paper*, Sydney: Allen & Unwin.

Demidenko, H. (1995a) 'Pieces of the Puzzle', *Meanjin*, 54.3: 430–6.

Demidenko, H. (1995b) 'All Peoples are Capable of Atrocities', *Sydney Morning Herald*, 27 June: 11.

Derkson, J. (1997–8) 'Unrecognizable Texts: From Multiculturalism to Anti-Systemic Writing', *West Coast Line*, 24.31, no. 3, Winter: 59–71.

Derrida, J. (1994) *Spectres of Marx: The State of the Debt, the Work of Mourning and the New International*, trans. Peggy Kamuf, New York: Routledge.

Dessaix, R. (1991) 'Nice Work If You Can Get It', *Australian Book Review*, February/March: 22–8.

Dibben, K. (1995) 'Author Mystery Deepens', *Sunday Mail* (Queensland), August 20: 3.

Dimic, M. (1990) 'Preface' and 'Canadian Literatures of Lesser Diffusion: Observations from a Systemic Standpoint', in J. Pivato (ed.) *Literatures of Lesser Diffusion*, Edmonton: Research Institute for Comparative Studies, University of Alberta.

Dimic, M. and M. K. Garstin (1988) 'Polysystem Theory', in E. D. Blodgett and A. G. Purdy (eds) *Problems of Literary Reception*, Edmonton: Research Institute for Comparative Studies, University of Alberta.

Dirlik, A. (1994) 'The Postcolonial Aura: Third World Criticism in the Age of Global Capitalism', *Critical Inquiry*, 20, Winter: 328–56; and in P. Mongia (ed.) *Contemporary Postcolonial Theory: A Reader*, London: Arnold.

Dixson, M. (1999) *The Imaginary Australian: Anglo-Celts and Identity – 1788 to the Present*, Sydney: University of New South Wales Press.

Docker, J. (1991) 'The Temperament of Editors and a New Multicultural Orthodoxy', *Island*, 48, Spring: 50–5.

Docker, J. (1994) 'Post Nationalism', *Arena Magazine*, February–March, 40: 3–4.

Doyle, B. (1989) *English and Englishness*, London: Methuen.

Drakulic, S. (1996) *Café Europa: Life After Communism*, London: Abacus.

Driedger, L. (ed.) (1987) *Ethnic Canada: Identities and Inequalities*, Toronto: Copp Clark Pitman.

D'Souza, D. and R. Macneil (1992) 'The Big Chill? Interview with Dinesh D'Souza', in P. Berman (ed.) *Debating P.C.: The Controversy over Political Correctness on College Campuses*, New York: Laurel.

Duffy, M. (2000) 'The Way They Were: Review of Cope and Kalantzis, *A Place in the Sun*,' *Weekend Australian*, 18–19 March: 11.

Edgerton, S. H. (1996) *Translating the Curriculum: Multiculturalism and Cultural Studies*, New York: Routledge.

Editorial (1995) 'Demidenko Still Needs to Explain', *Weekend Australian*, 26–7 August: 20.

Egan, S. and G. Helms (1999) 'The Many Tongues of Mothertalk: Life Stories of Maruy Kiyoshi Kiyooka', *Canadian Literature*, 163: 47–77.

Ehrenreich, R. (1992) "What Campus Radicals?", in P. Aufderheide (ed.) *Beyond P.C.: Toward a Politics of Understanding*, Minnesota, MN: Graywolf Press.

Elam, D. (1997) 'Sister Are Doing It to Themselves', in D. Looser and E. A. Kaplan (eds) *Generations: Academic Feminist in Dialogue*, Minneapolis: University of Minnesota Press.

Essed, P. and D. T. Goldberg (eds) (2002) *Critical Race Theories*, Oxford: Blackwell.

Fanon, F. (1952/67) *Black Skin, White Masks*, New York: Grove Press.

Faust, B. (1997) 'Let the Sweeping Dogmas Lie', *Australian*, 10 December: 38.

Fee, M. (1993) 'Canadian Literature and English Studies in the Canadian University', *Essays in Canadian Writing*, 48: 20–40.

Fekete, J. (1994) *Moral Panic: Biopolitics Rising*, Montreal–Toronto: Robert Davies Publishing.

Fernández, E. (1992) 'P.C. Rider', in P. Berman (ed.) *Debating P.C.: The Controversy over Political Correctness on College Campuses*, New York: Laurel.

Fish, S. (1992) 'There's No Such Thing as Free Speech and It's a Good Thing, Too', in P. Berman (ed.) *Debating P.C.: The Controversy over Political Correctness on College Campuses*, New York: Laurel.

Fishman, J. (1996) 'Introduction', in J. A. Fishman, A. W. Conrad and A. Rubal-Lopez (eds) *Post-Imperial English: Status Change in Former British and American Colonies, 1940–1990*, Berlin: Mouton De Gruyter.

Fishman, J. A., A. W. Conrad and A. Rubal-Lopez (eds) (1996) *Post-Imperial English: Status Change in Former British and American Colonies, 1940–1990*, Berlin: Mouton De Gruyter.

Fleras, A. and J. L. Elliott (1992) *Multiculturalism in Canada: The Challenge of Diversity*, Scarborough: Nelson Canada.

Fong, D. (2000) 'Aliens', unpublished essay (quoted with permission).

Foucault, M. (1988a) *History of Sexuality: The Care of the Self*, trans. Robert Hurley, New York: Vintage.

Foucault, M. (1988b) *Technologies of the Self: A Seminar with Michel Foucault*, Luther H. Martin, H. Gutman and P. H. Hutton (eds) Amherst, MA: University of Massachusetts Press.

Fox-Genovese, E. (1992) 'Untitled Statement', in P. Aufderheide (ed.) *Beyond P.C.: Toward a Politics of Understanding*, Minnesota, MN: Graywolf Press.

Frankenberg, R. and L. Mani (1996) 'Crosscurrents, Crosstalk: Race, "Postcoloniality" and the Politics of Location', in S. Lavie and T. Swedenburg (eds) *Displacement, Diaspora, and Geographies of Identity*, Durham, NC: Duke University Press.

Frankenberg, R. (1993) *White Woman, Race Matters: The Social Construction of Whiteness*, Minneapolis: University of Minnesota Press.

Fraser, M. (1995) 'The Begetting of Violence', *Meanjin*, 54.3: 419–29.

Freud, S. (1919/1985) 'The Uncanny', in A. Dickson (ed.) *Art and Literature*, vol. 14. *The Penguin Freud Library*, trans. J. Strachey, London: Penguin Books.

Frow, J. and M. Morris (1999) 'Two Laws: Response to Elizabeth Povinelli', *Critical Inquiry*, 25.3: 626–30.

Gaonkar, D. P. (ed.) (2001) *Alternative Modernities*, Durham, NC and London: Duke University Press.

Garber, M. (1992) 'Phantoms of the Opera: Actor, Diplomat, Transvestite, Spy', in *Vested Interests: Cross-Dressing and Cultural Anxiety*, New York: Routledge.

Garner, H. (1995) *The First Stone*, Sydney: Picador.

Garner, H. (1996) 'The Fate of *The First Stone*', in *True Stories: Selected Non-Fiction*, Melbourne: Text Publishing, 169–78.

Gatens, M. (1996) *Imaginary Bodies*, London: Routledge.

Gates, H. L. Jr. (1990) 'Critical Remarks', in D. T. Goldberg (ed.) *Anatomy of Race*, Minneapolis: University of Minnesota Press.

Gikandi, S. (1996) *Maps of Englishness: Writing Identity in the Culture of Colonialism*, New York: Columbia University Press.

Gilroy, P. (1987) *There Ain't No Black in the Union Jack: The Cultural Politics of Race and Nation*, London: Routledge.

Gilroy, P. (1993a) *The Black Atlantic: Modernity and Double Consciousness*, Cambridge, MA: Harvard University Press.

Gilroy, P. (1993b) 'It Ain't Where You're From, But Where You're At', in *Small Acts*, London: Serpent's Tail.

Gilroy, P. (2000) *Against Race: Imagining Political Culture Beyond the Color Line*, Cambridge, MA: Belknap/Harvard University Press.

Gitlin, T. (1992) 'On the Virtues of a Loose Canon', in P. Aufderheide (ed.) *Beyond P.C.: Toward a Politics of Understanding*, Minnesota, MN: Graywolf Press.

Globe & Mail (1994) 'Rape Routine in Ethnic Cleansing', 3 June: A.6.

Goldberg, D. T. (ed.) (1990) *Anatomy of Racism*, Minneapolis: University of Minnesota Press.

Goldberg, D. T. (1993) *Racist Culture: Philosophy and the Politics of Meaning*, Blackwell: Oxford.

Goldberg, D. T. (1994) 'Introduction: Multicultural Conditions', in D. T. Goldberg (ed.) *Multiculturalism: A Critical Reader*, Oxford: Blackwell.

Goldie, T. (1989) *Fear and Temptation: The Image of the Indigene in Canadian, Australian and New Zealand Literatures*, Kingston, Ontario: McGill-Queen's University Press.

Gordon, A. (1997) *Ghostly Matters: Haunting and the Sociological Imagination*, Minneapolis: University of Minnesota Press.

Gordon, A. and C. Newfield (eds) (1996a) *Mapping Multiculturalism*, Minneapolis: University of Minnesota Press.

Gordon, A. and C. Newfield (eds) (1996b) 'Introduction' and 'Multiculturalism's Unfinished Business', in A. Gordon and C. Newfield (eds) *Mapping Multiculturalism*, Minneapolis: University of Minnesota Press.

Gordon, T. and W. Lubiana (1992) 'The Statement of the Black Faculty Caucus', in P. Berman (ed.) *Debating P.C.: The Controversy over Political Correctness on College Campuses*, New York: Laurel.

Goto, H. (1994) *Chorus of Mushrooms*, Edmonton: NeWest Press.

Graham, D. (ed.) (1994) *Being Whitefella*, Fremantle: Fremantle Arts Centre Press.

Green, A. (1999) *The Fabric of Affect in the Psychoanalytic Discourse*, trans. Alan Sheridan, London and New York: Routledge.

Gregory, D. (1994) *Geographical Imaginations*, Cambridge, MA and Oxford: Blackwell.

Greif, S. (ed.) (1995) *Immigration and National Identity in NZ: One People, Two Peoples, Many Peoples?*, Palmerston: Dunmore Press.

Grewal, I. (1994) 'Autobiographic Subjects and Diasporic Locations', in I. Grewal and C. Kaplan (eds) *Scattered Hegemonies*, Minneapolis: University of Minnesota Press.

Grewal, I. and Kaplan, C. (eds) (1994) *Scattered Hegemonies*, Minneapolis: University of Minnesota Press.

Grinberg, L. and R. Grinberg (1989) *Psychoanalytic Perspectives on Migration and Exile*, New Haven, CT: Yale University Press.

Grosz, E. (1994) *Volatile Bodies*, Bloomington: Indiana University Press.

Gunew, S. (1993a) 'Multicultural Multiplicities: US, Canada, Australia', in D. Bennett (ed.) *Cultural Studies: Pluralism and Theory*, Melbourne: University of Melbourne Press.

Gunew, S. (1993b) 'Culture, Gender and the Author-function', in J. Frow and M. Morris (eds) *Australian Cultural Studies: A Reader*, Sydney: Allen & Unwin.

Gunew, S. (1993c) 'Against Multiculturalism: Rhetorical Images', in G. L. Clark, D. Forbes and R. Francis (eds) *Multiculturalism, Difference and Postmodernism*, Melbourne: Longman Cheshire.

Gunew, S. (1994a) *Framing Marginality: Multicultural Literary Studies*, Melbourne: Melbourne University Press.

Gunew, S. (1994b) 'Irreducible Difference: Race, Ethnicity, Feminism', in S. Gunew and A. Yeatman (eds) *Feminism and the Politics of Difference*, Sydney: Allen & Unwin.

Gunew, S. (1996) 'Multicultural Multiplicities: Canada, USA, Australia', in F. Loriggio (ed.) *Social Pluralism and Literary History: The Literature of the Italian Emigration*, Ottawa: Guernica.

Gunew, S. (1999) 'The Melting Pot of Assimilation: Cannibalizing the Multicultural Body', in S. Lim, L. Smith and W. Dissanayake (eds) *Transnational Asia Pacific: Gender, Culture and the Public Sphere*, Champaign, IL: University of Illinois Press.

Gunew, S., L. Houbein, A. Karakostas-Seda and J. Mahyuddin (eds) (1992) *A*

Bibliography of Australian Multicultural Writers, Geelong, Australia: Deakin University Press (Centre for Studies in Literary Education).

Gunew, S. and K. Longley (eds) (1992) *Striking Chords: Multicultural Literary Interpretations*, Sydney: Allen & Unwin.

Gunew, S. and A. Yeatman (eds) (1993) *Feminism and the Politics of Difference*, Sydney: Allen & Unwin.

Gunew, S. and F. Rizvi (eds) (1994) *Culture, Difference and the Arts*, Sydney: Allen & Unwin.

Gunnarsson, S. (1993) *The Diary of Evelyn Lau*, Toronto: Canadian Broadcasting Commission.

Gunning, M. (1995) 'Jury Still Out on the Talents of Evelyn Lau', *Vancouver Sun* (Weekend Sun), 2 September: D13.

Hage, G. (1993) 'Republicanism, Multiculturalism, Zoology', *Communal Plural*, 2: 113–37.

Hage, G. (1998) *White Nation: Fantasies of White Supremacy in a Multicultural Society*, Annandale, NSW: Pluto Press.

Hagedorn, J. (ed.) (1993) *Charlie Chan is Dead: An Anthology of Contemporary Asian American Fiction*, New York: Penguin.

Hall, S. (1995) 'New Ethnicities', in B. Ashcroft, G. Griffiths and H. Tiffin (eds) *The Post-Colonial Studies Reader*, New York: Routledge.

Hall, S. (1996a) 'When Was "The Post-Colonial"? Thinking at the Limit', in I. Chambers and L. Curti (eds) *The Post-Colonial Question*, London: Routledge.

Hall, S. (1996b) 'Cultural Identity and Cinematic Representation', in H. A. Baker Jr., M. Diawara and R. L. Lindeborg (eds) *Black British Cultural Studies: A Reader*, Chicago, IL: University of Chicago Press.

Hall, S. and P. du Gay (eds) (1996) *Questions of Cultural Identity*, London: Sage.

Haraway, D. (1991) *Simians, Cyborgs, and Women: The Reinvention of Nature*, London: Free Association Books.

Harel, S. (2002) (unpublished paper) 'Trauma and "métissage": The American Journey of Julien Bigras', delivered at the *Transculturalisms Canada Symposium*, University of British Columbia, February.

Harris, T. (1984) 'On *The Color Purple*, Stereotypes and Silence', *Black American Literature Forum*, 18.4: 155–61.

Harvey, D. (1998) 'The Body as an Accumulation Strategy', *Environment and Planning D: Society and Space*, 16: 401–21.

Harvey, M. (1992) 'Politically Correct is Politically Suspect', in P. Aufderheide (ed.) *Beyond P.C.: Toward a Politics of Understanding*, Minnesota, MN: Graywolf Press.

Henderson, G. (1995a) 'Playing with the Truth in this Work of "Faction"', *Sydney Morning Herald*, 27 June: 11.

Henderson, G. (1995b) 'Faction, Fiction or Propaganda: Ozlit Should be Blushing', *Sydney Morning Herald*, 22 August: 13.

Henderson, G. (1995c) 'Literary Judges Who Don't Want to be Judged', *Sydney Morning Herald*, 12 September: 13.

Ho, R. (1994) 'Site-Seeing Vancouver, Positioning Self', in P. Delany (ed.) *Vancouver: Representing the Postmodern City*, Vancouver: Arsenal Press.

Hobsbawm, E. and T. Ranger (eds) (1983) *The Invention of Tradition*, Cambridge: Cambridge University Press.

Hoffman, E. (1989) *Lost in Translation: A Life in a New Language*, New York: Dutton.

Hoffman, E. (1993) *Exit Into History*, New York: Viking.

Hoffman, E. (1998) 'Life in a New Language', in M. Zournazi (ed.) *Foreign Dialogues: Memories, Translations, Conversations*, Annandale, NSW: Pluto Press.

Hoffman, E. (1999) 'The New Nomads', in A. Aciman (ed.) *Letters of Transit: Reflections on Exile, Identity, Language, and Loss*, New York: New York Public Library.

Holborow, M. (1999) *The Politics of English: A Marxist View of Language*, London: Sage.

Hollinger, D. (1995) *Postethnic America: Beyond Multiculturalism*, New York: Harper Collins.

Hongo, G. (1995a) *Volcano: A Memoir of Hawai'i*, New York: Alfred A. Knopf.

Hongo, G. (ed.) (1995b) *Under Western Eyes: Personal Essays from Asian America*, New York: Doubleday.

Howard, J. (1997) 'Address', in *Multicultural Australia the Way Forward*, Melbourne, Australia: Department of Immigration and Multicultural Affairs National Multicultural Advisory Council.

Hudson, W. and D. Carter (1993) 'Reframing the Issues', in W. Hudson and D. Carter (eds) *The Republicanism Debate*, Sydney: New South Wales University Press.

Hutcheon, L. and M. Hutcheon (1996) *Opera: Desire, Disease, Death*, Lincoln: University of Nebraska Press.

Hwang, D. (1988a) *M. Butterfly*, New York: Penguin.

Hwang, D. (1988b) 'Afterword', in *M. Butterfly*, New York: Penguin.

Ignatieff, M. (1994) *Blood and Belonging*, Toronto: Penguin.

Indyk, I. (1995a) 'Literature, Lies and History', *Weekend Australian*, 21 August: 26–7.

Indyk, I. (1995b) 'Letter', *Australian Book Review* #174, September: 3–4.

Irving, H. (1997) *To Constitute a Nation: A Cultural History of Australia's Constitution*, Melbourne: Cambridge University Press.

Jagose, A. (1993) 'Slash and Suture: Post/Colonialism in "Borderland/La Frontera: The New Mestiza"', in S. Gunew and A. Yeatman (eds) *Feminism and the Politics of Difference*, Sydney: Allen & Unwin.

Jameson, F. (1998) 'Preface', in F. Jameson and M. Miyoshi (eds) *The Cultures of Globalization*, Durham, NC: Duke University Press.

Janaczewska, N. (1995) *The History of Water*, Sydney: Currency Press.

JanMohammed, A. R. (1992) 'Worldliness-without-World, Homelessness-as-Home: Toward a Definition of the Specular Border Intellectual', in M. Sprinker (ed.) *Edward Said: A Critical Reader*, Oxford: Blackwell.

Jost, J., G. Totaro and C. Tyshing (eds) (1996) *The Demidenko File*, Melbourne: Penguin.

Kamboureli, S. (ed.) (1997) *Making a Difference: Canadian Multicultural Literature*, Toronto: Oxford University Press.

Kamboureli, S. (2000) *Scandalous Bodies: Diasporic Literature in English Canada*, Ontario: Oxford University Press.

Kaplan, A. (2001) 'Trauma, Aging and Melodrama (With Reference to Tracey Moffatt's *Night Cries*)', in M. DeKoven (ed.) *Feminist Locations*, New Brunswick, NJ: Rutgers University Press.

Kaplan, A. (2003) 'Traumatic Contact Zones and Embodied Translators', in E. A. Kaplan and B. Wang (eds) *Trauma and Modernity: Histories of Transnational Cinema*, Hong Kong: Hong Kong University Press.

Kaplan, A. and D. Looser (eds) (1997) *Generations: Academic Feminists in Dialogue*, Minneapolis: University of Minnesota Press.

Karpinski, E. C. and I. Lea (eds) (1993) *Pens of Many Colours: A Canadian Reader*, Toronto: Harcourt Brace Jovanovich.

Keating, A. (1998) '(De)Centering the Margins? Identity Politics and Tactical (Re)Naming', in S. K. Stanley (ed.) *Other Sisterhoods: Literary Theory and U. S. Women of Color*, Urbana and Chicago: University of Illinois Press.

Keefer, J. K. (1996) 'Who's Afraid of Josef Svorecky? The "Reactionary" Immigrant Writer in a Multicultural Canada', in I. Mavor (ed.) *Ethnic Literature and Culture in the U. S. A., Canada, and Australia*, Frankfurt: Peter Lang.

Kimball, R. (1992) 'The Periphery v. the Center: The MLA in Chicago', in P. Berman (ed.) *Debating P.C.: The Controversy over Political Correctness on College Campuses*, New York: Laurel.

Kincaid, J. (1991) 'On Seeing England for the First Time', *Transition* #51: 32–40.

King, M. (ed.) (1991) *Pakeha*, Auckland: Penguin.

Kingston, M. H. (1989) *Tripmaster Monkey: His Fake Book*, London: Pan/Picador.

Kiyooka, R. (1975) *Transcanada Letters*, Vancouver: Talon Books.

Kiyooka, R. (1997a) *Mothertalk: Life Stories of Mary Kiyoshi Kiyooka*, D. Marlatt (ed.), Edmonton: NeWest Press.

Kiyooka, R. (1997b) *Pacific Windows: Collected Poems of Roy K. Kiyooka*, R. Miki (ed.) Burnaby, British Columbia: Talonbooks.

Kiyooka, R. (1997c) 'Dear Lucy Fumi', in *Mothertalk: Life Stories of Mary Kiyoshi Kiyooka*, Edmonton: NeWest Press.

Koestenbaum, W. (1993) *The Queen's Throat: Opera, Homosexuality and the Mystery of Desire*, New York: Vintage.

Kokkinos, A. (1998) *Head On*, Melbourne: Great Scott Production.

Kondo, D. (1997) *About Face: Performing Race in Fashion and Theater*, New York: Routledge.

Kornreich, J. (1996) 'Selling Her Soul', *Women's Review of Books*, 13.6, March.

Koshy, S. (2000) 'The Fiction of Asian American Literature', in J. Yu-wen, S. Wu and M. Song (eds) *Asian American Studies: A Reader*, New Brunswick, NJ: Rutgers University Press.

Kostash, M. (1991) 'Eurocentricity: Notes on Metaphors of Place', in S. Hryniuk (ed.) *Twenty Years of Multiculturalism*, Manitoba: St John's College Press.

Kostash, M. (1993) *Bloodlines: A Journey in Eastern Europe*, Toronto: Douglas & McIntyre.

Kostash, M. (1994) 'You Check Your Colour at the Door', *Globe & Mail*, 9 May: A19.

Kostash, M. (2000) *The Next Canada: In Search of Our Future Nation*, Toronto: McClelland & Stewart.

Koutsoukis, J. (1995) 'Helen Darville "Set Out to Distort"', *Age*, 29 September.

Kristeva, J. (1982) *Powers of Horror*, New York: Columbia University Press.

Kristeva, J. (1984) 'My Memory's Hyperbole', in D. C. Stanton (ed.) *The Female Autograph*, Chicago, IL: University of Chicago Press.

Kristeva, J. (1991) *Strangers to Ourselves*, New York: Columbia University Press.

Kumar, A. (1997) 'Conditions of Immigration', in M. Hill (ed.) *Whiteness: A Critical Reader*, New York: New York University Press.

Kürti, L. (1997) 'Globalisation and the Discourse of Otherness in the "New" Eastern and Central Europe', in T. Modood and P. Werbner (eds) *The Politics of Multi-culturalism in the New Europe: Racism, Identity and Community*, London: Zed Books.

Kymlicka, W. (1998) *Finding Our Way: Rethinking Ethnocultural Relations in Canada*, Toronto: Oxford University Press.

Langton, M. (1993) *'Well, I Heard It on the Radio and I Saw It on Television . . .'*, Sydney: Australian Film Commission.

Laplanche, J. and J.-B. Pontalis (eds) (1973) *The Language of Psycho-Analysis*, trans. Donald Nicholson-Smith, New York: Norton.

Lau, E. (1989) *Runaway: Diary of a Street Kid*, Toronto: HarperCollins.

Lau, E. (1990) *You Are Not Who You Claim*, Victoria, BC: Porcépic.

Lau, E. (1992) *Oedipal Dreams*, Toronto: Coach House.

Lau, E. (1993) *Fresh Girls and Other Stories*, Toronto: HarperCollins.

Lau, E. (1994a) *In the House of Slaves*, Toronto: Coach House.

Lau, E. (1994b) 'Why I Didn't Attend the Writing Thru Race Conference', *Globe & Mail*, Toronto, 9 July.

Lau, E. (1995) *Other Women: A Novel*, Toronto: Random House.

Lee, B. and J. Wong-Chu (eds) (1991) *Many-Mouthed Birds: Contemporary Writing by Chinese Canadians*, Vancouver and Toronto: Douglas & McIntyre.

Lee, R. G. (1991) 'The Woman Warrior as an Intervention in Asian-American Historiography', in S. G. Lim (ed.) *Approaches to Teaching Kingston's "The Woman Warrior"*, New York: Modern Language Association of America.

Lee, S. (1990) *Disappearing Moon Café*, Vancouver and Toronto: Douglas & McIntyre.

Legge, K. (1995a) 'The Demidenko Affair', *Weekend Australian* (Review), July, 1–2: 15–16.

Legge, K. (1995b) 'Demidenko: A Crisis of Identity', *Australian*, 21 August: 2.

Lim, S. G.-l. (1993) *Nationalism and Literature: English-Language Writing from the Philippines and Singapore*, Quezon City: New Day.

Lim, S. G.-l. (1994) *Writing S.E. Asia in English: Against the Grain, Focus on Asian English-language Literature*, London: Skoob Books.

Lim, S. G.-l. (1996a) *Among the White Moon Faces: An Asian-American Memoir of Homelands*, New York: The Feminist Press.

Lim, S. G.-l. (1996b) 'Reticence and Resistance: A Conversation', *The Women's Review of Books*, XIII, 10–11, July: 24–5.

Lim, S. G.-l. (1997) 'Immigration and Diaspora', in K.-K. Cheung (ed.) *An Interethnic Companion to Asian American Literature*, New York: Cambridge University Press.

Lim, S. G.-l., M. Tsutakawa and M. Donnelly (eds) (1989) *The Forbidden Stitch: An Asian American Women's Anthology*, Corvallis, OR: Calyx.

Lim, S. G.-l. and A. Ling (eds) (1992) *Reading the Literatures of Asian America*, Philadelphia: Temple University Press.

Lim, S. G.-l., F. Cheong and L. Kwa (2002) 'Singapore on My Mind', *The Women's Review of Books*, XIX, 10–11, July: 24–5.

Linteau, R. (1992) 'The Italians of Quebec: Key Participants in Contemporary Linguistic and Political Debates', in R. Perin and F. Sturino (eds) *Arrangiarsi: The Italian Immigration Experience in Canada*, Montreal: Guernica.

Lloyd, D. (1994) 'Ethnic Cultures, Minority Discourse and the State', in F. Barker *et al.* (eds) *Colonial Discourse/Postcolonial Theory*, Manchester: Manchester University Press.

Loewald, U. (1994) 'Feminism and Colonialism', in S. Hawthorne and R. Klein (eds) *Australia for Women: Travel and Culture*, Melbourne: Spinifex Press.

Loriggio, F. (1990a) 'History, Literary History, and Ethnic Literature', in J. Pivato (ed.) *Literatures of Lesser Diffusion*, Edmonton: Research Institute for Comparative Studies, University of Alberta.

Loriggio, F. (1990b) 'Italian-Canadian Literature: Basic Critical Issues', in C. D. Minni and A. F. Ciampolino (eds) *Writers in Transition*, Montreal: Guernica.

Loriggio, F. (1996) 'Introduction', in F. Loriggio (ed.) *Social Pluralism and Literary History: The Literature of the Italian Emigration*, Ottawa: Guernica.

Losche, D. (1996) 'Badtjala Woman – Fiona Foley's *Native Blood* and *Native Hybrid*', in *Colonial Post Colonial*, Melbourne: Museum of Modern Art at Heide.

Lowe, L. (1996) *Immigrant Acts*, Durham, NC: Duke University Press.

Lucashenko, M. (1997) *Steam Pigs*, St Lucia: University of Queensland Press.

Lum, C. M. K. (1996) *In Search of a Voice: Karaoke and the Construction of Identity in Chinese America*, Mahwah, NJ: Lawrence Erlbaum.

Lyotard, J.-F. (1986) 'Defining the Postmodern', in L. Appignanesi (ed.) *Postmodernism*, London: Institute for Contemporary Art.

MacLaren, I. S. and C. Potvin (eds) (1989) *Questions of Funding, Publishing and Distribution*, Edmonton: Research Institute for Comparative Studies, University of Alberta.

MacLaren, I. S. and C. Potvin (eds) (1991) *Literary Genres*, Edmonton: Research Institute for Comparative Studies, University of Alberta.

Malouf, D. (1986) *12 Edmonstone Street*, Harmondsworth: Penguin.

Malouf, D. (1994) *Remembering Babylon*, New York: Random House.

Mamet, D. (1992) *Oleanna*, New York: Vintage.

Manne, R. (1995) 'The Great Pretender', *Age*, 26 August: 7–8.

Manne, R. (1996) *The Culture of Forgetting*, Melbourne: The Text Publishing Co.

Maracle, L. (1990) 'Just Get in Front of a Typewriter and Bleed', in S. Lee, L. Maracle, D. Marlatt and B. Warland (eds) *Telling It: Women and Language Across Cultures*, Vancouver: Press Gang.

Marr, D. (1995) 'Australia's *Satanic Verses*', *Sydney Morning Herald*, 26 August: Spectrum 4A.

Martin, L. H., H. Gutman and P. H. Hutton (eds) (1988) *Technologies of the Self: A Seminar with Michel Foucault*, Amherst, MA: University of Massachusetts Press.

McClary, S. (1991) *Feminine Endings: Music, Gender, and Sexuality*, Minnesota: University of Minnesota Press.

McClintock, A. (1995) *Imperial Leather*, New York: Routledge.

McLean, I. (1998) *White Aborigines: Identity Politics in Australian Art*, Melbourne: Cambridge University Press.

Mead, J. (ed.) (1997) *Bodyjamming: Sexual Harassment, Feminism and Public Life*, NSW: Random House.

Mead, K. (1998) 'Writer's Snake Claim', *Australian*, Wednesday 21 October: 5.

Mignolo, W. (1998) 'Globalization, Civilization Processes, and the Relocation of Languages and Cultures', in F. Jameson and M. Miyoshi (eds) *The Cultures of Globalization*, Durham, NC: Duke University Press.

Miki, R. (1994) 'From Exclusion to Inclusion', *Canadian Forum*, September: 4–8.

Miki, R. (1998) *Broken Entries: Race, Subjectivity, Writing*, Toronto: The Mercury Press.

Miki, R. (2002) 'Unravelling Roy Kiyooka: A Re-assessment Amidst Shifting Boundaries', in J. O'Brian, N. Sawada and S. Watson (eds) *All Amazed. For Roy Kiyooka*, Vancouver: Arsenal Pulp Press/Morris and Helen Belkin Gallery/Collapse.

Milner, A. (1991) *Contemporary Cultural Theory: An Introduction*, Sydney: Allen & Unwin.

Minni, C. D. (1990) 'Interview', in J. Hesse (ed.) *Voices of Change*, Vancouver: Pulp Press.

Minow, M. (1997) *Not only for Myself: Identity, Politics, and the Law*, New York: The New Press.

Mishra, V. (1996) 'Postmodern Racism', *Meanjin*, 55.2: 346–57.

Mishra, V. and Bob Hodge (1993) 'What is Post(-)colonialism?', in P. Williams and L. Chrisman (eds) *Colonial Discourse and Postcolonial Theory: A Reader*, London: Harvester Wheatsheaf.

Miska, J. (1990) *Ethnic and Native Canadian Literature: A Bibliography*, Toronto: University of Toronto Press.

Mitchell, S. (1994) 'Passport to Criminal Pasts', *Weekend Australian*, 12–13 November.

Miyoshi, M. (1993) 'A Borderless World? From Colonialism to Transnationalism and the Decline of the Nation-State', *Critical Inquiry*, 19, Summer: 726–51.

Miyoshi, M. (1998) '"Globalization", Culture, and the University', in F. Jameson and M. Miyoshi (eds) *The Cultures of Globalization*, Durham, NC: Duke University Press.

Modjeska, D. (2000) 'The Rush of Memoir. Pt. 1 A Writ Served', *Australian Review of Books*, 5.6: 6–7.

Mohan, R. (1995) 'Multiculturalism in the Nineties: Pitfalls and Possibilities', in C. Newfield and R. Strickland (eds) *After Political Correctness: The Humanities and Society in the 1990s*, Boulder, CO: Westview Press.

Mohanty, C. (1991) 'Under Western Eyes: Feminist Scholarship and Colonial Discourses', in C. T. Mohanty, A. Russo and L. Torres (eds) *Third World Women and the Politics of Feminism*, Bloomington: Indiana University Press.

Modood, T. and P. Werbner (eds) (1997) *The Politics of Multiculturalism in the New Europe: Racism, Identity and Community*, London: Zed Books.

Mootoo, S. (2001) *The Predicament of Or*, Vancouver, WA: Polestar.

Morley, D. and K.-H. Chen (eds) (1996) *Stuart Hall: Critical Dialogues in Cultural Studies*, London and New York: Routledge.

Morris, M. (1998) *Too Soon Too Late: History in Popular Culture*, Bloomington: Indiana University Press.

Morrison, T. (1992) *Playing in the Dark: Whiteness and the Literary Imagination*, Cambridge, MA: Harvard University Press.

Mowatt, R. V. (1992) 'What Revolution at Stanford?', in P. Aufderheide (ed.) *Beyond P.C.: Toward a Politics of Understanding*, Minnesota, MN: Graywolf Press.

Mukherjee, A. (1988) *Towards an Aesthetics of Opposition: Essays on Literature, Criticism and Cultural Imperialism*, Ontario: Williams-Wallace.

Mukherjee, A. (1994) *Oppositional Aesthetics: Readings from a Hyphenated Space*, Toronto: TSAR.

Mukherjee, A. (1998) *Postcolonialism: My Living*, Toronto: TSAR.

Mukherjee, B. (1997) 'American Dreamer', *Mother Jones*, January/February.

Mura, D. (1996) *Where the Body Meets Memory: An Odyssey of Race, Sexuality and Identity*, New York: Doubleday.

Murray, H. (1996) *Working in English: History, Institution, Resources*, Toronto: University of Toronto Press.

Nairn, T. (1981) *The Break-Up of Britain*, London: Verso.

National Multicultural Advisory Council (1999) *Australian Multiculturalism: For New Century*, Canberra: AGSP.

Ng, R. (1993) 'Sexism, Racism and Canadian Nationalism', in S. Gunew and A. Yeatman (eds) *Feminism and the Politics of Difference*, Sydney: Allen & Unwin.

Nnaemeka, O. (1994) 'Bringing African Women into the Classroom: Rethinking Pedagogy and Epistemology', in M. R. Higonnet (ed.) *Borderwork: Feminist Engagements with Comparative Literature*, Ithaca, NY: Cornell University Press.

North, S. (1996) 'Asia Town: What Will the Future Hold for a 50-percent-Asian Vancouver?', *Vancouver Magazine*, 29.7, November: 46–58.

Oakley, B. (1995) 'Staying Power Wins Author a Literary Marathon', *Australian*, 2 June.

Oboe, A. (ed.) (2003) *Mongrel Signatures: Reflections on the Work of Mudrooroo*, Amsterdam: Rodopi.

O'Brian, J., N. Sawada and S. Watson (eds) (2002) *All Amazed. For Roy Kiyooka*, Vancouver: Arsenal Pulp Press/Morris and Helen Belkin Gallery/Collapse.

O'Connor, T. (1998) 'Race', *Brisbane Courier-Mail*, 28 March: 24.

O'Hearn, C. Chiawei (ed.) (1998) *Half and Half: Writers on Growing Up Biracial and Bicultural*, New York: Pantheon.

Okihiro, G. Y., M. Alquizola, D. F. Rony and K. S. Wong (eds) (1995) *Priviliging Positions: The Sites of Asian American Studies*, Pulman, WA: Washington State University Press.

Ong, A. (1999) *Flexible Citizenship: The Cultural Logics of Transnationality*, Durham, NC: Duke University Press.

Onufrijchuk, R. (1988) 'Post-modern or Perednovok: Deconstructing Ethnicity', in I. Angus (ed.) *Ethnicity in a Technological Age*, Edmonton: Canadian Institute of Ukrainian Studies, University of Alberta.

Padolsky, E. (1990) 'Establishing the Two-Way Street: Literary Criticism and Ethnic Studies', *Canadian Ethnic Studies*, 22: 22–37.

Palumbo-Liu, D. (ed.) (1995) *The Ethnic Canon: Histories, Institutions and Interventions*, Minneapolis: University of Minnesota Press.

Palumbo-Liu, D. (1999) *Asian/American: Historical Crossings of a Racial Frontier*, Stanford: Stanford University Press.

Papastergiadis, N. (1998) *Dialogues in Diaspora: Essays and Conversations on Cultural Identity*, London: Rivers Oram Press.

Pathak, Z. and R. S. Rajan (1992) 'Shahbano', in J. Butler and J. W. Scott (eds) *Feminists Theorize the Political*, New York: Routledge.

Pavlyshyn, M. (1995) 'Ukrainians Reject Stereotype Image', *Weekend Australian*, 16–17 September.

Peel, J. (1995) 'Letter', *Sydney Morning Herald*, 12 September: 12.

Pennycook, A. (1998) *English and the Discourses of Colonialism*, London: Routledge.

Perera, S. (1994) 'Recalcitrant Subalterns (and Other Multicultural Monsters)', unpublished paper delivered at the University of Hong Kong.

Perrin, C. (ed.) (1998) 'In the Wake of Terra Nullius (Special Issue)', *Law, Text, Culture*, 4.1, Autumn.

Perry, R. and P. Williams (1992) 'Freedom of Hate Speech', in P. Berman (ed.) *Debating P.C.: The Controversy over Political Correctness on College Campuses*, New York: Laurel.

Phelan, P. (1998) 'Introduction: The Ends of Perfromance', in P. Phelan and J. Lane (eds) *The Ends of Performance*, New York: New York University Press.

Philip, M. N. (1992) *Frontiers: Selected Essays and Writing on Racism and Culture 1984–1992*, Stratford, Ontario: Mercury Press.

Philip, M. N. (1995) 'Signifying: Why the Media Have Fawned over Bissoondath's *Selling Illusions*', *Border/Lines Magazine*, 36: 4–11.

Phillipson, R. (1992) *Linguistic Imperialism*, Oxford: Oxford University Press.

Pile, S. (1996) *The Body and the City: Psychoanalysis, Space and Subjectivity*, New York: Routledge.

Pivato, J. (ed.) (1990) *Literatures of Lesser Diffusion*, Edmonton: Research Institute for Comparative Studies, University of Alberta.

Poizat, M. (1992) *The Angel's Cry*, Ithaca, NY: Cornell University Press.

Povinelli, E. (1999) 'The Cunning of Recognition: A Reply to John Frow and Meaghan Morris', *Critical Inquiry*, 25.3: 631–7.

Povinelli, E. (2002) *The Cunning of Recognition: Indigenous Alterities and the Making of Australian Multiculturalism*, Durham, NC and London: Duke University Press.

Powell Street Revue and Chinese Canadian Writers' Workshop (1979) *Inalienable Rice: A Chinese and Japanese Canadian Anthology*, Vancouver: Intermedia Press.

Pratt, M. (1992) *Imperial Eyes: Travel Writing and Transculturation*, London: Routledge.

Prior, N. (1996) *The Demidenko Diary*, Melbourne: Reed Books.

Quan, A. and J. Wong-Chu (eds) (1999) *Swallowing Clouds: An Anthology of Chinese-Canadian Poetry*, Vancouver: Arsenal Pulp Press.

Radhakrishnan, R. (1996) *Diasporic Mediations: Between Home and Location*, Minneapolis: University of Minnesota Press.

Rajan, R. S. (ed.) (1993) *The Lie of the Land: English Studies in India*, Delhi: Oxford University Press.

Ram, K. (1996) 'Liberal Multiculturalism's "NESB Women": A South Asian Post-colonial Feminist Perspective on the Liberal Impoverishment of "Difference"', in E. Vasta and S. Castles (eds) *The Teeth Are Smiling: The Persistence of Racism in Multicultural Australia*, Sydney: Allen & Unwin.

Rattansi, A. (1995) 'Just Framing; Ethnicities and Racisms in a "Postmodern" Framework', in L. Nicholson and S. Seidman (eds) *Social Postmodernism: Beyond Identity Politics*, New York: Cambridge University Press.

Rée, J. (1998) 'Cosmopolitanism and the Experience of Nationality', in P. Cheah and B. Robbins (eds) *Cosmopolitics: Thinking Freely Beyond the Nation*, Minneapolis: University of Minnesota Press.

Renan, E. (1990) 'What Is a Nation?', in H. Bhabha (ed.) *Nation and Narration*, London: Routledge.

Riemer, A. (1996) *The Demidenko Debate*, Sydney: Allen & Unwin.

Robbins, B. (1998) 'Introduction Part I: Actually Existing Cosmopolitanism', in P. Cheah and B. Robbins (eds) *Cosmopolitics: Thinking Freely Beyond the Nation*, Minneapolis: University of Minnesota Press.

Roberts, G. and I. Makler (1995) 'A Fictional Life: The Fertile Mind of Helen Darville', *Sydney Morning Herald*, 26 August: 27.

Roedinger, D. (2002) 'Whiteness and Ethnicity in the History of "White Ethnics" in the United States', in P. Essed and D. T. Goldberg (eds) *Critical Race Theories*, Oxford: Blackwell.

Rose, G. (1999) 'Performing Space', in D. Massey, J. Allen and P. Sarre (eds) *Human Geography Today*, Cambridge: Polity Press.

Roy, P. (1998) 'Whitebread Music for White-bred Folks', *Globe & Mail*, 22 June: A14.

Ruddock, P. (1997) 'Address', in *Multicultural Australia the Way Forward*, Melbourne: Department of Immigration and Multicultural Affairs National Multicultural Advisory Council.

Ruthven, K. K. (2001) *Faking Literature*, Cambridge: Cambridge University Press.

Saghal, G. (1992) 'Secular Spaces: The Experience of Asian Women Organizing', in G. Saghal and N. Yuval-Davis (eds) *Refusing Holy Orders: Women and Fundamentalism in Britain*, London: Virago.

Said, E. (1992a) 'Figures, Configurations, Transfiguration', in A. Rutherford (ed.) *From Commonwealth to Post-Colonial*, Denmark: Dangaroo Press.

Said, E. (1992b) 'The Politics of Knowledge', in P. Berman (ed.) *Debating P.C.: The Controversy over Political Correctness on College Campuses*, New York: Laurel.

Said, E. (1993) *Culture and Imperialism*, London: Chatto & Windus.

Said, E. (1994) *Representations of the Intellectual*, New York: Pantheon.

Said, E. (1999) *Out of Place: A Memoir*, New York: A. Knopf.

Said, E. (2000) *Reflections on Exile and Other Essays*, Cambridge, MA: Harvard University Press.

Salecl, R. and S. Zizek (eds) (1996) *Sic 1: Gaze and Voice as Love Objects*, Durham, NC: Duke University Press.

Salvatore, F. (1991) 'The Italian Writers of Quebec: Language, Culture and Politics', in J. Pivato (ed.) *Contrasts: Comparative Essays on Italian-Canadian Writing*, Montreal: Guernica.

Salvatore, F. (1998) *Fascism and the Italians of Montreal. An Oral History: 1922–1945*, Toronto: Guernica.

Sandoval, C. (1991) 'U.S. Third World Feminism: The Theory and Method of Oppositional Consciousness in the Postmodern World', *Genders*, 10, Spring: 3–24.

Schaffer, K. (1995) *In the Wake of First Contact: The Eliza Fraser Stories*, Melbourne: Cambridge University Press.

Scott, J. (1992a) 'Campus Communities Beyond Consensus', in P. Aufderheide (ed.) *Beyond P.C.: Toward a Politics of Understanding*, Minnesota, MN: Graywolf Press.

Scott, J. (1992b) 'Multiculturalism and the Politics of Identity', *October*, 61, Summer: 12–19.

Sebesta, J. A. (1999–2000) 'Singing Scholarship, Dancing History, and Acting Theory: Academic Conferences as Sites of Performance', *On-Stage-Studies*, 22: 52–63.

Sedgwick, E. K. and A. Frank (1995) *Shame and Its Sisters: A Silvan Tompkins Reader*, Durham, NC: Duke University Press.

Sharpe, J. (1993) *Allegories of Empire: The Figure of Woman in the Colonial Text*, Minneapolis: University of Minnesota Press.

Shohat, E. (ed.) (1998) *Talking Visions: Multicultural Feminism in a Transnational Age*, New York: New Museum/MIT Press.

Shohat, E. and R. Stam (1994) *Unthinking Eurocentrism: Multiculturalism and the Media*, London: Routledge.

Silvera, M. (ed.) (1994) *The Other Woman: Women of Colour in Contemporary Canadian Literature*, Toronto: Sister Vision Press.

Silverman, M. (1992) *Deconstructing the Nation: Immigration, Racism and Citizenship in Modern France*, London: Routledge.

Silvermann, K. (1988) *The Acoustic Mirror: The Female Voice in Psychoanalysis and Cinema*, Bloomington: Indiana University Press.

Simon, S. (1996) 'National Membership and Forms of Contemporary Belonging in Québec', in International Council for Canadian Studies (ed.) *Language, Culture and Values in Canada at the Dawn of the 21st Century*, Ottawa: Carleton University Press.

Slattery, L. (1995) 'Our Multicultural Cringe', *Australian*, 13 September.

Smith, D. (1991) 'The New MacCarthyism', *Canadian Dimension*, September: 8–13.

Smyth, J. (1994) 'Sikh Group to Fight Legion Headgear Ban', *Globe & Mail*, 6 June.

Sollors, W. (1986) *Beyond Ethnicity: Consent and Descent in American Culture*, New York: Oxford University Press.

Sollors, W. (ed.) (1996) *Theories of Ethnicity: A Classical Reader*, New York: New York University Press.

Spettigue, D. O. (1969) *Frederick Philip Grove*, Toronto: Copp Clark.

Spivak, G. C. (1988) 'Can the Subaltern Speak?', in C. Nelson and L. Grossberg (eds) *Marxism and the Interpretation of Culture*, London: Macmillan.

Spivak, G. C. (1992a) 'Teaching for the Times', *MMLA Journal for the Mid-West Modern Language Association*, 25.1, Spring: 3–22.

Spivak, G. C. (1992b) 'Acting Bits/Identity Talk', *Critical Inquiry*, 18, Summer: 770–803.

Spivak, G. C. (1996) 'Transnationality and Multicultural Ideology: Interview', in D. Bahri and M. Vasudeva (eds) *Between the Lines: South Asians and Postcoloniality*, Philadelphia: Temple University.

Stam, R. (1997) 'Multiculturalism and the Neoconservatives', in A. McClintock, A. Mufti and E. Shohat (eds) *Dangerous Liaisons: Gender, Nation, and Postcolonial Perspectives*, Minneapolis: University of Minnesota Press.

Stasiulis, D. (1993) '"Authentic Voice": Anti-racist Politics in Canadian Feminist Publishing and Literary Production', in S. Gunew and A. Yeatman (eds) *Feminism and the Politics of Difference*, Sydney: Allen & Unwin.

Stimpson, C. (1992) 'On Differences: Modern Language Association Presidential Address 1990', in P. Berman (ed.) *Debating P.C.: The Controversy over Political Correctness on College Campuses*, New York: Laurel.

Stoetzler, M. and N. Yuval-Davis (2002) 'Standpoint Theory, Situated Knowledge and the Situated Imagination', *Feminist Theory*, 3.3: 315–33.

Stratton, J. (1998) *Race Daze: Australia in Identity Crisis*, Annanadale, NSW: Pluto.

Stratton J. and I. Ang (1994) 'Multicultural Imagined Communities: Cultural Difference and National Identity in Australia and the USA', *Continuum*, 8.2 (Critical Multiculturalism issue): 124–58.

Suleri, S. (1992a) *The Rhetoric of English India*, Chicago, IL: Chicago University Press.

Suleri, S. (1992b) 'Woman Skin Deep: Feminism and the Postcolonial Condition', *Critical Inquiry*, 18, Summer: 756–69.

Sykes, R. (1997) *Snake Cradle: Autobiography of a Black Woman*, Sydney: Allen & Unwin.

Sykes, R. (1998a) *Snake Dancing*, Sydney: Allen & Unwin.

Sykes, R. (1998b) 'In the Public Interest?', *Weekend Australian*, 24–5 October: 27.

Syson, I. (1995) 'Judging the Judges', *Age*, 26 September.

Tabakoff, J. (1999) 'It's Hasta la Vista, as "Ethnic" Says Adieu', *Sydney Morning Herald*, 10 April.

Talib, I. S. (2002) *The Language of Postcolonial Literatures*, London and New York: Routledge.

Taylor, C. (1994) 'The Politics of Recognition', in C. Taylor and A. Gutman (eds) *Multiculturalism: Examining the Politics of Recognition*, Princeton, NJ: Princeton University Press.

Taylor, C. and A. Gutman (eds) (1994) *Multiculturalism: Examining the Politics of Recognition*, Princeton, NJ: Princeton University Press.

Taylor, D. H. (1996) *Funny, You Don't Look like One: Observations from a Blue-Eyed Ojibway*, Penticton, BC: Theytus.

Taylor, D. H. (1999) *Further Adventures of a Blue-Eyed Ojibway: Funny, You Don't Look like One/Two*, Penticton, BC: Theytus.

Taylor, D. H. (2002) (unpublished paper) 'My Adventures in Paddling and Portaging the Rivers of Aboriginal Theater', delivered at the *Transculturalisms Canada Symposium*, University of British Columbia, February.

Tessera (1992) 'Other Looks: Representation, Race and Gender', 12, Summer.

Tomkins, S. (1995) *Shame and Its Sisters: A Sylvan Tomkins Reader*, E. Kosofsky Sedgwick and A. Frank (eds) Durham, NC: Duke University Press.

Toohey, P. (2002) 'Snapshots of a Fractured Nation', *Weekend Australian*, 4–5 May: 19–23.

Trinh, T. M. (1989) *Woman, Native, Other: Writing Postcoloniality and Feminism*, Bloomington: Indiana University Press.

Tsiolkas, C. (1995) *Loaded*, Sydney: Random HouseVintage.

Tuzi, M. (1997) *The Power of Allegiances: Identity, Culture, and Representational Strategies*, Toronto: Guernica.

Vasanji, M. G. (1999) 'Foreword', in N. Aziz (ed.) *Floating the Borders: New Contexts in Canadian Criticism*, Toronto: TSAR.

Vasta, E. and S. Castles (eds) (1996) *The Teeth Are Smiling: The Persistence of Racism in Multicultural Australia*, Sydney: Allen & Unwin.

Verdicchio, P. (1997) *Devils in Paradise: Writings on Post-Emigrant Cultures*, Toronto: Guernica.

Viswanathan, G. (1989) *Masks of Conquest: Literary Study and British Rule in India*, New York: Columbia University Press.

Wah, F. (1996) *Diamond Grill*, Edmonton: NeWest Press.

Wah, F. (1997–8) 'Speak My Language: Racing the Lyric Poetic', *West Coast Line*, 24.31.3, Winter: 72–84.

Wah, F. (2000) *Faking It: Poetics and Hybridity*, Edmonton: NeWest Press.

Walker, A. (1988) 'In the Closet of the Soul', in *Living by the Word: Selected Writings 1973–87*, San Diego, CA: Harcourt, Brace, Jovanovich.

Wallace, M. (1992) 'Untitled Statement', in P. Aufderheide (ed.) *Beyond P.C.: Toward a Politics of Understanding*, Minnesota, MN: Graywolf Press.

Walwicz, A. (1989) *Boat*, North Ryde, NSW: Angus & Robertson.

Ware, V. (1992) *Beyond the Pale: White Women, Racism and History*, Verso: London.

Wark, M. (1995) 'Revamp the Culture Club', *Australian*, 13 September.

Weir, L. and S. Richer (eds) (1995) *Beyond Political Correctness*, Toronto: University of Toronto Press.

Werbner, P. (1997) 'Afterword: Writing, Multiculturalism and Politics in the New Europe', in T. Modood and P. Werbner (eds) *The Politics of Multiculturalism in the New Europe: Racism, Identity and Community*, London: Zed Books.

West, C. (1992) 'Diverse New World', in P. Berman (ed.) *Debating P.C.: The Controversy over Political Correctness on College Campuses*, New York: Laurel.

West, C. (1993) *Race Matters*, Boston, MA: Beacon Press.

Widdowson, P. (ed.) (1982) *Re-reading English*, London: Methuen.

Willett, C. (ed.) (1998) *Theorizing Multiculturalism: A Guide to the Current Debate*, Oxford: Blackwell.

Willinsky, J. (1994) *Empire of Words: The Reign of the OED*, Princeton, NJ: Princeton University Press.

Willinsky, J. (1998) *Learning to Divide the Worlds: Education at Empire's End*, Minneapolis: University of Minnesota Press.

Wilson, R. and W. Dissanayake (eds) (1996) *Global/Local: Cultural Production and the Transnational Imaginary*, Durham, NC: Duke University Press.

Wilson, R. (1997) *Bringing Them Home: Report of the National Inquiry into the Separation of Aboriginal and Torres Strait Islander Children from Their Families*, Sydney: Stirling Press.

Wommersley, J. M. (1995) 'A Double Exposure' (letter), *Age*, 24 August.

Wong, J. (1996) *Red China Blues: My Long March from Mao to Now*, Toronto: Doubleday/Anchor.

Wong, J. (1997) 'Evelyn Lau Gets Perfect Grades in the School of Hard Knocks', *Globe & Mail*, 3 April: A11.

Wong, J. (1999) *Jan Wong's China*, Toronto: Doubleday/Anchor.

Wong, S. (1992) 'Stereotypes and Sensibilities', in P. Aufderheide (ed.) *Beyond P.C.: Toward a Politics of Understanding*, Minnesota, MN: Graywolf Press.

Wong, S.-l. C. (1993) *Reading Asian American Literature: From Necessity to Extravagance*, Princeton, NJ: Princeton University Press.

Wongar, B. (1994) *Raki*, Sydney: Angus & Robertson.

Wu, J. Yu-Wen Shen and M. Song (eds) (2000) *Asian American Studies: A Reader*, New Brunswick, NJ: Rutgers University Press.

Young, I. (1990) *Justice and the Politics of Difference*, Princeton, NJ: Princeton University Press.

Young, R. (1990) *White Mythologies: Writing, History and the West*, Routledge: London.

Yu, S. and A. MacKenzie (2000) 'Sexy Asian Men?', *Rice Paper*, 6.10, Spring.

Yúdice, G. (1995) 'Neither Impugning nor Disavowing Whiteness Does a Viable Politics Make: The Limits of Identity Politics', in C. Newfield and R. Strickland (eds) *After Political Correctness: The Humanities and Society in the 1990s*, Boulder, CO: Westview Press.

Yuval-Davis, N. (1994) 'Identity Politics and Women's Ethnicities', in V. Moghadam (ed.) *Identity Politics and Women: Cultural Reassertions and Feminisms in International Perspective*, Boulder, CO: Westview Press.

Zizek, S. (1989) *The Sublime Object of Ideology*, London: Verso.

Zizek, S. (1996) '"I Hear You With My Eyes": or, the Invisible Master', in R. Salecl and S. Zizek (eds) *Sic 1: Gaze and Voice as Love Objects*, Durham, NC: Duke University Press.

Zizek, S. (1997) 'Multiculturalism, or, the Cultural Logic of Multinational Capitalism', *New Left Review*, 225, September/October: 28–51.

Index